I Don't
Believe in
Astrology

To all of you who, for almost five decades, have sought me out and invited me to sit next to you as you opened up to your depths and shared your life story. I have loved listening to you.

I adore humans—I carry an unabashed love for the victors who made it through their pain, and as well for the perpetrators who created it. Evil has no power over compassion. My prayer is that we as a species will survive this narrow entrance into the next age, and that many more of us will touch the sweet spot of humility.

With the long view intact, we come to understand our humanness as an unfolding experiment that is about to turn a corner. I pray this book inspires compassion as you and your observer look at yourself and others. This is the doorway to the golden age. The future of our children is depending on us.

Astrology is assured of recognition from psychology, without further restrictions, because astrology represents the summation of all the psychological knowledge of antiquity.

—CARL JUNG

God doesn't play dice.

—ALBERT EINSTEIN

Contents

FOREWORD   1

INTRODUCTION   3

PART I. PSYCHOLOGICAL ASTROLOGY AND THE NATURE OF THE UNCONSCIOUS MIND

1. Falling in Love with Your Fate   13
2. Astrology Through the Lens of Psychology   22
3. The Observer and the Gremlins   32
4. How Astrology Works: Elements, Modes, Signs   43
5. The Planets   53
6. The Twelve Houses   69
7. Esoteric Astrology: Saturn and the Rising Sign   86

PART II. UNDERSTANDING YOURSELF AND OTHERS

8. The Psychology of Aries: I Am   107
9. The Psychology of Taurus: I Have   120
10. The Psychology of Gemini: I Think   134
11. The Psychology of Cancer: I Feel   147
12. The Psychology of Leo: I Will   164
13. The Psychology of Virgo: I Analyze   178
14. The Psychology of Libra: We Balance   191
15. The Psychology of Scorpio: I Desire   206

16. The Psychology of Sagittarius: I Seek   220
17. The Psychology of Capricorn: I Use   231
18. The Psychology of Aquarius: I Know   245
19. The Psychology of Pisces: I Dream   259
20. The Thirteenth Sign   273

APPENDIX I: Debra Silverman Resources   281
APPENDIX II: Find Your Saturn Sign   285
ACKNOWLEDGMENTS   287
ABOUT THE AUTHOR   292

I Don't
Believe in
Astrology

Foreword

I FEEL LIKE THIS BOOK was written for me. For most of my life I was proud that I didn't believe in astrology. This is not because I'm some materialist reductionist who thinks everything is woo-woo. I have a crystal in my pocket right now!

But the reason I didn't believe in astrology is the out-of-the-box explanation of my natal chart didn't really fit. Or rather, I felt like it could fit everyone. Like an amateur Penn & Teller, I was convinced that all this nonsense about astrology was just the cognitive bias called the Barnum effect writ large.

Underneath that intellectualism was another hidden motivation. I didn't want anything to limit the possibilities of where I decided to take my life. I wanted to make my own stars, not let some intergalactic zodiac box me in.

When I met Debra Silverman, I told her, "I don't believe in astrology." She said, "Great, that's the title of my next book!" We had a good laugh about it, but it didn't change my belief. I nonetheless agreed to sit down with her for her flagship Four Elements reading. And it changed my life.

The superficial reading of my natal chart indeed didn't really fit. But as we dove deeper into the complexities of the houses, positions, and the entirety of my chart, certain guiding principles of my essence started to be revealed. The king skeptic was retreating under the pursuit of the queen of astrology.

Then, after two hours, it was checkmate. In understanding my inherent nature, I wasn't limited—I was expanded. I clarified my mission and purpose on a deeper level and understood my inherent vulnerabilities. This information is invaluable.

I hope that in reading this book you will start to have the same experience. I invite you to engage with curiosity and creativity. And maybe, just maybe, this book will change your life like my first reading with Debra changed mine.

—*Aubrey Marcus*

Introduction

Astrology has an honorable history in every nation or race of people on the face of the earth that has attained any degree of civilization. Even the enemies of astrology cannot deny that fact.

—LUKE DENNIS BROUGHTON, *Elements of Astrology*, 1898

LET ME GUESS.

(1) You don't really believe in astrology, though you kind of wish you did. You're curious about whether I can change your mind.

Or (2) You have begun to believe in astrology, yet you want more information to enhance your belief in the influence of the stars in your life.

Either way, you've come to the right place. I call this book (and my podcast) *I Don't Believe in Astrology* because I, too, was once a skeptic. Over time, that has changed. I have witnessed firsthand, over decades of professional practice applying both psychology and astrology, exactly what astrology is capable of. I am now a firm believer.

Something brought you here—some inkling, curiosity, or feeling that there's more to astrology than a personality sketch or a glib forecast for the day. What you know so far might not feel quite substantial enough for you to really lean in. I bet you have flirted with your sun sign. Maybe you've had a reading and been surprised at the accuracy. Perhaps you *want* to believe in a starry world where life finally makes sense.

Astrology is controversial. It might seem overly abstract or fanciful. Astrology to me is nothing less than medicine, a life-changing tool that makes a huge difference, even if you don't believe in it.

Think about it: you don't have to believe in something for it to work. I'll bet you believe in true love, even if it has disappointed you at times. You believe in gravity, even though you might not understand it. You trust the lights will come on when you flick the switch without being able to explain it. Belief and understanding are not required for love or gravity or electricity to do their thing.

The same is true of astrology. You don't have to understand it. It's there for you, no belief required. Over time, and with the help of this book, you will find out how useful this timeless body of wisdom truly is. You don't have to believe in astrology—astrology believes in you.

You are not a mistake. No one pushed you onto the bus called life—it's a volunteer position. We are here on assignment. Even if you don't believe that (yet), it doesn't matter because it will become obvious to you eventually that everyone has a purpose and life lessons that are seeking them out.

There are issues that will keep showing up in life until you learn your lessons. This is a book about how to turn your confusion into purpose. It's a book about the negative voices in your head, that restless sense of dissatisfaction, the feeling of not being sure of who you really are. Do you wonder if you're living your purpose, whether you're living the right life, whether you're with the right partner, whether you're in the right job? Everyone has that inner voice that tells them they are doing something wrong, or should be doing something differently, or should become someone better.

The voices in your head—I call them gremlins—are saboteurs. They say the meanest things about you! They bring you down until you finally get fed up, hit the crisis point, and at last hear the quieter, kinder, more compassionate voice—the voice I call your observer. Astrology shows you the path through the forest of gremlins into the light of the observer, where those negative voices finally grow quiet enough for the truth to come through.

Astrology shows you who you really are and says, "Hey, this is you, and it's okay. You have permission to be a daydreamer (Pisces), or ambitious (Capricorn), or strong (Aries). There are reasons you value freedom over relationships (Aquarius), or financial security over frivolous shopping (Taurus), or talking over listening (Gemini). It's natural for you to obsess about the meaning of life (Sagittarius), or have a morbid curiosity about death (Scorpio), or feel best when your whole family is under one roof (Cancer), or be in love with romance (Libra), or try to get all the attention (Leo). You don't need to fight it. It's just you being you."

Astrology turns on self-awareness. If you are a Virgo, astrology will teach you that you tend to criticize yourself. Bringing that into your awareness helps you to ease up and understand how important it is for you to be precise, attend to details, and check off your to-do list. The voice of your observer (I'm going to show you how to find and hear it) will say, "Yep, you criticize yourself. Don't worry. You're okay." Then if someone tells you, "Hey, relax, it's not that important," you'll know enough about yourself to know that for you, it *is* important, and that's okay, too. You love the small stuff. You'll know you've got the observer turned on when you learn to laugh at yourself a little, and genuinely be able to say to yourself, "Oh, there I go again. That's so me!"

There are struggles inherent in each of the twelve signs. Find your struggle, and you will discover what you are here to learn. You're not here by accident. There is a curriculum, and a folder in the home office with your name on it. Astrology provides the keyhole to peek through, to see what your lessons are. It's a relief to know your challenges are happening for a reason, and most of all, to understand that you're not to blame.

A client once told me she got ten years' worth of therapy out of one astrology reading. With this book, I hope to help you gain that same benefit—it's an efficient route to self-knowledge and relief from your gremlins.

Guess what else: the things you think are wrong with you are your strengths. This is the ultimate truth about astrology: it changes what you thought was wrong. That may feel counterintuitive. You are going to find out how the lessons inherent in your struggles take you to the high road of your astrology chart—the road to your highest self. There are repetitive behaviors that follow you around. That's a good thing, not a bad thing. Those behaviors are your signposts. They are at the heart of understanding your sign and yourself.

As you probably see by now, this isn't a typical astrology book. This is a psychology-of-you book, utilizing astrology as the guiding light, the framework. The signs are a way to talk about your idiosyncrasies and show you that you don't have to feel bad about your so-called faults.

There is nothing wrong with you. You are a divine being who volunteered to take on this lifetime with the exact personality you have. I promise that is the truth. What a wonderful thought: you are exactly as you were meant to be.

ASTROLOGY AS MEDICINE

I understand why people resist and misunderstand astrology as a pseudo-science. It's just plain strange that the position of the sun would influence your personality, that the moon's position would describe the nature of your emotional temperament, and that the other planets would influence different aspects of your life. I know it sounds woo-woo, and we have been programmed to deny woo-woo. I certainly have. If you don't identify with all things mystical or you are suspicious of magical thinking, I am right there with you. Why *would* you believe in astrology? Think about this: people once said all these same things about psychology—

some still do. People often keep their therapy a secret or are embarrassed to admit they tried it, and since not everyone gets results, they may decide it doesn't work. Yet consider how many people therapy has helped.

I went to graduate school to study clinical psychology. My career has involved working with people of high standing in our society—serious people who live in a world of professionalism and tangible accomplishments. I'm a practical person who has been devoted to teaching and healing since a very young age. I pride myself on changing people's lives. I focus on results. The goal for a healer is to assist someone with a problem or pain by taking them through a process so that at the end of the session, they walk out with a plan. I have noticed that most of my clients feel better at the end of a good astrology session. That's a constant.

In almost five decades of being in practice, it's still amazing to me how far I move someone along in a therapy session with their astrological chart in my hands, as compared to doing "ordinary" talk therapy. When people come to me complaining that they just aren't right, I show them how untrue that is. I say, "Yes, I hear you, and guess what? I can explain all of this by looking at your chart. It's all right here."

The single most significant influence astrology has is the immediate and dramatic way it changes the way you speak to yourself. It shifts the voices in your head. You become more forgiving and tolerant of yourself and others.

There will always be skeptics. Recently a client told me that when she told her father, who is a doctor, that she was coming to see me, he started screaming at her. This was completely out of character for him. He told her, "Those people are quacks! No daughter of mine is wasting her money on astrology!" This happens. Her father was embodying the voice of the critic, the voice that defaults to simple logic that often operates in left-brained people who only trust what they can prove. Fortunately, my client was able to hear her own voice. She left our session realizing many truths about herself. She understood that what she really wanted was to leave a job that made her unhappy and go back to school. She couldn't have gotten to that place listening to the voice of her father. Instead, she was able to hear her truth—all because of astrology.

The preconceptions, doubts, questions, or cynicism people bring into my office quickly evaporate when they feel seen and understood, sometimes for the first time. I love the skeptics. I love it when they get to the end of a session and they say, "How do you know all this? You know me so well. You know me better than I know myself!" They leave with profound insights into their character—with stars in their eyes and a softer heart.

ABOUT THIS BOOK

This isn't one more spiritual book filled with theories. It's not going to tell you to buy expensive green drinks, take some newfangled supplement, or encourage you to collect crystals. The truth is that when your "human" gets triggered, the crystals aren't going to help you. You could be meditating every day and still have gremlins.

There is an epidemic on this planet of anxiety, depression, addiction, all things that describe the personality seeking comfort or some kind of relief from the gremlins. The billion-dollar industries of therapy, biohacking, and self-help can all be reduced to a single question: Are you at peace with who you are? I can guarantee you are going to say no, and that is why you are reading this book.

The function of this book is to give you access to the voice of compassion that knows you are okay, lovable, and a beautiful soul. Learning about yourself in this book will increase your self-awareness and give you access to a kinder inner voice. Who doesn't need that? The reason people love astrology is because they get insights about themselves that are so different from what their inner critic tells them. Once the observer is turned on, you will have the musculature to activate your positive inner voice through the practice of channeling the observer—and just like that, the gremlins will have nothing on you.

In part 1, you'll learn about the unfriendly nature of the human condition and how it is not your fault. You are built to sabotage yourself. You will discover how to use psychology with astrology. You'll learn how to identify the specific gremlins that come with your chart. You'll learn the technology of how to tap the power of your observer to access the high road of your character. This is how you fall in love with the crazy thing called life.

Part 2 consists of 13 chapters, one for each sign, and a special chapter just for the thirteenth sign, which I won't tell you about just yet. Each chapter will include a psychological analysis of the sun sign, a profile of someone with this sign, what this sign looks like on the low road and on the high road, how this sign can best work with the observer (you'll learn about this concept in part 1), what your life lesson is if you are this sign, what medicine will help you, and what it looks and feels like if your moon, Mercury, or Saturn is in this sign, or if this is your rising sign. At the end of each chapter, you'll get a special meditation just for you, and then I'll sum it all up by telling you about the sign's essence.

Just so you know, not everyone relates to their sun sign. In fact, this is one of the main reasons some people don't believe in astrology. There are good reasons why you might not be a pure example of your sun sign. It might be your moon or your rising sign showing up with a stronger influence. If you have multiple planets in a different sign (a stellium), that sign takes precedence. The planets themselves also have their own qualities and were in certain houses at the time of your birth. All that colors the expression of your sun sign (I'll tell you more about these influences in part 1). Astrology is complex, with many factors at work. You don't need to understand at the level of a professional astrologer. What matters is that the themes in your chart will explain you to yourself, and help you to understand others.

There is no one you know who doesn't have a mental health issue that plagues them. It is a universal song that is remedied with awareness, although never completely corrected. We live this life managing and healing the voices in our heads, which are simply described by the twelve signs. It will become almost funny when you see how obvious it is what your internal dialogue repeats. It becomes endearing that the very things that are driving you crazy—and they really are—are your best friends. Every single one of your crises is a doorway to your awakening. Similarly, all your gremlins are reciting the broken records that are your alerts, your SOS to say, "I must need help because the same things keep happening to me."

Astrology is a doorway into a chamber of timeless wisdom. Your soul is waiting for you to become conscious of your assignment. While it might seem mystical or like a Disney movie that a book could magically bring you closer to your soul, that is my hope for this book. Who has ever given you permission slips to understand yourself and be yourself? That is the ingredient irritating your system, causing you discomfort and that underlying sense of dissatisfaction. While you may think you've got a spiritual practice going, until you fall in love with your unique soul and the requirements that come with it, you're fooling yourself.

So come on in! It's so bright and meaningful inside this sacred conversation. My Gemini personality wants you to play with me, and I just want you to jump in right now and begin this process. So let's go!

PART I

Psychological Astrology and the Nature of the Unconscious Mind

As long as man struggles with his mortality, he is affected by the myriad mutations of heaven and earth. Astrology is the study of man's response to planetary stimuli. The stars have no conscious benevolence or animosity; they merely send forth positive and negative radiations. Of themselves, these do not help or harm humanity, but offer a lawful channel for the outward operation of cause-effect equilibriums.

—Paramahansa Yogananda, *Autobiography of a Yogi*

1

Falling in Love with Your Fate

Have you ever asked yourself: What am I here for? What am I supposed to be in this life? If you have, you have begun to live in a new way. It is my deep belief that the function of astrology is to help men and women, who have begun to ask questions concerning the purpose and meaning of their own lives, to find answers to these questions. Astrology has little real value to offer to people who do not ask such questions.

—Dane Rudhyar

IT'S A SETUP. YOU COULDN'T get it right, even if you tried.

We're all guilty—of being human. We sabotage ourselves. We don't act in our own best interest. We break people's hearts, and our hearts get broken. We leave, and are left. We betray, and are betrayed. Someone you know will cheat, get addicted, ghost people. We insist on acting in ways that are not in our own best interest, make us feel bad, and set us up to question who we are as individuals and even as a species. At worst, these existential questions plague us with no satisfying answers. It is how we are wired. Human nature has a strange and nonsensical operating system.

Here's a thought: What if it's not anybody's fault that we are a bad design? Not your parents', not your partner's, not your life choices', and not your fault that your mind doesn't move directly to comfort, wisdom, or clear answers? Wouldn't that be a relief?

When I was in my twenties in graduate school for clinical psychology, I remember at the very beginning of the program I was in a room with about fifty other students. The professor asked us why we wanted to study psychology. I raised my hand and said, "Because I want to know why we don't do the things that are good for us. Why don't we exercise? Why don't we eat well? Why don't we do what will set us free? Why don't we quit the job we hate? Why don't we leave the relationship that's not healthy?" I really wanted to know. It was the reason I chose psychology—*why don't we humans do what will make us happy?*

Psychology never answered that question completely . . . astrology did. The answer to that question is simple: it's our design faults. It's the way we are wired. People are so stupid, they don't even know they're smart. And that's just dumb! The good news is that it's not fatal.

We are evolving. You wouldn't be reading this book if you didn't have an appetite to learn and grow. However, no matter how evolved we get, inside everyone's mind lives unconscious impulses keeping us from doing what's good for us. We can't explain why it's so easy to slide into laziness, depression, or anxiety—those saboteurs arrive and we surrender. We can't help it—human nature by design has a natural propensity to go to the lowest level and let gravity take over. It's the kid who steals the candy and says, "I couldn't help it!"

Let's be honest: it takes so much effort to take the high road. We doubt our instincts and our decisions. We are not designed to immediately forgive or to feel joy easily. We tend to blame before we forgive—forgiveness is a learned skill and blame is an automatic behavior. Forgiveness doesn't come naturally.

Here are some examples of the human condition and our faulty design (I'll point out more throughout the book):

★ **Peace eludes us:** The first and most important design fault is that the human mind cannot sustain peace. We struggle. We have a hard time getting along with each other. We live for drama. Think about it: the people we pay the most, actors and athletes, are the ones who create drama for us to watch. We fear differences. We judge each other, often uncharitably. We gossip. We're nosy—popular culture and social media are based on that truth.

We especially talk badly, internally, about ourselves. Is there anyone who doesn't live with a negative voice in their head that self-doubts, even degrades and demeans? Those voices get loud, whether it's the voice that criticizes what you see in the mirror first thing in the morning, or the one that keeps you up in the middle of the night, worrying about what happened or what's to come. We worry—oh, how we worry! We worry about whether we're doing the right thing, making the right decision, making the most out of our lives, doing what we should be doing or doing something we shouldn't be doing; whether we are really loved or loving well enough; whether we are wasting our lives. We are consistently unsettled. The universal inner dialogue is too often riddled with fear, judgments, and busyness. That's just nuts!

★ **Forgiveness doesn't come naturally—blame and shame do:** For so many, apologizing is not natural. We immediately blame the other, and walk away with a grudge. We aren't designed to take responsibility for our lives. We aren't built to own our humanness. We make mistakes. Rather than admitting to them, we tend to turn to blame, denial, addiction, escapism, and secret shame.

It's someone else's fault that the relationship failed, the addiction developed, the job was lost, the accident happened, the childhood was ruined. Think of the child who spills the juice and when his mother turns around, points at his brother and says, "He did it!" leaving the mother perplexed because nobody will take responsibility. In a moment, everyone is angry, caught in the web of human nature. Blame is simply part of the human condition. It's way too easy to point the finger rather than accept that our imperfections might have something to teach us about compassion.

★ **We are pathologically insecure:** Another strange design fault are our inherent feelings of insecurity. Everyone has them. We feel watched and judged, if not by others, then by the voices inside our heads—that running commentary that creates and encourages insecurities. Even with therapy and meditation, too often the results are disappointing. Many give up when the effort doesn't feel worth the results. And so we return to the broken record that something is wrong with us. We *must* be bad because we are unhappy. What kind of logic is that? (Taurus, Virgo, and Cancer are the signs most susceptible to insecurity.)

★ **We learn the hard way:** Often, it takes a tragedy, like a serious illness or a brush with death, to change behavior or attitude. In my early twenties, I was introduced to the books of Alice Bailey—they were the first stop on my spiritual journey. In her book *Initiation, Human and Solar,* she wrote (I am paraphrasing) that the goal of this game called life is to go through initiations—better known as crises—to see if you will allow your soul to intervene. In other words, the purpose of crisis is to see whether or not you will wake up, seek your soul, and turn these lessons into a joyful practice of full acceptance. Welcome to planet Earth, where you will be presented with meaningful lessons over and over again, disguised as your personal trauma drama, until you finally get the message—whether you like it or not. It's the only way we really learn. Too bad no one informed you (until now).

★ **We prioritize instant gratification:** We choose instant gratification over patience. We are not built for future pacing. We go for immediate pleasure rather than preparing for what's to come. I find it so strange that we as a collective cannot look generations ahead to contemplate the implications of our actions for our children's children. Humans do not come programmed with the long view or a trustworthy impulse control. (Aries, Leo, and Sagittarius are most likely to fall prey to this one.) Humans are consumption machines.

★ **We resist change:** Think about the past and your ancestors; they struggled just like you. Their hearts got broken, they got sick, they did things they regretted, they got hurt, they lived unhappily. Here we are, generations later, doing exactly the same things. The sins of our fathers and mothers follow us around. We resist changing the story. We resist change altogether. We may read books about how to change. In reality, it's easy to contemplate and hard to do. Dare I say that as a species, we are lazy, impulsive, and naturally lack wisdom? (Taurus, Cancer, and Scorpio really resist change!)

★ **We have triggers:** If I look at your chart, I will know exactly how to push your buttons. For a Virgo, I just make a mess and leave it. For a Gemini, I refuse to talk. For a Leo, I ignore you. For an Aries, I disagree with you. For an Aquarius, I tell you you're just like everybody else. For a Cancer, I insult your family. Once the ego is triggered by your family member, your boss, your mean friend, or someone on the internet, any wisdom you might have been studying or good habits you've been trying to implement go right out the window.

Think about driving a car, getting cut off, and how quickly your higher self is eclipsed by your reactivity. Do you flip someone off or swear at them in a rage? All it takes is for someone to prod the tender spots in your psyche and I guarantee you will take it personally. You know that idea that you shouldn't take anything personally? Bullshit. Everyone does. An air sign will push feelings away entirely and replace them with denial. She'll say, "I don't even care." Or perhaps you act out with destructive behavior—typical of the fire sign—that for a moment soothes the pain, like spending money, or escaping with the help of drugs and/or alcohol. Maybe you stonewall like an earth sign, or break down in tears like a water sign. We are built to be triggered, rather than built for wisdom.

Wait a minute. Is it really so bad? Is there no hope? Of course there is hope. Our human design may be inefficient, frustrating, and nonsensical. Don't worry. There is a method to the madness.

You were created as an experiment in the name of evolution: souls arrive and enter a classroom called planet Earth, programmed to experience great dissatisfaction, sadness, disharmony, and illness. The question is: Can humans still love, regardless of what life hands them?

The formula works like this: you have to get it wrong to get it right. Everything that's wrong with you is included in your curriculum. It's like the game show *Jeopardy!*. You get the answer, reflected by your life's drama. The question is, "What does life want me to learn?" The minute you realize that your issues are not going away, that there is always something in human nature challenging us, you then begin answering the question, "What are my assignments?" Astrology helps with this answer. Your chart describes your assignment. The ultimate challenge is to accept exactly what's been handed to you with gratitude. It sounds straightforward. I assure you, it's not.

Understanding and acceptance arrive upon realizing that (1) we're all in this together and (2) every single person you know, bar none, has secret issues and parts of themselves they really don't like. As an astrologer psychotherapist, I'm telling you: this reality is not going away. The sooner you realize that you came down here with an agreement to take on the human condition, the quicker you come to peace. Acceptance arrives when there is no longer resistance to your particular life situation. That's when the healing begins.

The evolutionary exercise that you signed up for is far beyond conscious memory. You don't remember that you agreed to take on the very things that bug the shit out of you. The moment you realize design faults are real and they are not going away . . . they go away. Once your awareness is on, you say, "I'm really quirky, I'm emotionally stunted, I don't like to feel human." Then you realize, "Wait a minute, wait a minute. Was that my assignment?" (said the Aquarian). Here is where free will begins. This is your "get out of jail free" card: acceptance of what is, without resistance.

If you're an air sign or an earth sign, you're going to verbally complain throughout your whole assignment. If you're a fire sign, you're indulging to avoid this conversation. Now we understand why you water signs are depressed—this reality feels so assaulting to you. "What do you mean I have to be in pain to heal? That makes me want to cry!"

Falling in love with your fate is the only way out. This is the purpose of life. Pretend this is your job description and you can't wait to go to work. The whole focus will change.

I spent so many years overthinking. Debra Silverman drove me nuts. I can't believe I lived with her for so long. And then one day I realized she's not going anywhere and that if I didn't accept the fact that I'm superglued to her, I would be miserable and so would she. (This is so Gemini.)

So I looked at my soul and said, "Deb, you little codependent, emotional, mushy little thing, we've got to get out of here." I was such an emotional being. I wouldn't have resisted my assignment all those years if somebody would have just told me what it was. "You are an emotional dependent and you must learn about being alone." I had to spend years and years in my thirties and forties and fifties being a complete idiot. It's embarrassing. I look back at myself and wonder what I was thinking.

Please don't try to make it okay and say, "Debra, we all love you!" I know—at that time, my immaturity was in full effect. I'm just sharing my raw human experience, and I'm proud to say that I'm a cute little human who had psychological wounds. I'm not embarrassed anymore. (Well, just a little.)

Human nature is embarrassing, at best. I promise you that as we unpack the psychology of your chart and we push those buttons, you're going to feel very self-conscious. I'm not here to make every sign sweet and saccharine-like. I'm here to speak to the truth of our shadows. That's where the gold is hidden.

We don't actually change until life is really bad. We can't get out of those repetitive patterns without enough discomfort. I'm sorry to tell you this. This is bad news. You will not change until you are in enough pain or so sick of your situation that you can't stand it anymore. They call that rock bottom. That's the evolutionary turning point.

We as a collective—the human race—are just about to hit that spot. There is going to be a shock wave, a wake-up call. There is civil war energy in the stars. It's all over the world. There will be radical change. It's going to reach a fever pitch, and we aren't going to like it.

This book will help you to better understand yourself and the motivations and qualities of others in this turbulent time. It will help you to see why things are happening the way they are, and why we react the way we do. Your assignments in this life are going to become clearer, as long as you have tools to recognize them. This book is about finding and learning how to use those tools.

I'm here to say (to all of humanity), "You're fucked up—and I still like you." The good news is, in no uncertain terms, no matter what happens next in this life and on this planet, you are contributing to human evolution with your story. It may feel embarrassing and humiliating. It may feel scary or startling or impossible to endure. You don't want to tell anyone that you're addicted to watching porn, or eating sugar, or obsessing over TikTok. You don't even want to tell anyone your political opinions. People are on edge, critical, judgmental, irrational. It's hard to know what to say or do anymore, and people are just trying to cope. I'm always shocked at the human capacity to accept discomfort without taking action.

Understanding astrology may interrupt your life because once you fall in love with your fate, you wake up and then you can't go back to sleep.

You'll want to stay awake. You'll see things in a new way. Your compassionate soul is committed to the evolution of our species, and you're about to have a front-row seat, so be ready. This is why you're here.

Your soul wants nothing more than to help, or you wouldn't be here. There are billions of souls standing in line in the waiting room, wanting to incarnate. Why do you think there are eight billion people on this planet and counting? It's because they longed to be included in this experience, right here, right now.

"I'll help!" volunteers the soul. "Pick me!" Then we get here with a backpack full of psychological rocks and forget what we promised to do because it's so heavy. We have to go through the whole process of suffering so we can remember.

The worse the pain, the greater the angst, the greater the contribution you're making to the planet. The bigger the story, the bigger the spirit. If you get out from underneath all that suffering, you are on the path to liberation. If not, just keep going.

Would you say this has been a bad experiment? Humans have not typically displayed the highest versions of themselves. The experiment hasn't worked that well. However, as an astrologer looking into the future, I have high hopes for the next version of humanity. I think they will be far superior to what we have now. It's coming. I see it in some of the people and children I've already met. Here comes the Aquarian Age!

There *is* hope, and we *can* overcome our faulty design. We need optimism and hope now more than ever. How do we find it? Through the intersection of astrology and psychology.

2

Astrology Through the
Lens of Psychology

In its penetration into our shared lexicon, astrology is a little like psychoanalysis once was. At mid-century, you might have heard talk of id, ego, or superego at a party; now it's common to hear someone explain herself by way of sun, moon, and rising signs. It's not just that you hear it. It's who's saying it: people who aren't kooks or climate-change deniers, who see no contradiction between using astrology and believing in science. The change is fueling a new generation of practitioners.

—CHRISTINE SMALLWOOD, "Astrology in the Age of Uncertainty,"
The New Yorker, October 21, 2019

I'M A GEMINI. I TALK a lot. I used to feel guilty and tell myself to stop talking. I was self-conscious. The worst thing you could say to me was: "Do you have to keep talking all the time?" My ego would defend, "That's not me. I'm not that Gemini." And I would stop talking . . . for a while. If I have an audience or I'm writing, I can go on and on. There were times my insecurities would shut me down and stop me from being me.

Then I found friends who also didn't stop talking. I had found my people. One day I realized, "You know what, Debra? You're a Gemini. So here's what we're going to do. You're going to use your skill set. You talk. You're also going to learn how to listen." That was a game changer. That broken record saying, "Stop talking so much," was really just a gremlin whispering in my ear. I gave up the guilt and shame and embraced who I am, and that came with the understanding that of course I need to talk—I could also learn to reciprocate. And wow, have I studied listening. I practice every day.

Every sign carries classical human nature dynamics that tend to operate on automatic. This is where we lose our free will. It's also where astrology and psychology intersect. Whatever your psychological issues are, whatever it is that bugs you (or your partner) about you, I guarantee it coincides with qualities in the signs. Here are twelve personality traits. Regardless of what sign you are, you may relate to these themes. See if any of these ring true for you. (It might not be your sun sign—you'll learn why later.)

★ **Wanna fight?** You are antagonistic and impulsive. You accidentally (or intentionally) offend people with your bluntness and then wonder why they don't like you. You have a lot of confidence, yet you exhaust people because your energy is so strong. People appear beige and unmotivated to you. You always have energy to get up and go. Hello, Aries!

★ **Something's wrong with me.** You feel inadequate and have low self-esteem. Sometimes you think you are boring, or too predictable. You're stubborn and immovable. You collect things. You long for comfort, security, and simple pleasures, yet you can't help thinking there is something wrong with wanting that. You live with insecurity about your body and your finances. Hello, Taurus!

★ **I can't stop moving!** You are hyperactive so you have trouble paying attention. You are always changing course—a different major, a different job, a new career. You have a hard time finishing things. You worry that you aren't really accomplishing anything. You talk without listening. Your mind is childlike and fickle to the point of feeling like you never really get focused, and you can carry internal discomfort with you. You display charisma and hide your self-consciousness. Hello, Gemini!

★ **Life hurts.** You feel the collective pain of the world. It's obvious you carry it in your body—you physically hurt for no apparent reason. You think you might have been born into the wrong family. You feel highly sensitive and you feel best when you are alone or at home with animals and the people you love the most. No strangers welcome! You feel like a lot of bad things have happened to you or your family, and you have sad stories to tell. Life feels harder than it should. Hello, Cancer!

★ **Look at me!** You have to be the center of attention and you crave external validation. Without it, you feel insecure and frustrated. You take a lot of effort to stand out and make a great first impression. Deep down, however, you wonder if anybody really knows who you are without the shine. Your opinions alienate people. You cannot blend or be soft when you are upset. It's just your nature to get all riled up. Hello, Leo!

★ **Good enough will never be good enough.** You are a perfectionist. You often try to fix things, clean things, correct things, and assist other people in doing things the right way. Still, you never really feel you're actually doing things well enough—or are good enough. Failure feels like a familiar poison to you. If only you could relax! You wake up in the night making lists so nothing is left behind . . . of course it won't be because you'll check your list one more time. Hello, Virgo!

★ **All I need is love.** You often think of yourself in relation to other people. Romance is your favorite distraction. You are an idealist, yet the reality of relationships slips away and rarely lives up to your expectations. You have artistic dreams and see the world through rose-tinted glasses. You never want to hurt. When you sense disharmony, it feels like a tragedy has occurred and you take responsibility and let the person off the hook way too soon. Hello, Libra!

★ **Going dark.** You can get preoccupied with the shadowy impulse in all of us. You can get stuck in an addiction to the dark side of human nature. Because you've seen the worst, you don't easily trust people. You protect yourself by staying guarded, seemingly aloof. You instinctively see through people and think like a detective. Trust no one! That is your motto. Hello, Scorpio!

★ **Everything's fine!** You always see the sunny side, even to the point of denial. If it's negative, if it's bad, if it has to be dealt with, you're more likely to sweep it under the carpet—until the crisis demands your attention. And if things get too intense? You're out of there—time for a trip, to travel, to get out of this world. Maybe it is a microdose or a fun adventure. Your young adulthood included drugs and indulgences, or if it didn't, you are making up for lost time now. You avoid pain with laughter at the expense of the sensitive people around. Hello, Sagittarius!

★ **I'm working on it.** You are ambitious, materialistic, goal-oriented, and a workaholic. You get the job done and you have extremely high standards for others, second only to the high standards you have for yourself. You are a know-it-all and think that if you aren't the best, you are wasting your life. You suffer from workaholic syndrome. If you are not working or making money, you go to the other extreme and find yourself lazy and down. You are an extremist: up for the job or down for the count. Hello, Capricorn!

★ **Emotions are overrated.** Let's be frank: you're a little weird. You don't feel like you quite belong and people don't seem to really understand you. You value freedom over connection and you have trouble feeling your feelings. Sometimes you think you must be from another planet—it just might be true. You were the smart kid who knew what was coming next. Design, style, art, and athletics always came way too easily. Your genius showed up during childhood and might feel hard to live up to. Hello, Aquarius!

★ **I'm not even here.** You feel *everything.* You are so sensitive. You feel disheartened and disenchanted with this reality, and you want to escape or retreat. Sometimes you wonder if you are here by mistake and why people are so cruel, especially to animals and the helpless. Hello, Pisces!

We all have the twelve signs within us. They are universal. Everyone has a physical body (Aries); everyone has to have resources and money (Taurus); everyone has to have a functioning mind to learn and speak (Gemini); everyone comes from a mother (Cancer); everyone longs to experience romantic love (Leo); everyone needs their health (Virgo); everyone has to relate to people (Libra); everyone will have a sexual impulse at some point in their lives (Scorpio); everyone, at some point, ponders the question, "What does it all mean?" (Sagittarius); everyone has to work (Capricorn); everyone is a little bit unusual in their own way (Aquarius); and everyone carries a wish or a dream (Pisces) to change this planet.

These are the twelve signs, and they are inherent in everyone because we come with essentially the same operating system. With a chart in front of a skilled astrologer, it becomes specific what themes, and what design faults, are unique to you.

ASTROLOGY + PSYCHOLOGY = UNDERSTANDING

Unlike other astrology systems, I'm often going to mention three concepts that link astrology and psychology: your ego, which is represented by your sun sign; your soul, which is expressed through your rising sign; and your life lessons, described by your Saturn placement. In all the other astrology books, you will hear that the sun, moon, and rising signs are the most important. I'm not disagreeing with that. In fact, I agree. Since we are doing psychology with astrology, we have a slightly different focus. Later, I'll also talk about the moon (emotions) and Mercury (mind). First, these three aspects of astrology—the sun, the rising sign, and Saturn—in my system are the most important for understanding the psychology of astrology.

The ego is personality, and it is represented by your sun sign. It's how you show up in the world. Your ego decides your preferences and opinions. It likes mustard and hates mayonnaise. It wants your hair cut a certain way, has opinions about people, and chooses a particular pair of shoes. It gets easily offended, loves praise, and prefers some people to others. If your ego isn't healthy, if you don't have self-esteem or clear boundaries, you will lose yourself. No one tells you how important your ego is. "Ego" has a negative connotation, yet it is the primary impulse that makes you, you.

The soul, on the other hand, is the part of you with very few needs or preferences. Represented by your rising sign, it is gentle, compassionate, generous, and it only wants to experience life fully. Everyone has a soul. Let's get the idea out of the way that you don't have one. Trust me, you do. In esoteric astrology, the soul reveals your highest purpose, and ideally, the ego is happily in service to the soul. However the soul, unlike the ego, is not demanding. Until you have a working relationship with your soul, you will be governed by your ego alone because it takes up all the airtime. This is the culprit responsible for your misery. The ego judges, is impatient, and is hardly ever happy. Unless you know how to activate the presence of your soul, your ego will run the show. Soulful people, no matter what happens to them, know how to surrender and fully accept their fate.

Here's an example to show the difference between the soul and the ego. Sting, who has been one of my clients for many years, is a Leo rising. In other words, his soul is a Leo. He will get on stage willingly, and turns into the masterful performer that he is, with the bass and his colorful outfits. He puts on an amazing show, and then goes quiet. He is not the guy in the room taking up all the space as he might be if Leo were his sun sign (ego). He is gracious and even a bit shy. He's always making sure (like the Libra sun sign that he is) that others are okay.

Madonna, on the other hand, is a Leo sun. She's comfortable being the most overt person in the room. She's happy to be the center of attention. She has no problem sharing her talent, on stage or off. Madonna exudes talent and showmanship like the sun projects light and warmth. Sting is quieter as a Leo rising because the rising sign is our private self— our soul—that we have to consciously activate and reveal. With the sun sign, it's a knee-jerk reaction. With the rising sign, it's a choice to find the high road. Sun sign Leos want to show off. Rising sign Leos can resist.

Your soul is the part of you that is open to every and any experience. No demands. It's not biased. Healthy, sick, tall, short, fit, out of shape, young, old—the soul loves you just the way you are. It's not looking to feed your ego or pacify your emotions. It simply longs to be in the glorious fulfillment of being alive. It doesn't even care whether you are a "success" or a "failure"—that's the ego's language. The soul is a slut. It will do anything, at any time, for anyone, just to get a lesson, just to learn something new in order to live this life with full conviction. Your soul is fully committed to life, no matter what's involved!

Everyone comes here to learn something. You promised your soul that in this life, you would learn lessons, and to be honest, the lessons are not usually easy. Psychology calls that resistance. The reason you go to a therapist is because you bumped into some part of yourself that cannot get comfortable dealing with resistance or conflict. It's inherent in the human condition that we will react to life with protection and fear as our first response—another design fault. Design faults work against all of us. The gremlin voices increase resistance, fear, and negativity. The avoidance of life lessons creates consequences.

Those life lessons come from Saturn, which represents your life lessons. You probably won't want to learn them—whenever I teach Saturn in my school, everyone says, "I hate that part of me," no matter what sign it's in. These are your lessons, nevertheless. Saturn is like the stern high school principal who insists you follow the rules or you won't graduate. Where Saturn was at your time of birth determines what lessons you came here to learn. I'll talk in more depth about Saturn in chapter 7.

You can begin to understand how astrology informs psychology in your own life by finding the repetitive patterns. What are the bothersome themes that follow you around? What are the challenges that keep coming up for you, that make you say, "Not this again!"? What is it you can't stop thinking about? What nibbles at you? What bump in the road can't you get over? Life is humbling. It brings us to our knees. (Saturn rules the knees.) We're all struggling in one way or another—not equally, to be fair, yet struggling nonetheless to find our soul's healing balm. There is a solution.

Once you know astrology, you see why you hate to be alone (Libra), or love it (Virgo)—and feel okay about that. You recognize your workaholic tendencies without excuses (Capricorn), or that you may be a little weird (Aquarius), or get bored easily (Gemini), or your naturally frugal tendencies (Taurus), or that you have trouble making decisions (Pisces), or why you are so sensitive (Cancer), or so easily frustrated (Aries), or so obsessed with all things spiritual (Sagittarius), or are naturally a little dark (Scorpio), or light and childlike (Leo).

Without astrology, we have no language to articulate our funny personalities. We have no context to understand our idiosyncrasies. Why do you always organize things when you are upset? Oh, you are an earth sign. Why do you stick your foot in your mouth and talk so loudly? I see, you are a fire sign. Why do you get so upset at the littlest thing? Aha, a sensitive water sign. Why do you have so much trouble staying in relationships? An air sign. Now I get it. Without this level of understanding, those qualities are just annoying.

You have to go inside, sit down next to your unconscious impulses, name them, become friends with them, and invite them to come with you to the other side of the street—a street called Awareness Avenue. This is where astrology and psychology intersect, and this is where the answers await you.

Astrology shows you exactly where your ego disrupts your life. It informs you why you do what you do and, used properly, it will assist you in falling in love with it. Astrology with psychology untangles the knots, criticisms, and distractions of the ego that drive you and your family nuts. Your angst is your liberation. Everything that bugs you about yourself, your family members, and your friends is a gift in disguise. Shocking!

CARL JUNG AND THE ASTROLOGY/ PSYCHOLOGY CONNECTION

. . . .

Modern psychology, born in 1930, addresses our primal instincts. Astrology, which is over four thousand years old, has known about the animal impulses in us all along. Astrology contains the wisdom psychology seeks. Early psychiatrists labeled the voices of our psyche to understand the dynamics of human nature. Freud introduced three words to describe the human psyche: ego, id, and superego. These represent our outward personality, our emotions and primitive drives, and our moral compass. Astrology has addressed this for millennia.

Carl Jung knew this—the father of modern psychology was an astrologer! He always had his patients' charts in front of him during their sessions. Jung was quietly both a scientist and a visionary seeking mystical experiences. He secretly integrated both into his practice as a doctor, a psychiatrist, and as an astrologer.

Both Freud and Jung believed we are driven by the unconscious mind. Jung studied archetypes based on astrology that influence the unconscious mind. He described the sun sign as the ego, and the influence of the other planets as elements of the personality that orbit around the ego, just as the planets orbit around the sun.

He sought—as astrology does—to bring unconscious programs into consciousness through therapy. He wanted, as he once wrote, to "free [people] from the compulsive quality of the foundations of [their] own character." When our archetypical influences become visible in the clear light of consciousness, we heal.

3

The Observer and the Gremlins

I have loved the stars too truly to be fearful of the night.
—SARAH WILLIAMS, *Twilight Hours: A Legacy of Verse,* 1868

IF YOU CAN TAKE JUST one practical application from this entire book, let it be the awareness of your observer. Everyone has an observer waiting in the wings. I call it the thirteenth sign—the nameless one. The observer is objective and has the power to step off the stage of your life and show you truth without judgment. It is a neutral mirror, the unbiased reporter. The observer merely tells what is.

Gremlins, on the other hand, are the biased, critical, even mean voices in your head. They are anything but objective. The gremlins will criticize you all day long. If you burn the toast, the gremlins say: "You idiot! Can't you even make toast?" The observer simply reports: "The toast is burnt." No blame. No shame. No judgment. Just the facts. It has no opinion, and it is the secret to your healing.

Let's say you're a thrifty Taurus or a homebody Cancer or a social butterfly Gemini. The gremlins criticize you, calling you stingy or boring or shallow. The observer counters that voice by saying, "You're good at saving money, Taurus." "You stay home if you want to, Cancer." "Look how friendly you are, Gemini." That is how you shift from the negative voices to a reframe.

MEET YOUR OBSERVER

Without the observer, you are a victim to the whims of your ego and the drama therein. Because the observer is neutral—think of the observer as Switzerland—it can help you to remain calm when things go wrong. Human nature is so reactive! What the observer does is discharge and unplug the reactivity fueled by your ego and your emotional body.

What is it that keeps us from activating the observer? Gremlins. They know your weak spots, and they aim directly at your vulnerabilities. They point fingers, insisting fault.

Gremlins specialize in interrupting. They have no manners. They are a nuisance. Can you imagine if your default voice excluded gremlins and was filled with trust and wisdom? Sorry. That's not happening. Design fault! Even when you're at the most enlightened, heightened state of peace, without careful practice, gremlins, like termites, can eat away at the foundation of a healthy psyche. Here's the good news: the more experienced you are, the easier it is to turn on the observer.

Now that I have had years of practicing turning on my observer, when someone gets angry at me, my observer smiles and says, "Oh, look. A bit of reactivity." I remember when I first learned this concept. I was living in Vancouver and I had a landlord who got into an argument with me. Right in the middle of the escalating rant, my observer kicked in and I thought, "I don't want to fight with him. I'm never going to win." So I calmly let him go on, then I said with neutrality, "Let's talk about this later." This dispelled the charge and he stopped. We were able to resolve our problem in a calmer, less emotional way.

Imagine your kid is throwing a tantrum and you are just about to lose your temper. Turn on your observer. Step apart from the situation, see it objectively. "Wait a minute. I'm the adult. What am I doing, matching the mood of this kid? I have the ability to stay calm," says your observer.

Imagine fighting with your partner. You both get angrier and angrier, each trying to outdo the other. Turn on your observer and you see how the two of you are escalating the tension. Then you choose to go in the opposite direction. You become quiet, kind, and understanding. Your partner won't know what just happened.

Another example: someone cuts you off on the freeway. You want to swear or even tail the person so you can give them a piece of your mind. You turn on your observer, see what you are doing, and realize you are putting yourself and others in danger, so you slow down and let it go.

This is, to be clear, a very unnatural reaction for a human to take. It's completely, instinctually counterintuitive to calm yourself down when your emotional body is reactive. You have to work the observer like a muscle, and it will get stronger. Everything in us wants to say, "Fuck off!" When you turn on the observer, you realize this is just adding fuel to the fire. You are matching someone else's low frequency rather than taking the high road.

This is how wars and divorces can be sidestepped, simply with the calmness of curiosity and kindness.

FEEL YOUR EMOTIONS, THEN TURN THE OBSERVER ON

· · · · · · · · · · · · ·

Knowing how to turn on your observer changes your life. It assists you to step off the emotionally charged situation and see it neutrally. This isn't easy when you're having strong feelings. When you know you need your observer and you just can't seem to turn it on, try this:

1. Put your hands over your heart and ask yourself: "What am I feeling?" You may feel nothing because you have shut off completely, or you may feel moody, or you may feel something stronger like anger, misery, or irritation. Just stop, pause, and feel it. Take your time.

2. Put your awareness on and tag the feelings. Know that you are allowed and entitled as a human to stay in your emotions. Ask yourself if you are indulging. If so, fine. You are allowed to indulge. Just notice.

3. Just feel it, no matter how intense it is.

4. When you've indulged long enough (you'll know), say out loud, "Observer on."

5. Ask yourself: What am I teaching myself right now? What am I supposed to be learning? Why does this keep happening? When you can set the emotion aside and really entertain these questions, you know you've turned on your observer.

NOTE: There is no blame involved here. You are responsible for what you are teaching yourself. No blame allowed.

Spoiler alert: you can't just go straight to the spiritual without walking through the valley of your stories and your reactivity. You have to move through the pain body. The side effects of bypassing or avoiding the emotional body are the source of every war (and divorce). If you are often in conflict, it may be because you didn't know how to inquire, identify the emotion, and take a breath.

Here's a vivid example of how I learned this lesson. I was kayaking to the ocean from a lagoon where the water was calm when, all of a sudden, waves surged toward me because the ocean is higher than the lagoon. It was loud and scary. Everything in me wanted to say, "No! I'm turning back!"

I was taught that if you lean to the right or the left, you'll tip. If you start paddling faster and go straight into the wave, you'll get through. When the waves came at me, I got scared and turned back to the beach. Yet ahead was where the dolphins were! I really wanted to see the dolphins, so finally I forced myself to go straight into the wave to get to the other side and it worked. A real-life analogy: the only way through is through.

The moral of the story: If you lean, resist, or pull back, you'll miss the opportunity to see the dolphins. Don't turn away. Rumi said, "The crack is where the light gets in." To face your gremlins, to paddle straight into the wave, you have to face your fear. Want to know my definition of FEAR? Forgetting Everything's All Right.

Over time, I've learned how to turn on my observer. I recognize situations that used to make me want to argue (I have moon in Aries). Whether it's an airport employee or a server at a restaurant or someone in my family, now my observer kicks in and I just think, "I wonder what God was thinking when they created that person."

All reactive human impulses come from the ego. Here's a harsh truth: your ego has you by the short-and-curlies. Your emotions have you all riled up. Your mind makes it worse. You can't *not* react when someone screams at you, and if you think you're going to get so spiritual that you'll never get triggered again, I have bad news for you. You will get triggered again. You're going to get angry. Welcome to the human race.

Develop the muscles to stop—hello, observer! Own that you are triggered, realize that you are pissed that someone insulted you, and realize that your ego is in an uproar. Then you take a moment, take a breath, and it's in that breath that the observer comes on.

Don't be surprised if your friends and family don't know how to react to you when you turn on the observer. They may try to keep you in that familiar territory where your ego rules the roost. When you have the free will to say, "I'm not doing this conversation," it's empowering beyond measure.

It's not natural. It's not easy. As an astrologer, I guarantee you, you are absolutely addicted to your drama. We all are. To get you out of that position, stop letting your ego lead. It's really heavy lifting, at first, until you've built up those muscles. It's just like going to the gym. In the beginning, you don't want to go, and then your muscles get stronger and all of a sudden, you realize, "Wow, look at what I'm bench-pressing now!" In other words, "Wow, I don't get triggered as much!"

The observer really is the secret sauce. The observer poses the neutral question: "Is there a reason to fight with this person when you will lose and the other person will also lose?" It's logic at the highest level. Let it be known: the emotional body operates with neither logic nor objectivity.

The observer offers access to the soul. It is the Rosetta stone—the key to translating a secret language. It is your soul, brought to you by your rising sign. The soul is constantly seeking the high road. The ego does not know how to laugh at yourself and see your quirks as endearing. Self-deprecation and humor are direct results of the observer. You will know your observer is on when you can laugh at yourself. We are such funny little human creatures. In this book, my calling myself out as an emotional mush-push was exactly that: my observer making fun of my ego. And it made me laugh!

Your ego is stuck to you like glue. There's the design fault again. Who pays that guy who talks shit about you all the time? "What am I supposed to be learning? How do I accept the unacceptable personality traits I have?" These questions are waiting in your back pocket. Without a trained observer, the Aries may not realize she can't help being pushy, the Cancer doesn't know it's okay to want to stay home, the Sagittarius won't see that he is supposed to travel, the Capricorn may not recognize that she can't help working so hard. Your observer takes you out of the cycle of criticism into self-acceptance.

The enlightened masters know that at the highest level of consciousness, most of this illusion called life is just a movie. We do yoga, we take meditation classes, you're reading this book—all with the hope of getting to the voice of your observer. You can't bypass your humanness! You can't even bypass the gremlins. It's a well-worn pathway in your brain. (It's called the amygdala.) Yet when you say, "Observer on," it's like telling the gremlins, "You are not in charge." It's like you put the gremlins (the mind) in a seat where they must be quiet for a time-out.

HOW TO TRAIN YOUR OBSERVER MUSCLES

. . . .

Turning on the observer when things get hard is an art form. At a time when you are feeling neutral (not upset, anxious, angry, or feeling any strong emotions), sit in a comfortable position and imagine that you have a camera pointing at you on your right side with a view of your profile.

Now, take the camera to your left side, looking at your profile from the other side.

Next, point the camera directly in front of you, as if you were going to take a selfie.

Then, point the camera at the back of your head. Notice what you are wearing.

After doing this, notice the shift in energy. Once the observer is on, practice this over and over again. It will get easier to see yourself, without judgment, from a higher perspective. Imagine you are seeing through the eyes of love or an angel, looking at your human nature. "Aren't these humans so interesting?"

The next time you get in an argument with your partner who just pissed you off *again*, turn the observer on. Say it out loud, like a commander: "Observer on." Here comes the free will button. "I'm so sorry, I got triggered. Can we take a breath?"

Can you imagine how many wars would be stopped if we all knew this technology?

(PS: Don't turn your observer on during the make-up sex! You never need your observer when making love.)

"WHY AM I HERE?" "WHERE IS MY LOVE?"

If there is one question I hear more than any other in my practice, it's "Why am I here?" second only to "Am I going to find love soon?" Let me tell you something, psychotherapist to reader: whatever you're doing, you're doing better than you think, and you're way further along your path than you know—or you wouldn't be reading this book.

Your soul is stalking you to fulfill your destiny. That's the pressure you are living with. It's so hard for most people to get over the thought that they're not doing what they came here to do. They're not with the right partner. They're not in the right job. It's an epidemic. A disease of discontent. One way to begin exploring your soul is to look to your rising sign.

Let me give you an example. A certified astrologer who fulfilled a rigorous training with me began with an earnest sincerity to be excellent at her job. She completed all levels at my school, then sat through fifty of the advanced classes I teach. Her soul demanded that she work harder than everyone else (Capricorn rising). All that time, she was looking over her shoulder, questioning if she was getting it right. As time went by, she received the highest scores from client feedback sheets. When I told her what a great job she was doing, she said, "I don't think so. There's so much more for me to learn."

I said, "Excuse me, Capricorn rising. Who sat through fifty advanced classes? Who does readings all day long? Who does constant research? When are you going to get that you are there?"

She shook her head and said, "I don't know. I'm not there yet."

That's when I realized her observer wasn't on. I encouraged her to reframe her ambition as a gift rather than a curse. Is it working? You'll have to ask her.

She was on the low road of Capricorn rising.

THE HIGH ROAD AND THE LOW ROAD

· · · · · · · · · · · · ·

Announcement: each sign has a high road and a low road. The high road is your higher self, and the low road is your gremlin's voice. The low road of Taurus is laziness. The low road of Capricorn is arrogance. The low road of Libra is codependence. The low road of Virgo is obsessive-compulsive disorder. The low road of Cancer is hypochondria. The low road of Aries is rage. You get the idea.

The high road of Leo is embodying great talent as a performer. The high road of Scorpio is helping others find their way out of darkness, as a therapist might do. The high road of Pisces is to be a creative genius. The high road of Gemini is brilliance in communication. The high road of Sagittarius is collecting wisdom and sharing it with others. The high road of Aquarius is to change the world through activism.

Ultimately, your high road leads you to your soul's desires.

A good friend of mine who is both a Buddhist and a student was sitting on a long flight to Europe. The woman next to him was telling him her story. She had just been divorced because her husband was having an affair. Her two girls and she were moving out, with so much resentment toward her husband. She was completely distraught that her husband had betrayed her.

My friend turned to her and said, "I'm going to take a sleeping pill. Before I do, I'm going to say this to you. Was it a good marriage?"

She said, "No."

He said, "Were you fighting all the time?"

"Yes."

He said, "How about you think about it like this. He has liberated you to find your life. He loved you enough to let you out of this marriage. The only way he could guarantee the nail in the coffin was to do something unforgivable. I want you to go tell your daughters that." Then he took his sleeping pill and fell asleep.

When he woke up later, she was staring at him, waiting for him to wake up. She said, "I just finished writing letters to both my daughters. You changed my life. Thank you so much! You're so right. I'm liberated. I didn't want to be with him anyway."

He stood in as her observer, allowing her to see that it was love that created the drama. Her marriage wasn't undermined because someone was out to get her. That slight adjustment gave her the gift to free her daughters from cursing their father, and allowed her to step away from the battle that was about to ensue. Gremlins neutralized.

We won't all meet our observer on a flight who can help us to see clearly. Still, we all have access to our observer with this practice I'm suggesting. In the meantime, I want you to write these things down right now:

I'm on schedule.

I'm doing the best I can.

Life has my back.

I am being supported.

To begin with, it's okay to lie to yourself. Even if you don't believe it (at first), just write it. Say it out loud. Repeat the words. Let astrology help you realize, if nothing else, that you are an embodied, spiritual human being. You are a member of what I call the lucky sperm club. The fact that you are even here, considering the number of sperm that wanted to incarnate and didn't make it, means you are incredibly lucky to have this life, this body, and your "stupid story" (everyone has a stupid story—that's the human condition).

I'm on schedule. I'm doing the best I can. Life has my back. I am being supported. I am in the process of learning exactly what I came here to learn. Just repeat it like a broken record, and be prepared for a miracle.

4

How Astrology Works

ELEMENTS, MODES, SIGNS

Normality is to be different. Every person is a different person. And one day you need to be aware of your difference. Aware that you are not the same as the others. That is to be normal.

—ALEJANDRO JODOROWSKY

THIS ISN'T A BOOK ABOUT teaching you to be fully versed in astrology (I have a school for that). This is a book about your soul, your observer, and the tools to access your true self. For that purpose, there is a language to learn. In the next few chapters, I will introduce you to the language required to understand the essential ingredients of your chart: the elements, modes, signs, planets, and houses. Astrology is the science of human nature distinctions. You'll soon see why your sun sign is never enough to fully describe you.

That being said, understand that these chapters contain superficial explanations of highly complex phenomena. This is not an astrology course. This is more like a glossary of terms, so when you get to part 2, you will know what I'm talking about enough to understand how the information applies to you.

GENERATE YOUR BIRTH CHART

The first step is to execute your chart. To do this, go to Astro.com and click on "Charts & Calculations," then "Chart drawing, Ascendant." Enter your birthdate, your place of birth, and the time you were born (if you don't know your birth time, use 12:00 p.m.). Here is an example of a birth chart:

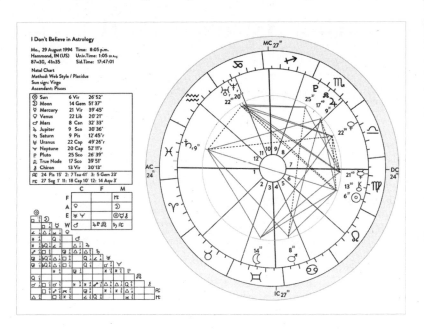

As you can see, a birth chart (also called a natal chart) looks like a pie with twelve pieces. This appears with Egyptian hieroglyphic symbols indicating where the planets were at your birth. Based on astronomy, this chart is executed with mathematic, predictable formulas that determine where each planet was at the moment of your birth. For some of you, this may be the first astrological chart you've ever seen.

That circle is a snapshot of the sky at the moment of your birth. Imagine your mother at the center of the circle, giving birth to you and looking up at the sky. The planets at the top of the chart were visible, and the planets below the center were not. Most important, whatever was at the eastern horizon establishes your rising sign. Grab a pen and write down your sun, moon, AC (rising sign), Mercury, Saturn, north node, and MC (midheaven).

THE FOUR ELEMENTS

The four elements are the foundation to all astrology. Knowing these is the simplest beginner's entrance to understanding personality types. I've written an entire book with no astrology in it, just based on the elements, called *The Missing Element.*

Each sign has its own element. The elements are the cheat sheet to astrology. Because there are twelve signs and four elements, there are three signs in each element:

★ **WATER:** Cancer, Scorpio, Pisces
★ **AIR:** Gemini, Libra, Aquarius
★ **EARTH:** Taurus, Virgo, Capricorn
★ **FIRE:** Aries, Leo, Sagittarius

Let's begin in water. We spend nine months in utero in the water element, allowing destiny, karma, genetics, your very body type, hair color, eye color—all to be determined by the mystery (Pisces) of water. It's the most abstract, nonlinear element. This is the element of the ultimate mystery of how you got your bloodline, what your psychology will be like, and what your gifts and curses are. In other words, "Why me?"

Think about water as the entrance of the day, just as it is the entrance of life. We begin every day by going to the bathroom, taking a shower, having a cup of tea, washing our face, brushing our teeth. That's the water cycle. This is a universal human doorway.

Welcome to the human race. We all have a mother (Cancer). We never speak of this, but we all arrived through an orgasm—at least one person had to have one (Scorpio). We all have a family of origin, whether we know them or not. This is essential for existence.

Water is the predominant element on planet Earth. This planet should be called Water. It's blue. In astrology, water is the element that is poetic, mystical, and loves the quiet (Pisces). It describes a personality type that has feelings, is intuitive, and is fascinated by all things magic. It's a spiritual element that includes the conversation about what is God, why am I here, and how do I explain what happens after death? Think mystery and awesomeness.

When a baby is born, it takes its first breath. Welcome, air. The energies of the stars are imprinted with our very own astrological chart. We are anointed with a name, we hear our first words, the sound of our mother's voice, and we begin consciousness.

Air is the element of the curious mind as it becomes acquainted with this reality. Air is filled with the desire to understand and learn (Gemini). When we enter school, we learn how to spell, read, write, use our minds, socialize, and get along with others (Libra). School can last anywhere from fourteen to twenty-five years. At worst, unexamined thoughts and assumptions about what reality is make for an "airhead" who follows societal dictates without questioning in the name of conformity and approval (Libra). At best, this is the inquisitive mind who carves out their individuality, researches and studies greater minds of the past, and cultivates advanced technologies and new societal values that will progress and evolve our species (Aquarius).

After schooling, we enter adulthood which includes practicality and "earthing"—our ability to manifest as productive citizens, seeking security and safety (Taurus). We start our career, and are now responsible for the realm of money, security, work, and time. So is birthed the desire to be perfect and to get it right (Virgo). Your job is to become grown-up, financially responsible, and to show your worth through your contribution to the world (Capricorn). It's common for earth personalities to feel like they have never done enough, to carry a feeling of inadequacy. And to judge themselves and others as either successes or failures.

If you are successful, in the last era of your life you have the gift of freedom to celebrate and enjoy your creation. This is the fire cycle. It's the zealot who's in love with life and shares their joy (Aries). During the fire cycle of older age, we become the teachers, pass on our wisdom, and participate in all that life has to offer (Sagittarius). You have your hobbies, grandkids come over, and you relish your progeny and the creation of your family line by loving your family the most (Leo). You celebrate—of course in reality, it doesn't always go that way. Even so, we have the option to embody the spirit of the fire cycle—even if we aren't actually free to do whatever we want.

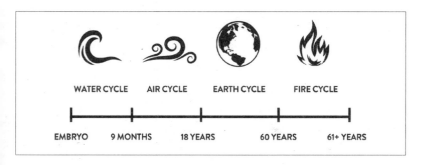

AIR AND FIRE, WATER AND EARTH

· · · · · · · · · · · ·

There is something in astrology called compatibility. It occurs as a dance between the elements. For example, air and fire get along well together. If you've ever blown on kindling to get a fire started, you know that when you add air to fire, the fire grows.

Similarly, water and earth get along well together. When

you put water on earth, earth flourishes with blossoms and fruit.

Mix up these pairs, however, and often, conflict occurs. Water squelches fire. Air disrupts earth. Study the elements of your most personal planets (sun, moon, rising, and Mercury). With complementary elements, you will feel harmonious. Conflicting elements cause confusion and discomfort. There is no right or wrong combination. These are all just karmic patterns put in place by your destiny.

THE MODES: FIXED, CARDINAL, MUTABLE

Each sign identifies with a mode: cardinal, fixed, and mutable. These categories distinguish yet another range of personality types. Each mode contains one sign from each element.

★ **Cardinal signs** are Aries, Cancer, Libra, and Capricorn. These people cannot follow. They are the leaders. They will not work for someone else. They are the starters who stand in the front saying, "Follow me!" The design fault for cardinal signs is they may be accused of being bossy, directive, and not good at taking instruction from people they don't respect.

★ **Mutable signs** are Gemini, Virgo, Sagittarius, and Pisces. Multitasking geniuses, they do many things at the same time, and yet suffer from thinking themselves wrong because they don't have sustained focus. Gifted with the ability to change on a dime, this can be misinterpreted as being fickle or noncommittal. Their design fault is a judgment that they cannot follow through or decide what they want. They judge themselves and suffer from a feeling of indecisiveness.

★ **Fixed signs** are Taurus, Leo, Scorpio, and Aquarius. A strong internal sense of groundedness, stability, and liability, they are not easily moved or persuaded. In their own minds, they think of themselves as prone to being stuck. In truth, they are stable and comforting to others, but not to themselves. Their design fault is that they feel like they never do enough, or think something is wrong with them because they are unable to be flexible and change easily.

THE TWELVE SIGNS

Here is a rundown of the dates associated with the sun signs, along with each sign's element, mode, and basic qualities, plus a body part—notice how these start at the top, with Aries ruling the head, and end at the bottom, with Pisces ruling the feet.

(Note that every four years misses a day because of leap year, so this chart is not always accurate—you have to look up what the dates are in the year you were born to be certain.)

SIGN	DATES	ELEMENT/ MODE	QUALITIES	BODY PART
Aries	March 21– April 19	Fire/Cardinal	Independent, assertive, willful	Head
Taurus	April 20– May 20	Earth/Fixed	Loyal, thrifty, grounded	Throat
Gemini	May 21– June 20	Air/Mutable	Social, curious, distractible	Arms
Cancer	June 21– July 22	Water/Cardinal	Intuitive, nostalgic, homebody	Stomach
Leo	July 23– August 22	Fire/Fixed	Passionate, talented, performer	Heart/ back
Virgo	August 23–September 22	Earth/Mutable	Attractive, organized, perfectionist	Colon
Libra	September 23– October 22	Air/Cardinal	Romantic, arty, mediator	Kidneys
Scorpio	October 23–November 21	Water/Fixed	Edgy, introverted, intense	Genitals
Sagittarius	November 22–December 21	Fire/Mutable	Adventurous, optimistic, inspiring	Thighs
Capricorn	December 22–January 9	Earth/Cardinal	Ambitious, traditional, clever	Knees
Aquarius	January 20–February 18	Air/Fixed	Eccentric, intellectual, futurist	Ankles
Pisces	February 19–March 20	Water/Mutable	Empathetic, dreamy, avoidant	Feet

THE TAROT CARD/ASTROLOGY CONNECTION

. . . .

I have studied the tarot at great length and fallen in love with the philosophy and the inherent message that comes with this magical resource. George Bernard said if he were ever to be stranded on a deserted island, the two books he would want would be the Bible and a tarot deck. The tarot deck is the complete story of human evolution. Are you ready for this next part?

The major arcana has twenty-two cards. In the fifteenth century, astrologers reserved a card for each of the twelve signs, and each of the ten planets. The funny thing is, at that time they only knew about seven planets. We didn't find Uranus until 1780, Neptune until 1890, and Pluto until 1930. Somehow, they knew enough in the fifteenth century to reserve three cards for the planets that hadn't been discovered yet! It's so remarkable. All we see with the human eye is as far out as Jupiter. We cannot see Uranus, Neptune, or Pluto. And yet, a card was left for each of them.

Yes. I am suggesting that the tarot deck was created with the foreknowledge that there would be twelve signs and ten planets. There is great value in studying those twenty-two cards. Any mystic will tell you the tarot is an ancient resource that must not be overlooked.

The tarot cards tell the story of human evolution, from the first card, the Fool, to the last card, the World. We begin with an act of folly—the fool, jumping off a cliff—and end with the world, which implies that everything you're going through is an echo chamber for all of humanity and your healing is the healing of all of us. This is why the cards are written. The tarot deck is a treasure of wisdom brought to us from time past, not unlike astrology, that deserves your attention. However, this book is not about the tarot, so let's carry on.

5

The Planets

By looking upward, I see downward.
　　　　　　　—Tycho Brahe, sixteenth-century astronomer

THERE ARE THREE PRIMARY INGREDIENTS in astrology: the planets, the signs, and the houses. Think of the planet as "what," the sign as "how," the house as "where." Like peanut butter, jelly, and bread, you need all three to hold the sandwich together. These three ingredients influence your chart.

Let's start with the first ingredient of the recipe: the planets.

Imagine a council of ten characters inside your head. Think of them as ten board members running your company. Each has a unique voice. They talk about different arenas in your life—your style, your feelings, your life lessons, your goals, and more:

★ The sun is your ego and life-force.
★ The moon is your emotions and internal world.
★ Mercury is your thought process and how you communicate.
★ Venus is love, and the parts of life you value and find delicious.

★ Mars is male energy and will.

★ Jupiter is fun, describing your joy and favorite things to do.

★ Saturn is the teacher of your life lessons, the disciplinarian, and karma.

★ Uranus is rebellion, weirdness, and genius.

★ Neptune is the dreamer and the inner mystic.

★ Pluto is power and passion.

Let's make a distinction. Having a Libra sun is different from having your moon in Libra or Mercury in Libra. Knowing the nature of each planet distinguishes their effects.

CONJUNCTIONS AND THE COMPLEXITY OF ASTROLOGY

Before I jump in, I want to be sure you understand that this chapter presents a superficial version of the planets. Don't make the mistake of thinking that this is the whole picture. Astrology is far more complex than just the sun sign or one planet at a time. This is another reason why your sun sign may not describe you.

For example, if two or more planets are very close together, we call that a conjunction. It's as if they are holding hands and working as one. Look at your chart and find your sun. It appears as a circle with a dot. Is there another planet standing next to it, within ten degrees? It's highly likely that Mercury is nearby because it always travels one sign in front, in the same sign, or one sign behind the sun. The sun and Mercury always travel together. The sun is your ego and Mercury is your mind, constantly in service to your ego. In fact, they are best friends.

Other planets may be close to your sun, which creates a significant influence. For example, if Pluto were in the same sign as your sun sign, which only happens once a year for ten days, Pluto will have a larger influence on your character than even your sun sign. No one ever tells you this. In traditional astrology, it's undervalued, but as a therapist, I believe it is a central figure in your character's development and expression. There is only one day in a year when Pluto and the sun are at the same degree. The talented and fascinating India Arie is a Libra with Pluto conjunct to her sun, at the exact degree. She is surely a Plutonian personality—powerful, steady, and hugely influential as an artist. Her presence onstage shifts the energy of the audience and the room; she is no ordinary performer.

Astrology is a complex puzzle. You can't isolate one piece to describe your entire personality and/or destiny. In India's case, this one piece of the puzzle certainly is a major influence. However, all ingredients have to be considered, or we end up doing cheap astrology. After almost five decades, I am not interested in cheap astrology.

You can't direct a symphony without studying music for years. All this to say that if you want a profound reading that has the power to change your life, go see a professional, seasoned astrologer. This is where astrology goes from superficial to profound. I have certified astrologers on my website; they have been rigorously trained. On second thought: come study with us! (See page 281.) Teaching you every aspect of astrology is beyond the scope of this book. Just know the sky's the limit, and this science is as old as the mountains. Getting the greatest impact from astrology requires some serious study.

SUN: YOUR LIFE-FORCE

Astrology does not prioritize the sun sign randomly. The sun is the primary influence in our lives, and everyone who has flirted with astrology knows their sun sign. Even my grandmother knew she was a Gemini.

Life centers around that giant fire. Without the sun, we don't exist. We dress in obedience to the seasons and the weather. Will you wear a coat or not? Bring an umbrella or not? Every single plant on Earth turns toward the sun. Without the sun, this entire reality would *poof*—disappear.

Your sun sign is the centerpiece of your character: the outward expression of your ego, the way you appear in the world. This is your instinctual, knee-jerk reaction. If your sun is in a water sign, you can't help but be sensitive. If you are an air sign, you can't help but be cerebral, a communicator, and a thinker. Earth signs are grounded and practical by nature, whether they want to be or not. Those with their suns in a fire sign are passionate, energetic, and loud. These are all generalizations. We just finished saying there is so much more, but stay with me.

The sun sign is consistent, easily identified, and predictable. If you were a company, the sun would be chairperson of the board, standing at the head of the table, setting the tone and running the show. The sun brings light and warmth, energy and radiance. Your chairperson needs attention and affirmation, praise and appreciation. Without it, your self-esteem goes out the window. The chairperson in your company, better known as the sun, will determine whether your company will grow and flourish or shrivel and shrink.

Every sign is ruled by a planet (or a star or a moon), and the sun rules Leo.

IN EVERY SUN SIGN IS ITS OPPOSITE

• • • • • • • • • • • •

Everything in this universe has an opposite—yin and yang, male and female, sun and moon, dark and light. No one ever tells you that within every sun sign is a shade of its opposite sign. For instance, if you are an Aquarius, you have a little Leo in you—a scientist at heart who secretly loves to sing. If you are a Gemini, you have a little Sagittarius in you—a friendly, talkative information junkie who secretly wants to run away from home and travel the world. If you are a Libra, you have a little Aries in you—a romantic at heart with a fiery temper. Just think how true it is for you and the people you know. (To see the opposite of your sign, consult the circular chart on page 44.)

MOON: YOUR EMOTIONS AND INSTINCTS

The moon comes up at night—therefore, it deals with our internal world, the part of us that is feminine, emotional, psychic, and intuitive. The moon influences the unconscious mind that reveals itself in the dreamtime. A well-trained dream interpreter uses the language of the moon, which can appear nonsensical, as a resource and messenger. I can guarantee you that dream analysis therapists often have a strong moon/water influence in their charts. (Hello, all of you Jungians!)

The *Farmer's Almanac* determines when to plant flowers, when the tide will come in and out. That data is based on the moon's cycles. The moon is the fastest moving "planet" in our solar system, which explains how a moody personality can change for no apparent reason. Humans are mostly water. Water never stops moving.

You cannot stop a mood with just a thought. You cannot say to someone having an intense emotional response, "Stop feeling." You have to wait for them to dry out. Moods don't change in response to logic. At worst, the moon's influence can show up as a depressive personality.

I look to your moon to determine your emotional body's response patterns. I always tell people, when you think of where your moon is, it will be determined by your response if I pushed you up against the wall. If your moon is in water, you will go quiet, maybe withdraw completely. If your moon is in an air sign, you will go up in your head and logically try to explain your feelings. An earth sign becomes practical: "Hold on, hold on, let's figure out how to solve this problem, we need results," disregarding the emotional experience. A fire sign gets pissed off—the emotional body instantly escalates into drama and anger.

The moon on your board of directors sits quietly in the corner, tracking everyone's emotions: "Uh-oh, I feel a change in the energy and I don't like where this is going." She probably pulled a divination card before the meeting started and sensed a problem about the meeting to begin with. She happily offers people water or coffee. She is maternal, carrying a package of Kleenex and essential oils in her bag.

The high road of the moon's expression is emotional wisdom. She's trustworthy, intuitive, knowledgeable about seasons and cycles; believes in astrology; and is in sync with the lunar cycles. The low road is moodiness, being swamped by sensitivity, and suffering from insomnia. "I'm nervous, I'm scared, I can't sleep, I think something's wrong. I wonder if I have an emotional disorder." The moon rules the sign of Cancer.

MERCURY: THE LIGHT OF YOUR MIND

Mercury represents the mind and its facility to work (or not). The mind is slippery. Think of a winged messenger, as in Greek mythology—the one that flies around at the speed of light. Mercury influences messages and communication devices. Mercury presents like a wild pack of monkeys jumping in the trees. Like Pac-Man, the mind is always hungry.

In the boardroom, Mercury stands at the front of the room, right next to the chairperson. Mercury has prepared a PowerPoint presenting the agenda, is carrying a device to record the meeting, and is making sure everyone is in attendance. He says everyone's name out loud.

Constantly asking questions, collecting information, Mercury says, "Just to make it clear, can you repeat what you just said, and then I'll say it back to you?" Then he turns to the secretary and says: "Write this down!"

At best, he's well-spoken and organized. The low road is being unprepared because he moves too quickly. He cannot make decisions so he asks everyone's opinion and gets distracted. Mercury rules both Gemini and Virgo.

MERCURY RETROGRADE

· · · · · · · · · · · · ·

People make faces and say, "Oh no! Mercury's in retrograde!" Such a fuss! Too much gets blamed on a planet. Mercury in retrograde is not bad. When Mercury is in retrograde, meaning it seems to move backward in relation to the spin of the Earth, it's an opportunity to do exactly what Mercury is doing: go backward. Time to review. Did you forget to follow through? Think about all the "re-" words: review, revisit, reconsider, return.

I purchased a house during Mercury retrograde. I admit I was a little concerned, as every astrologer screams, "Don't do it!" It's hard to say to your lender, "Let's wait three weeks because, you know, Mercury." When timing is of the essence, when life presents an opportunity, you may have to act. I was careful about the paperwork, going back over it a few times. The funny part is, I sold that house two years later for a great profit. Surprise, nothing bad happened!

Mercury retrograde doesn't insist that you're going to get it all wrong. It invites you to be meticulous and conscientious. People say technology often seems to fail during Mercury retrograde. Could this be a sign to pause and check your work? The simple message of Mercury retrograde is stay awake and aware.

VENUS: BEAUTY AND LOVE

Venus rules your taste buds, what tickles your fancy, and your best, most favorite things. It's about love affairs and the delicious parts of life. Venus is sweetness, beauty, and artistry. Money, food, values, and security all come under her domain. She is about soft sheets, good smells, and sweet kindness. Distinct from masculine Mars energy, Venus traditionally represents feminine energy.

Venus is the HR director for the company. She breezes into the boardroom dressed to the nines, looks around, and notices that no one arranged lunch. With Mercury's help, she gets a list of everyone's orders and comments that they certainly could have booked a nicer, five-star hotel for the board meeting. She has ideas about how to do it better next time. She truly wants to hear how everyone is doing. Before she arrived, she looked over the values of the company because she wanted to know: Does it have enough heart? Is the company operating from an ethical framework? Do the employees love their jobs? Are they each in their area of expertise? Venus wants to make it all right for everyone.

The high road of Venus is to have solid, harmonious relationships and true caring. The low road of Venus is to live with disharmony, to be gossipy and judgmental, and to be vain—to never pass up a mirror.

Venus rules Taurus and Libra.

MARS: POWER AND ENERGY

Mars, the red planet, rules warriors. Mars addresses your ability to apply your personal power, to be fearlessly direct, and comfortably assertive. The position of Mars describes how you are going to use male energy, physical prowess, and athletic ability. It's the get-up-and-go planet.

Mars walks into the meeting with boots on, looking like Superman. He's ready to take over. He wants to focus the group energy and be direct by getting straight to the point. He might have a gavel to slam on the table, demanding everyone's attention. "Order in the boardroom!" says Mars, "And do it quick!" There is nothing vague about this energy—it is goal-oriented, always on task, and imbued with life.

The high road of this energy is to seek efficiency and clear direction. High-road Mars easily gets things done. The low road is to be overly dramatic, insensitive, harsh, and arrogant, while disregarding other people's feelings. This can be an interrupter who may be unaware that they are being obnoxious. Mars rules Aries.

OUTER PLANETS

. . . .

One of the single most influential indicators of a personality trait that stays with an individual for their entire lifetime is when an outer planet is standing next to the sun. By outer planet, I mean Jupiter, Uranus, Neptune, and Pluto. Most people don't have an outer planet next to their sun. It's the exception to the rule. Don't be upset if you don't have this. However, if you do, it is a signature that describes a person's uniqueness throughout their entire lives.

In our school, we spend elaborate time unpacking this. Just take a look at your chart to see if any outer planet is standing next to the circle with the dot (the symbol for the sun).

You may notice some personal planets next to the sun. Don't worry about that. Venus and Mars often travel with the sun, which is also not relevant. What really matters is those planets that stay in the same sign for a year or more. When the sun hits that particular planet, there is a vivid, specific distinction that will help to explain why you are the way you are. Please take the time to look at your chart. It's a determining factor to understanding someone at the deepest level.

JUPITER: FUN AND FAVORITES

Jupiter is so huge that 1,300 planet Earths could fit inside, and according to the latest count, Jupiter has ninety-two moons. It's no surprise that Jupiter is the planet of all things large. I describe Jupiter as a big, jolly Santa Claus—round and fat, giving gifts and eating too much, shouting, "Ho, ho, ho!" Jupiter loves to spend money, play, and travel. If Jupiter is in a favorable position in your chart, you have really scored in your lifetime. It means you were born under a lucky star. What gets you excited, what are the things you effortlessly love? Jupiter knows God loves you. Experience this life fully!

In the company meeting, Jupiter is the one who gets everyone excited for the company retreat or the holiday party. They motivate and inspire. They tell jokes and make everyone laugh—the class clown of the boardroom.

High-road Jupiter can be quite funny. One-liners are their specialty. The low road of a Jupiterian personality is to be indulgent, overly opinionated, self-righteous, or to subscribe to a narrow belief system, such as thinking only your religion can provide salvation and everyone else is going to hell. Jupiter rules Sagittarius.

SATURN: THE TASKMASTER

Serious Saturn arrives right on time, always carrying a watch and a slightly displeased expression. This planet is referred to as the old man of the zodiac, who determines what you must do to fulfill your purpose and keep your promise to your soul.

Saturn upholds rules of conduct. If you don't follow through, there will be consequences. You might argue. It won't do any good. Saturn is ruthless and unforgiving. This is the realm of facts, societal expectations, all things solid and weighty—Saturn rules mountains, buildings, and teeth. It is the realm of rules, regulations, and law. Try getting a driver's license without your ID. Out of the question! That's Saturn in full force.

Difficult and stern Saturn constantly questions you: What are you doing with your time? Why did you come to this planet? What is your purpose? Are you on task? Are you following instructions or avoiding your destiny? At worst, Saturn is about hardship and karma—if you don't follow the rules, failure is the consequence. Saturn tests your mettle. How strong are you? Do you have a backbone? And did you pay your taxes?

I spend a lot of time encouraging students and clients to pay attention to this influence. To me, it is the most important influence in the zodiac. Our school focuses strongly on studying the element, the sign, and the house your Saturn is in.

Saturn is the COO, the organizer who comes into the meeting wearing a suit and holding a briefcase. Taking over the meeting, Saturn says, "We have goals to meet. We have a timeline. We have an agenda. We have deliverables." Saturn kicks ass and takes names. "Show me the progress report, the comps, and the projections."

The high road of Saturn echoes Nike's phrase: just do it. Have discipline, be accountable, be responsible, and always be on time. High-road Saturn is honorable and offers recognition where recognition is due. As the COO, Saturn says, "This company is doing really well. Projections are on target. We're on schedule. Good work, everyone!"

The low road of Saturn is judgmental, crotchety—the grumpy grandparent who thinks nobody and nothing is ever good enough. Even when it's your best effort, low-road Saturn says you could have done so much better.

When you accept Saturn's lessons, your company will be successful, your profit margin increases, and public acclaim is yours. You'll get more esoteric information about Saturn in chapter 7.

Saturn rules Capricorn.

URANUS: YOUR ECCENTRIC SIDE

Uranus influences uniqueness, eccentricity, and astrology because you have to be willing to think outside the box to believe in astrology. Uranus is definitely outside the box. Uranus was discovered during the French Revolution, when the bourgeoisie suddenly got sick of being poor and went off to completely dismantle the wealthy. The French Revolution was radical, and heads were flying. Around the same time, shiploads of disenfranchised people arrived to find a new land. A group of them got together and said, "Hey, we have some new ideas! Freedom of speech! Freedom of religion! Anybody can live here! Forget about the king!" They threw the tea in the harbor and started a revolution. A country was born.

Another paradigm-shifting change that happened around when Uranus was discovered was the harnessing of electricity. Uranus influences surprise and electric shocks. It's the unknown factor you didn't see coming. Uranus rules intuition—for example, knowing when the phone is going to ring or getting flashes of the future. You think of someone, and suddenly they arrive at your door. That's the Uranian influence.

Uranus rules rebelliousness and nonconformity. When Uranus influences you, you cannot follow. It wouldn't surprise me if you wanted to be an astrologer. You take the road less traveled. No following the leader. You're too busy changing the world! Perhaps you wonder what's wrong with you. This personality type feels very separate from mainstream humanity.

Uranus walks into the meeting wearing unmatching clothes, sporting tattoos and unusual hair (think Einstein). Standing on their head, a

Uranian sees things from a completely different perspective, which can open up minds to new possibilities. I have Uranus at the top of my chart (this is called the midheaven, which describes your professional life). Correspondingly, I have a crazy career. I'm not a normal astrologer and I'm not a normal psychotherapist. I break the rules in both categories. I've always been a rebel, professionally. For a long time, I felt separate until I realized it was the influence of Uranus—and an asset to being a trailblazer.

The low road of Uranus is to live in the future without concern about bringing anyone along. They have a high-strung nervous system. These are rebels without a cause who have the impulse to be contrary. They reject all things "normal" just to be different. Anxiety, nervous system disorders, and ADHD go hand in hand with low-road Uranian energy. They shake their foot under the table, can't stop moving, and can't find calm.

High-road Uranus is fascinated with technology and new innovative ideas that support a kinder version of humanity. A nontraditional leader who sits in a circle instead of standing at the head of the class, they don't want to control. They want to share the leadership role so as not to continue the old hierarchy. You can witness high-road Uranus in humanitarians, team players, and philanthropists doing their best work.

Uranus rules Aquarius.

YOUR MIDHEAVEN AND YOUR CAREER

. . . .

The midheaven is at the very top of your chart, marked "MC." Identify the sign on the top of the chart and ask yourself if that flavor/sign shows up in your career. For example, in addition to having Uranus at the top of my chart, I have Cancer on the midheaven. Cancer is the sign of the mother and of nurturing. I'm the quintessential Jewish mother with my clients. Every session, I try to figure out how to soothe and offer comfort. The flavor of your midheaven describes your highest calling in your work.

NEPTUNE: YOUR OTHERWORLDLY SIDE

Neptune was discovered at the turn of the century, in the 1890s, when anesthetic was invented. When you are under, where do you go? Who knows! Anesthesia dulls out whatever part of your brain registers pain, yet nobody can completely explain how it works. That's so Neptune—explaining the unexplainable.

Neptune influences altered states, being out of body, and all things otherworldly that allow you to take a break from the mundane world: classical music, fine art, ballet—all the high arts. It also rules alcohol, marijuana, and drugs—the means to escape this world. Having this strong influence explains a high sensitivity to that which we cannot see: the invisible realm, mediumship, dead people, and other dimensions, including the new lingo for that: the multiverse.

Neptunians pick up other people's energy and are affected by subtle smells and sounds. Think crystals, or incense and candles in a temple or a church. Every New Age bookstore that has champa burning displays a Neptunian influence.

In the boardroom, Neptune is the creative director. These are the people who create fantasy worlds beyond most people's imaginations. Neptune energy is behind movies. Think about it: you watch a movie called *The Wizard of Oz*. You meet Dorothy and her friends, and you feel like these characters are real. You worry about Toto. You marvel at how the horse changes colors. You hold your breath as the witch melts. You've been captured. Willingly, you suspend reality, and off you go to another world. Take off your seat belt—you're in Neptune land! When you come back down with a thump to the dense physical plane, you never feel quite as comfortable as you did in the diffuse dreamworld. The lights come on and you think, "Did that even happen?"

The high road of Neptune is a visionary/seer who loves to create through any and all art forms. Neptune inspires the extremely gifted artist or filmmaker who can create visually stunning scenes, or the musician who elicits emotional reactions without words. This personality type is a connoisseur of life.

The low road of Neptune is confusion, illusion, and ambivalence. They may be without ambition, overly indulgent, addicted, or lost in space. Low-road Neptune doesn't like this reality; they just want to be high all the time. At worst, they like to stay in their bedrooms, can be paranoid, and are escape artists.

Neptune rules Pisces.

PLUTO: YOUR UNCONSCIOUS MIND

Now for our last planet, and don't you dare say it's not a planet! A hundred astronomers tried to demote Pluto. Why? Because Pluto rules the human shadow, the land of the gremlins. Human nature avoids the shadow. As a collective, we fear it. Therefore, there was an attempt to deny Pluto's status. Pluto will not be denied.

Pluto is so far away that scientists only viewed it for the first time in 1930 at Lowell Observatory in Flagstaff, Arizona. Originally, they detected Pluto by its electromagnetic field alone. They knew something was there even though they couldn't see it, which I find amusing and a perfect metaphor for Plutonian energy. We may not be able to see Pluto. Even so, it wields significant influence.

Pluto represents the power of the unconscious mind, discovered during a time when Hitler, Freud, and Einstein were all dealing with invisible forces. We never had a word for the unconscious mind until Freud coined the term in the 1930s. He introduced us to this notion that there is something invisible that can make or break our psyches. Hitler captured a continent by manipulating the dark side of human nature. Einstein figured out that the smallest particle that could not be seen by the human eye could destroy or create via nuclear power. These are all in the realm of invisible worlds. For better or for worse, Pluto lives in the dark.

Imagine Pluto as an Italian director who comes into the room wearing dark sunglasses, his shirt unbuttoned revealing a hairy chest, wearing a gold medallion. He sits there and doesn't talk. He's a little scary, a little attractive, and completely intense. What's he doing in the company boardroom? Nobody knows, and everybody is afraid to ask. Maybe he's a silent partner.

Plutonians have healthy constitutions. They are made of steel. Pluto is so far out, so small and so cold, and yet there are no limits to its power. You could use that power to focus on health, creativity, and results, or to be destructive, dark, and violent. I could write a whole book on how to deal with your Plutonian energy. It changes people's lives. Pluto's placement reveals what your passion is. Guess where my Pluto is? In the house of astrology.

The high road of Pluto is a powerful leader who has the best interest of the collective in mind. They are magnetic, strong, with a capacity to heal—a surgeon who takes something bad out of you. "This is going to hurt, and you're going to thank me later." The low road of Pluto is a control freak who doesn't talk and wants to have it their way. They are inconsiderate and judgmental—boy, oh boy, does Pluto control with their intimidating expressions without saying a word.

Pluto rules Scorpio.

These have been the planets, brought to you by astrology. That brings us to the twelve houses.

6

The Twelve Houses

The houses deal with things mundane and material; with the objective mind and environmental affairs.
—LLEWELLYN GEORGE, *A to Z Horoscope Maker and Delineator*, 1910

THIS IS WHERE ASTROLOGY STARTS to get a little complicated. Every time I teach the houses in a beginner's class, students always look confused. I want you to understand how the houses influence your chart, especially the position of your sun. I also don't want you to get confused. To simplify, the house your sun sign is in provides the theme for your entire lifetime. That theme never goes away. It never changes. I'll use myself as an example.

For much of my life, I was the little goody-goody, the cheerleader, the social butterfly—qualities often associated with Gemini. That aspect of my personality took the front seat. I'm good at socializing. But secretly, socializing has always been a great strain. In college, I paid attention to who laughed at my jokes because it was less effort for me to keep up that cute, friendly façade if I knew who was easiest to please. When I got married and had a family, I maintained my smiley and bouncy personality. The cheerleader and goody-goody were never too far away from my driver's seat.

That secret, over time, wore me out. To push down and hide your true nature is exhausting. They call that pushing down "depression." I maintained my attractive mask, guaranteeing I would fit in and play the game that every extrovert excels at, and yet I couldn't understand why socializing sometimes felt like nails on a chalkboard, costing me pure effort.

When I finally found my way to my first therapy session, I spilled the truth: I was not as happy as I appeared. I was not as bouncy as people thought. Actually, I carried a deep sadness that felt more real to me, and more cumbersome, than the lighthearted qualities everyone saw. Somehow, that lightheartedness didn't extend all the way inside, although you sure couldn't tell by looking.

When I discovered my sun was in the eighth house, ruled by Scorpio, which is the house of introversion, it all made sense. I needed someone to listen deeply to me, to keep my secrets, and to show me how to heal. I was a Scorpio in disguise. I received therapy and then became a therapist. Scorpio qualities are useful for being a therapist, a doctor, a surgeon, or any kind of healer. First, eighth house people often need healing for themselves.

Other ways my sun in the eighth house shows up—where I have Scorpio tendencies—is that I have always had an interest in death. What a morbid topic for a cheerleader, or a social butterfly who is trying to comfort others and make them feel safe. I long to go deep with people, and I get a lot of fulfillment from doing so. I am happy to talk about what no one else talks about: your pain, love, sex, money. Helping people deal with their secrets, the things they least want to show, even to themselves, is my specialty.

What kind of Gemini would ever be interested in doing that? The kind with the sun in the eighth house. I can follow anyone into the depths of their pain without ever dropping my pom-poms.

Your birth time establishes the house positions in your chart. Find out what house your sun was in when you were born (you can see this on your chart—see the example on page 44), and you'll know where your sign thrives.

FIRST HOUSE

Aries rules the first house. This is the house of the self. You are all about the physical: your appearance, life-force, and ego. Understanding and accepting that your life's theme is to be self-involved will alleviate any guilt you feel about focusing on yourself—you can't help it! Even if you are a sweet little Cancer whose whole life is about the family, if your sun is in the first house, you need time to go into your own space. While adjusting and compromising for others all the time is in your Cancerian nature, the first house modifies that. You need to take care of yourself.

Another first house quality is to be active. You need to get up and go. Movement is your medicine. Even if you are a Taurus and you want to stay home baking cookies, if your sun is in the first house, you're going to dance to music while the cookies are baking. First house people are also independent and self-sufficient. There is no person with sun in their first house who doesn't (loudly) say to their spouse, "Stop telling me what to do!"

Even if you are a Capricorn and a traditionalist, you do not want others' opinions. The first house carries an assertive, aggressive, athletic energy. It's liberating to have a first house personality. They want to lead, not follow, yet they don't look behind them, so they get called self-centered. The truth is, they simply don't need to merge with others to find their identity. Quite the opposite. They are here to distinguish themselves through their independent personalities.

Sun in the first house is your permission slip to let go of the guilt of not following. You need to be yourself, all the way, no compromising. You have permission to ask: Who am I? How do I stay true to myself? How do

I not conform to other people's expectations of me? What will allow me to have physical, athletic, assertive, direct energy that is not influenced by another?

If the first house were a real house, the props in the house would be a mirror, boxing gloves and a punching bag, self-help books, workout gear, gym shoes, a tennis racquet, and a bicycle.

If you have three or more planets in the first house, I know that during this lifetime you've come here to feel sovereignty and independence. You are running the ship. You are not here in this lifetime to do anything other than to discover your own will, and while that sounds selfish, it's exactly the promise you made, that you would distinguish yourself from the other and you would enjoy it, guilt-free.

SECOND HOUSE

Taurus rules the second house. This house is related to possessions, money, investments, earthbound hobbies, and anything that is grounded, heavy, and materially valuable. If you have your sun in the second house, you lean toward old-fashioned values. Second house types love to collect things and put a lot of value on their possessions, which bring them comfort. They don't want newfangled computers. They are more interested in antiques, especially family heirlooms. They care less about worldly accomplishments and more about stability, sustainability, and survival.

The second house brings practicality, home, and comfort to your sun sign. Maybe your mom left you a beautiful ring and it makes you feel good to wear it every day. Second house energy is earthy and tribal—they live to a steady drumbeat. They like to play the same songs over and over, watch the same movies over and over, and are attached to their routines. They are a little rumpled and messy and they like things that way. They love comfort food, and they feel most secure when they have enough money in the bank, fresh flowers in the house, and a lot of pillows. They are rhythmic and stable, bringing a sense of security to others. And the beat goes on.

Even if you are a versatile Gemini who loves variety and change, if your sun is in the second house, you may love to read old books or frequent used bookstores. A Scorpio in the second house might be a banker or an insurance agent, dealing with money in a way that makes other people feel secure. A bossy Aries might run a retirement home, managing everyone's things. Capricorn in the second house is absolutely solid and stable—the family executor. If you have Aquarius in the second house, you might be fascinated with cryptocurrency—the futurist with an interest in money. A Cancer in the second house will bake for the family.

Second house people have a system. They are grounded and repetitive. They move at a slow and steady pace. Eventually, they get it done.

I know someone who was a Pisces in the second house. She worked with seniors and was always talking about her deceased parents. She invented an entire imaginary life around her dead relatives and wrote a book about the things they told her. She escaped into a dreamworld, as a Pisces loves to do. Because of her second house, her stories were all about her ancestors and how they made her feel secure. She didn't want to forget them.

The props in the second house would be a drum; stacks of coins; checkbooks and financial statements; big, heavy, comfortable furniture; jewelry; and of course, some chocolate. It smells delicious in the second house.

If you have three or more planets in the second house, I know that you came here to learn about value, stability, and a spirituality that is rooted and grounded in nature. Gardening and music are essential.

THIRD HOUSE

Gemini rules the third house. This is the house of the marketer, communicator, and trendsetter. Third house people are great journalists and short story writers (novels take too long). People with their sun in the third house love to learn and have a fascination with thoughts, intellect, and the passionate consumption of information. They move fast and talk to everyone, whether they know them or not. They are very attached to their siblings and love to tell stories about their families. They like technology and marketing, thinking up newer, faster ways to get things done. They are networkers. The third house brings a smart, quick, talkative energy to your sun sign.

I have a friend who has a Scorpio sun in the third house. She says she doesn't like people (Scorpio), yet her phone rings all day long and she knows everyone in town. A Capricorn in the third house might work for a cell phone corporation or be some kind of professional in the field of communication, like an editor or a marketer. They might make money off the internet. Pisces in the third house might do poetry slams or write science documentaries—the third house is the house of theater and brings a shy, poetic Pisces out of her shell. Aries in the third house could invent new communication devices or create a new kind of social media. When they tell a story, they're likely to perform and embellish it, or they will be an anchor person on television. A third house Sagittarius might write about and study world religions and tell everybody about what they learned, or become a motivational speaker.

The tricky part about third house people is that unless they are an earth sign or a Scorpio, they aren't very thorough. You can never be sure if they actually know what they're talking about in depth, or if they just skimmed the book and skipped to the end. They will definitely be entertaining and make friends everywhere they go. They think of friends as their siblings.

The props in the third house are a computer, brain games, magazines, a library pass, textbooks, documentaries, writing tools, and a thick address book filled with everyone's contact information.

If you have three or more planets in the third house, I know that you came here to learn how to communicate and connect with people and to stay close to your siblings, even if they are not siblings by blood.

FOURTH HOUSE

Cancer rules the fourth house. This is the house of family, traditions, ancestry, and lineages. Fourth house people are quintessential caretakers. Even if they are an Aries, they visit their grandpa every week, take care of their mother, stay home with the sick child . . . and they actually enjoy it! They are homebodies—they would rather you come to their house than go to your house. They will take care of you, give you the medicine you need, advise you on the foods you should be eating, and they'll bake something for you to take home with you. They tend to be introverted and save everything that makes them nostalgic or reminds them of their memories or family. They are the archivers of the family history and love to explore genealogy. They are also historians and natural psychologists.

I have a friend who is a Capricorn in the fourth house. He is a well-known therapist with a PhD. He does workshops where he talks about unconscious motives and asks: Is this a past life issue or a current life issue? He talks about unconscious motives and how to change the psychological inheritance (he might call it karma) you received from your family. He believes that if you break negative patterns in your family, you won't come back in the next life with the same issues.

Family is important to fourth house people. Geminis love to be around people, yet a Gemini in the fourth house only loves to be around people if they all have the same last name. A Capricorn in the fourth house might be a professional home builder. If you put a Sagittarius in the fourth house, they may love the *idea* of travel, read books about travel, research the newest, best suitcases. In reality, they rarely get around to actually going anywhere unless they bring the whole family along. A Libra in the fourth house could be a divorce lawyer, do family trusts, or be a successful mediator.

Props in this house are old family photos; cookbooks; a box of tissues; cuddly blankets and soft sheets; family heirlooms; a subscription to an ancestry research site; and books about the psychology of archetypes, birth order, mythology, and astrology. There will always be some kind of comfort food simmering on the stove. They think about the next meal right after they finish the last one.

If you have three or more planets in the fourth house, I know that you came here to learn about the psychology of human nature, and to make peace with your family dynamic.

FIFTH HOUSE

Leo rules the fifth house. This is the house of romance, art, drama, games, and children. Fifth house people are full of excitement and exuberance. They are high drama, high voltage, full of physical energy, and they love attention. They are always in motion. No matter your sun sign, if it's in the fifth house, you will be a little more dramatic, a little more outgoing, and a little more excited about everything.

I have a brother who is a double Scorpio (sun and moon), both in the fifth house. When he meets people, he tells them his entire life story of how he was addicted to heroin and how his dad went to prison. You would think a Scorpio would keep all of that a secret. Because he's in the fifth house, the drama of his life overrides any ideas of hiding. He wants to share it with everyone. What kind of Scorpio reveals all the family dynamics? The kind who needs to get everyone's attention and loves entertaining.

Even a Taurus in the fifth house will tell you all about the story of the love they had for their grandmother. They can't help making things a little more dramatic and colorful. A Cancer in the fifth house is going to be loud, entertaining, and a show-off. If Gemini is in the fifth house, they are talented at writing or acting. They need a lot of attention and they easily come up with ideas. It's always a holiday in the fifth house.

This house would have a stage set up for karaoke and lots of kids running around playing. There might be a closet full of brightly colored costumes and hats. The atmosphere is loud, dramatic; everyone is celebrating something, and somebody is always falling in love. There's never a dull moment in the fifth house.

People with three or more planets in the fifth house are here to truly embrace the wonder and vitality of being alive in this body, in this time, on this planet.

SIXTH HOUSE

The sixth house is ruled by Virgo. This is the house of health, service, details, and numbers. Sixth house people like to organize things and keep everything straight. I like to hire sixth house people. They bring with them the ability to create systems and implement them. I have a Taurus in the sixth house working for me right now. She loves organizing, spreadsheets, and helping me with taxes. She sits in the corner and counts. Really? Okay, go ahead and count.

This house is all about creating order out of chaos. If you have a lot of planets in the sixth house, you are probably fascinated by health and wellness. Sixth house people like to do special diets and cleanses. They are sometimes hypochondriacs. A sixth house person might decide to eat only seaweed with brown rice or green drinks that have no dairy. They love new technologies for longevity and anti-aging—they may be biohackers. They are often administrators or accountants.

This is the house of plants and herbal medicine. I know a Sagittarius in the sixth house who traveled all over the world finding exotic plants, extracting the essential oils, and selling them on the internet. A Capricorn in the sixth house would be good at making money from a health-related business. A Gemini in the sixth house could easily be a health coach or run seminars to teach people about natural remedies. An Aries in the sixth house creates pioneering new ways to get or stay healthy. Terence

McKenna was a Scorpio in the sixth house. He was an ethnobotanist and a pioneer in the healing properties of psilocybin.

Props in the sixth house might include health tracking devices, cabinets full of vitamins and herbal remedies, spreadsheets and sharpened pencils, stacks of bins and shelves for organizing, diet plans and food lists, and a lot of plants.

If you have three or more planets in the sixth house, you came here to learn about how to take care of your health and others'.

SEVENTH HOUSE

Libra rules the seventh house. This is the house of harmonizing, partnering, and looking for relationships. Seventh house people fall in love with everyone, whether it's their employees, their friends, or their next romantic interest. They live on a bicycle built for two.

Seventh house people tell stories. They exaggerate. I have a good friend with her sun in the seventh house who tells stories about things we did together. Her stories make me wonder if we were actually in the same place at the same time because her version doesn't resemble what actually happened at all. Seventh house people create idealistic, romantic versions of everything.

Beauty in their environment is important to them. Seventh house people have an incredible aesthetic sense and a lot of style. Many seventh house people are artists or designers. An Aquarian in the seventh house knows how to put things together that you would never think would go together. A Capricorn in the seventh house might be an artist who actually makes money at it. They might have a beautiful home with only the best, most expensive furniture.

People with their sun in the seventh house are good communicators and may be involved in careers having to do with the law, justice, and mediation. They listen well and talk well, all in the name of harmony, so they make excellent marriage counselors. They are good at collaborating, and partnership is important for them because no matter what sign they are, they are Libras in disguise.

Props in the seventh house would be a judge's gavel, books about the law, relationship self-help books, romance novels, and a beautiful collection of heart figurines.

If you have three or more planets in the seventh house, I know you came here to learn how to have healthy relationships.

EIGHTH HOUSE

Scorpio rules the eighth house. This is the house of change and transformation, birth and death, sex and money. This house is strong, intense, and secretive—it rules death and taxes. It's the house of the things people don't want to talk about.

If your sun is in the eighth house, you may have a fascination with true crime or abnormal psychology. You may get money without knowing why—it is the house of inheritance, trust funds, and a fearlessness about large amounts of money. It's also the house of therapists. The eighth house is about digging deep into the unconscious mind.

The eighth house contains a magnetic force, almost like a vortex. It's full of all that is taboo: evil, deviance, the paranormal, secrets, violence, addiction, and darkness. The eighth house is like the twilight zone—it's a little scary, and you kind of like it. You don't tell anybody you live there. Eighth house people even keep secrets from themselves. I remember watching a trial of a serial killer who didn't want to hear the testimony about the things he did because he said it was "too disturbing." That's classic eighth house.

Props in the eighth house might be psychological thriller films, ghost stories, heavy philosophical books (anything by Nietzsche), a Ouija board, a collection of antique guns or swords, and maybe even some sex toys (in a hidden drawer). The eighth house would be full of secret passageways and library walls that spin around to reveal hidden rooms. It's scary in there, and also thrilling.

If you have three or more planets in the eighth house, I know you came here to bring people who are stuck in the dark back into the light.

NINTH HOUSE

Sagittarius rules the ninth house. This is the house of life purpose, philosophy, rationality, and the search for truth through religion, contemplation, travel, and the attainment of knowledge. I think of people in this house as having a megaphone. They like to tell everyone the latest spiritual update on what Jesus, Mohammed, and the Buddha are up to. They travel the world and have a passport with a lot of stamps on it. They love to move energy through their bodies—Kundalini yoga is their favorite kind of yoga.

This is the house of publishing—in fact, my agent has a strong ninth house. Ninth house people love to share information and distribute it around the world and across different languages. Ninth house people often study abroad. They are attracted to all things multicultural and pick up other languages easily.

If your sun is in the ninth house, you are a spiritual seeker, travel calls to you, and you can't help telling the truth, even if it's not in your best interest. Even a shy Taurus who doesn't like to talk may tend to be blunt and direct when they do speak up.

Any earth sign in the ninth house will feel the pull to travel in an earthy way, like volunteering on an organic farm in South America. Carlos Castaneda was a Capricorn in the ninth house. He was a sociologist who was interested in shamanic practices before that was trendy. That love of travel can be confusing for a Cancer in the ninth house, who wants to stay home and at the same time, has a compulsion to run away.

Props in the ninth house might include a suitcase for traveling, passports, books on philosophy and world religions, yoga mats, documentaries about other cultures, and meditation apps.

If you have three or more planets in the ninth house, I know you came here to seek truth, no matter where you have to go to find it.

TENTH HOUSE

Capricorn rules the tenth house. This is the house of social status, ambition, success, and fame. Tenth house people are focused on their careers and achieving their highest purpose. What did you come here to do? This question echoes throughout the tenth house.

Tenth house people are natural leaders. Many presidents and CEOs have their sun in the tenth house. This personality type has to be successful, wants to be famous, excels at a young age, and can't do anything other than be the best. They sometimes get burned out because they are ambitious at such a young age. Then they make a big comeback. For example, Donald Trump has his sun in the tenth house. He was famous on television and in business, then we didn't hear about him for a while . . . then he reemerged and became the president.

Tenth house people tend to be traditionalists, workaholics, and like to know the rules. They often had difficult childhoods, then overcame their obstacles to become successful. Even a playful Gemini will be ambitious and have high standards if they have their sun in the tenth house.

Props in the tenth house would be business suits just back from the dry cleaner, an expensive briefcase, a high-end computer, VIP passes, keys to the Porsche, and a detailed business plan. Tenth house people only want the best and can't tolerate mediocrity.

If you have three or more planets in the tenth house, I know you came here to learn how to work hard for your rewards.

ELEVENTH HOUSE

Aquarius rules the eleventh house. This is the house of community, the future, friendship, activism, and humanity. Eleventh house people cannot follow the crowd. They go in a different direction. The eleventh house is about technology that connects people and disseminates information. Surely some eleventh house character invented social media.

If your sun is in the eleventh house, you may collect eccentric people. You put less value on money and possessions, and more value on futuristic ways of living in intentional communities or communes focused on permaculture and regenerative agriculture. You might be an environmental activist, a vegan, or a scientist developing new technology to make the future better.

Eleventh house people are all about community and service to the collective. They are humanitarians who feel driven to help others. I know a Cancer woman with her sign in the eleventh house who adopted children with extreme handicaps. My son has Aries in the eleventh house. A few years ago when the weather got really cold, he went out and spent a lot of money on wool socks to hand out to homeless people. A Libra in the eleventh house is a quintessential scientist with a big vision for bringing people together.

Props in the eleventh house would include all the latest technology, community event schedules, political rally flyers, quirky clothes, vegan food in the fridge, and maybe an appointment card for a visit with a tattoo artist.

If you have three or more planets in the eleventh house, I know you came here to think outside the box and change the world with your humanitarian spirit.

TWELFTH HOUSE

Pisces rules the twelfth house. This is the house of the mystic, the unconscious mind, creativity, emotion, and all things that go on beneath the surface. Twelfth house people are hard to interpret. If your sun is in the twelfth house, it definitely explains why you don't relate to your sun sign. Sun signs in the twelfth house feel more diffuse and less obvious. You may not feel completely comfortable in this world, and you may have a connection to other worlds—maybe you talk to dead people, see angels, or feel vibrations other people can't feel. It's a house of alternate realities. They have no sense of time.

One of the best astrologers in my school is a Sagittarius in the twelfth house. A typical Sag loves to travel. A twelfth house Sag may never leave the house. Twelfth house people want to stay in their bedrooms, turn on Netflix, make sure they have some really good spiritual reading material, and get annoyed if anybody comes into the room wanting them to go do something. There can be alcoholism or drug addiction in the twelfth house because of the need to escape from the so-called real world.

A Capricorn I know who has his sun in the twelfth house is a successful builder. When he walks into people's homes, he tells me he feels the storylines of the people in the room. He once turned to a client and said, "Your grandfather's here." Water signs feel comfortable in the twelfth house, while the other elements feel disoriented or disconcerted in the twelfth house. A naturally talkative Gemini will feel drawn to silence. A conscientious Virgo may be confused about the impulse to run away from their responsibilities. A dramatic Leo may suddenly want to avoid the spotlight.

I had a client who was a double Virgo with her sun in the twelfth house who never felt like a Virgo because the twelfth house diluted her Virgo traits. She felt like she was in a dream she couldn't shake off. The twelfth house has that distracted, dreamy sort of creativity. It's the house of music—all types, including celestial music. The best photographers and filmmakers often tend to be twelfth house people. They are easily inspired and moved by beauty, colors, and music. This is a great house for an astrologer because they don't need proof to accept, believe, and feel the truth of mystical information. They have empathy for others and feel what other people feel.

The props in a twelfth house would be incense, tarot cards, books on magic, dream interpretation guides, incense, glowing stars on the ceiling, poetry, romance movies, bottles of wine, and probably all the Harry Potter books.

If you have three or more planets in the twelfth house, I know you came here to explore and discover what lies beyond the boundaries of this earthly realm.

PUTTING IT ALL TOGETHER

As you are looking at all these different influences, remember this:

- ★ **The planet tells you *what*.** What energy is this? Is it your life-force sun energy, your emotional moon energy, your Mercury mind energy, your stern Saturn energy?
- ★ **The sign tells you *how*.** How will that energy show up? Will that sun energy show up like an airy Gemini? Will that moon energy show up like a fiery Aries?
- ★ **The house tells you *where*.** Literally, like a house—what is your address? What arena will this energy show up in? Are you in the house of communication, of dreams, of work, of love?

It's tricky to figure out how to interpret it all (that's what professional astrologers are for). However, unpacking your chart allows you to understand how all these subtle influences contribute to the complex person you are.

STELLIUMS

· · · · · · · · · · · ·

When there are three or more planets in either the same sign or the same house, that is called a stellium in astrology, and it shows you what your theme is. That theme is screaming your name. If you have three or more planets in Capricorn, your Capricorn energy will be especially strong. You might be a successful CEO of a Fortune 500 company. If you have three or more planets in the first house, you have a particularly strong Aries energy because Aries rules the first house. You might be a professional athlete or a leader of some sort. Note that you might have a stellium in one or more of the houses and also in one or more of the signs. Your life can have multiple themes that may harmonize or conflict.

7

Esoteric Astrology

SATURN AND THE RISING SIGN

The value of astrology, then, is not its power to predict what the gods have in store for humans, but its ability to reveal the godlike powers that reside in the depths of a human being.

—GLENN PERRY, PhD

THIS CHAPTER IS GOING TO step away from traditional astrology and discuss two indicators essential to esoteric astrology: the rising sign and Saturn. This is an important way in which my astrological model is different. I've been practicing as a full-time astrologer for almost five decades. Over this time, with years of hands-on clinical work, I have decoded the means to touch your heart, penetrate your veneer, and reveal what's beneath the mask of your persona. I focus on your gremlins, channeling your observer, and handing you the medicine your soul craves as it waits in the wings for you to notice.

Most astrology books are based on exoteric astrology, which exclusively addresses the outer world—it speaks to your ego, which assists you in fulfilling agreed-upon societal expectations to fit in, be an adult, and create a life of security and safety; to find a spouse and have children while achieving some kind of success. The primary goal of the ego is to pressure you into accumulating large doses of societal approval. Your ego wants to check off the list of requirements for who you are "supposed to be," while cultivating self-esteem robust enough to convince you that you are a good person. "I'm doing just great. My goals are to be wealthy, shiny, successful, in a long-term relationship, and if I'm really lucky, achieve some sort of fame or acknowledgment of my worth." Hello, ego.

The focus of esoteric astrology is much different. Esoteric astrology (a term Alice Bailey originated) is about your connection with your inner world. This philosophy directs you to listen to the quiet voices inside, whispering to you. This is the voice of your soul.

In popular astrology, the rising sign describes the way you look and how people see you. In esoteric astrology, the body represents your soul. In other words, the body doesn't lie. You get gut reactions. That's the difference. In esoteric astrology, we describe the rising sign as access to your soul. It's called the rising sign and/or the ascendant, both suggesting a rising up to the higher parts of yourself. Notice that there are two words, so we don't mistake the rising sign as a superficial indicator, but rather as a source of elevation. In my system, it's the ultimate goal to aim for the rising sign.

I also emphasize a distinction on the significance of Saturn. In esoteric astrology, Saturn is the taskmaster in charge of the lessons you are here to discover through effort. You will have discipline, which is what Saturn requires. The words "discipline" and "disciple" have the same root. What is a disciple? A being who serves God because they are in love with their creator.

I love Saturn. I find it easy to exercise discipline because I know who I work for. It's a spiritual focus that Alice Bailey called the hierarchy—"the group of spiritual beings on the inner planes who are the intelligent forces of nature and who control the evolutionary processes." My soul and I are playing a team sport, and Saturn is the coach. This is the single variable that has changed my life, had me fall in love with my fate, and freed my soul. I want this for you, so in this chapter we're going to wander into esoteric astrology territory.

My goal as an astrologer and psychotherapist is to counsel you to reach the high road of your chart, as described by your rising sign and the position and element of your Saturn. This is why we always discuss the high road and the low road. I am here to aim you at your high road. Of course I use the whole chart in all its complexity. However, these two ingredients are the primary indicators that take you directly to your soul.

My entire practice begs these questions: What did this soul sign up for? What is stalking you? What does life want you to learn? Astrology helps you turn on your observer. Think about it: the astrologer's point of view is to see you from a distance, looking back with objectivity and neutrality. This is why astrology reduces your emotional reactivity and negativity, quieting the gremlins to a minimum so you can hear the voice of your soul.

My favorite moments in a reading—and this happens a lot—are when clients cry because they finally feel seen. I become the voice of their higher self (or observer), which sees through the eyes of love. However, sometimes I have to call my clients out. "Stop that ego impulse, you're not supposed to be constantly traveling around, hiding from yourself. Settle down and get grounded." Or I might say the opposite: "Let go of that job already! Security is not what you promised your soul. You're supposed to be a free spirit, moving around all the time."

How do I know this? From the position of Saturn and/or the rising sign. These two are the keys to sourcing answers from your higher self. The rising sign echoes your soul's guiding voice. All astrology describes the ego. That's its function. Make no mistake—esoteric astrology is the fast track to your soul.

ABOUT ESOTERIC ASTROLOGY

Alice Bailey wrote a lengthy book called *Esoteric Astrology,* and another called *Esoteric Psychology.* Her twenty-four books prepare us for the Golden Era, which she called the Aquarian Age. It was Alice Bailey who coined the term "New Age." These eras each last approximately 2,100 years. We recently moved from the Piscean Age into the Aquarian Age. There is no actual date when the Aquarian Age began. My suggestion is that it started in the 1960s, when our world's values radically changed. Alice Bailey channeled this, alerting us in the 1920s that we were about to turn a corner, pass over a threshold on a planetary level, and begin a new version of humanity. Her books were a wake-up call, preparing us each to identify our unique role through astrology and esoteric laws.

She said the Aquarian Age would arrive when science began to support metaphysics. That's how we would know we are in what she called the New Age, which is now happening. We are there. Science backs up many things we used to think were mystical or supernatural, from quantum physics and string theory to the existence of beings on other planets. I don't think it is a coincidence that information is now coming out that extraterrestrial beings have been communicating with us for years. (As an astrologer, I'm allowed to say this because I talk about the planets all day long.) Her predictions are coming true.

Alice Bailey channeled that the purpose of the Aquarian Age was to dismantle our current societal matrix, which is far too filled with ego and greed, in order to create a new template based on higher spiritual values. Hello, Aquarian Age! Can we finally leave the wildfire of our egos behind?

It was in the Piscean Age that Buddha, Jesus, and Mohammed appeared with a mission: to learn about love and to keep an open heart. It seems the Piscean Age failed. Look around: our reality is not based on nonattachment or love. In fact, all of humanity is based on fear and greed.

Gremlins live off fear. They eat it for breakfast. The ego instills in us that we "should" be doing something big, that we ought to be productive, financially successful, and highly esteemed. The Piscean Age didn't work out so well. Take two. Let's see if we can do better in the Aquarian Age.

Alice Bailey says that in the New Age, values will be about service and love without the need for recognition, greed, and glamour. In her world, love is the centerpiece. Achievements, in esoteric law, are not measured on the outer plane. Rather, they are measured on the inner. If someone is suffering, according to Alice Bailey, they are serving humanity by taking on collective pain. Suffering is not at all a sign of failure. Think of Nelson Mandela, Mother Teresa, Martin Luther King, the Dalai Lama. They took on our collective karma without flinching.

These high spiritual beings are recognized as the ones who give and serve freely with no ego or needs of their own. This may be true of you, even if you don't realize it. If your life feels painful or flat or if you think you are a failure, think again. From the soul's point of view, this couldn't be further from the truth. Measuring your life by an external ruler, or according to how you rate on society's terms, is not the esoteric assessment. So often, people have no idea the size of the contribution they've made until they see themselves through the eyes of God.

In my early days as an astrologer, I spent a lot of time with other people's charts, studying to identify the details of what they came to learn in this lifetime. I have seen many who have had the hardest lives, suffering abuse, deprivation, mental health issues, addiction. These people are unrecognized heroes who are carrying the weight of the human condition without knowing it.

Toby is a Pisces. He spent fourteen years living with his wife, who had a rare disease that was eventually fatal. Shortly after they married, she got sick. He served and nursed her to her last breath. When it was over, he went off to a cabin in northern British Columbia to live by himself. He lives alone to this day, smiling and emanating peace. He is fulfilling the promise of his Cancer rising and Pisces sun. He is a double water sign, which promises to serve selflessly, to be comfortable living a life of quiet. He is performing a soul-filled life. Alice Bailey would approve.

So many misinterpret the loners and the shy personality types to be inactive or useless. That is so far from the truth, according to the soul. They are taking on the collective karma for the benefit of us all. Toby is doing a spiritual life. He is a very evolved being disguised as a shy man, not for any other reasons than simply to be his true self. He is following his soul's calling. This is the goal of everyone's lifetime.

Most likely, you don't know the karma you carry with your family, your partner, your closest friends, even your dog or cat. There are unwritten debts to be paid, unspoken lessons to be learned, and your soul is up for all of it. Your crises and struggles are more than just obstacles to overcome. They are the backdrop by which you get to practice spiritual principles. In your soul's eyes, you show up just as the great ones do. There is no difference. We are in this together. We are all one. That sounds so spiritual, but it's also true.

Your soul has enlisted you into the service of the collective with specific assignments according to your chart that you probably don't like or even understand. The crisis that surrounds you, or the trauma you grew up with, even that awful relationship, happened in order to teach you how to break your heart and then heal. This is how we all contribute to the evolution of our species. The soul never tires of heartbreaks. To the soul, heartbreak is the heart breaking open, and that's the ultimate goal: those who stay in love the longest win. This is why I call the soul a slut—because it is willing to take on any kind of pain, without resistance.

We need to reframe the ego in the context of the soul's mission so our souls can finally bring us peace, calm, a soothed nervous system, and the divine order of this place.

You cannot be an astrologer and not realize, as Einstein said, that God doesn't play with dice. Astrology is as trustworthy as the sun coming up tomorrow and the moon moving through the heavens in its perfectly predictable order. I firmly believe (and have seen it in so many readings) that your chart explains why you are here and what you are here to learn. Specifically, studying your Saturn and exploring the high road of your rising sign will bring you to this wisdom.

SATURN: THE ENFORCER (AKA THE COP, THE SCHOOL PRINCIPAL, OR THE TASKMASTER)

Anyone who knows me knows I have a lot of discipline. I had no idea why I took life so seriously, especially being a lighthearted Gemini. The deeper I studied, the more I realized I had a lot of Saturnian influences in my chart. This explains why I hate to be a minute late, why I can't ignore a text and always answer within half an hour, why I use my words with precision, and why I follow through with whatever I promise—especially when I don't want to. I've come to love Saturn. I credit my success to my obedience to that old man called Saturn.

Saturn rules rules. In fact, Saturn makes up the rules! I didn't understand that this is the keyhole to success in a big way until my second Saturn return (page 95). This is when I opened up my astrology school. I became a CEO. I learned business and applied Saturnian values to my company. I began looking at spreadsheets and now I know what a profit margin and a P&L are. A schedule is sent to me daily that I must follow. Welcome to Saturn.

When I teach Saturn, people don't like hearing what they've come to learn. They almost always say, "Oh, I don't like that lesson." I wish this weren't true. We accrue spiritual merit by working through hard lessons. This is exactly what contributes to the evolution of humanity, and everyone has an assignment. Design fault: you may have imagined life would be easy. As M. Scott Peck said in the first line of his book *The Road Less Traveled*: "Life is difficult."

Warning: the complaining gremlins that tell you how bad you're doing always stand next to Saturn because who in the world wants to endure hard lessons like mental illness, heartbreak, financial ruin, betrayal, addiction, or worse? Saturn seems harsh. Would you believe me if I said Saturn has your best interests in mind? All Saturn is asking of you is to accept your fate, play this game called life according to the rules, and do it with consideration, kindness, and love. When in doubt, just do the next right thing. That's how you make friends with Saturn. I'm sorry. It's so hard, but it's true.

So, what are the rules?

For starters, be on time. Get up and exercise. Be disciplined. Pay your taxes and your bills. Save your receipts. Clean out your car. Eat real food from the earth. Be simple. Share. Forgive. Drink fresh water. All the things that take effort are required (unless of course you are a Capricorn or have a well-aspected Saturn in your chart). The laws of Saturn say once you have paid your dues and you are good at something by being consistent (Saturn is all about consistency), you will be rewarded. Work hard, even when you don't want to—especially when you don't want to. That's the key.

As you're reading this, you will feel the resistance—95 percent of the people I work with say, "I don't have any discipline" (which by the way, isn't true; just getting up every day, brushing your teeth, and making it through this dense reality shows discipline). No one ever tells you that you have reason to be depressed, exhausted, and weary. Saturn rules bones, teeth, government, and buildings—all the substantial, heavy factors of this life. This is a Saturn-ruled planet. It's heavy here and Saturn constantly asks you to work.

These are hard truths—immovable laws. Saturn is ruthless. Saturn is watching. You don't need a rule book. We all know what's best for us: eating properly, exercising, ending unhealthy relationships . . . remember when I said I was in graduate school asking the question, "Why don't we do what's good for us?" The answer is because we don't have a good relationship with Saturn.

Here is a great example: Sting has Saturn on the sun (remember, we said the planet standing next to the sun trumps the sun sign). I have never seen a more disciplined man. He plays bass and practices constantly. Every single show before he sings, he does the exercises to warm up his voice, and he's so consistent. He shows up just as shiny today as he did forty years ago. He is the definition of an old soul who complies with Saturn's demands and has reached internal and external success by being committed to follow-through, meditation, and his own inner calling.

If you don't fulfill your promise in this lifetime, don't worry—you can try again the next time around. That's karmic astrology. Our relationship with Saturn follows us around from life to life.

Saturn drives some of you crazy. You think you're getting it wrong and you're not doing enough, and it's not true. You're an extremist. There is nothing moderate about this influence. Obeying Saturn is just as uncomfortable as neglecting Saturn (without the consequences). Find your Saturn sign quickly by looking up your birth year in the chart on page 285.

The element of your Saturn gives us a clue as to what you are here to learn in this lifetime:

If Saturn is in water (Cancer, Scorpio, Pisces), you are here to learn how to feel your feelings, set boundaries, and be vulnerable. Saturn challenges you, after your heartbreaks, to get up and try again—to not allow your emotional realm to freeze and turn to ice. Saturn asks you to regain your faith in love and people, no matter what's happened to you.

When Saturn is in air (Gemini, Libra, Aquarius), relationships and communication are your lessons. Relationships may seem challenging and you may resist them or settle. Either you've had too few, or too many, or your relationships have been dysfunctional, so your mind constantly judges who you're with or intellectualizes, justifying why you should leave. At best, you are built for relationships, community, friendships, and relating to others.

When Saturn is in earth (Taurus, Virgo, Capricorn), money, resources, or security might be your lesson. You had money and lost it, or you've never been financially secure enough and you deem yourself a failure. Heads up: the soul has no concern for money as the determinant of your success. The real question is, do you respect the physical realm? Do you care for your money? Do you care for your body? Do you care for this earth? Are you willing to accept what the world sees as a lowly job in order to bring security to your family and those who depend on you, without complaining? Are you willing to be successful and acknowledge your abilities?

If Saturn is in fire (Aries, Leo, Sagittarius), you are here to be seen. Your temper is either subdued or out of control. Perhaps you were once shamed on stage (literally or metaphorically), or you have always been too afraid to take the spotlight. Your life lesson is to stand up and be noticed. Be bold. Say the things that aren't easy to say. If you left your passions behind because you didn't get the applause you expected, don't give up. Do what you do because you love it, not because you're seeking affirmation from the outer world.

People working with me have often said that I have a very intense work ethic. My answer is: I know that I came to this planet to assist in preparing for the Aquarian Age. I respect Saturn. I just wish I could tell Alice Bailey in person that I listened to everything she said.

SATURN RETURN

Saturn carries a timepiece in his grandpa-like vest pocket. Every seven years, Saturn comes back around and demands you change something about your life. If you agree, change will be easy. If you resist, uh-oh . . . here come the repercussions. This is at the core of that astrological phenomenon called Saturn return.

The first time Saturn was at a ninety-degree angle to where it was when you were born, you were seven years old. This is the first step toward individuation. You begin your schooling, learn how to read and write, and begin conforming.

Every seven years, Saturn makes its mark. It comes around again at fourteen. Did you feel confused at fourteen? Of course you did. No one is exempt from teenage awkwardness.

Saturn hits again between twenty and twenty-two (an astrologer can tell you exactly when these Saturn transits are affecting you). This is the time most people go out into the world, either to complete their education or to start their career. This is often when the first knock-knock of destiny calls your name. Alice Bailey addressed this: if you are destined to follow a spiritual path, you'll get your first call around twenty-one. Many famous people got discovered at this age. India Arie started her spectacular career. Barbra Streisand was in the musical *Funny Girl* at twenty-one, which launched her career. I'm not sure it's appropriate to put my name right here with these two giants, but it is true that I was twenty when I first discovered the work of Alice Bailey and began my practice.

Destiny happens at your first official Saturn return, when Saturn literally returns to the exact spot it was at your moment of birth. This is between twenty-eight and thirty and it lasts about two and a half years. At Saturn return, change is imminent. You'll feel the pressure of Saturn's insistence. People often get married, get divorced, have a baby, lose a loved one, or experience some combination of those events around this time.

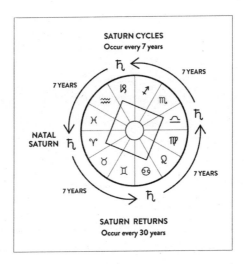

Here's an illustration. A young man got married early, in his twenties, to his college sweetheart. He wasn't madly in love, yet he cherished her and she loved him. The marriage was sweet and solid, yet he found himself feeling complacent in a life that was expected. He spent seven years relatively content yet restless and unchallenged. Try as he might to let go, he couldn't seem to get himself to end the marriage . . . until the entrance of his Saturn return. The moment Saturn entered his sign at zero degrees, he filed for divorce. He traveled, he studied, and, true to his Gemini rising, he was able to start anew and remake his life.

Every time I ask someone, "What happened between twenty-eight and thirty," they have a story to tell—and suddenly I look like a magician. Calling out someone's Saturn return is the ultimate astrology parlor trick. In my experience, it is 99 percent accurate. At a seminar in Los Angeles, there were twenty people in the room. We went through every single person, and each one had something dramatic happen. I believe in astrology because of this consistent indicator.

The day I knew for sure that Saturn return was real was in 1982. I was giving a reading for a general in the US Army. He was a full-blown Aries with Saturn in Capricorn, a giant man with beautiful energy and a type-A personality. For some reason, I gave him both the year and the exact month of his Saturn return, which I don't normally do. I asked: "What happened in May 1961?"

His eyes bulged. "I was flying home from Vietnam, so upset with what I'd experienced. I heard this crazy thought in my head: How can I bomb Washington, DC? I went AWOL. I couldn't kill one more person. When the plane landed, I went straight to a psychiatrist and said, 'I need help.'"

Before that day, this man was a nonbeliever. He had come at his wife's insistence. This really drove it home for him and me: astrology is real.

One of the magic ingredients of our school is that I teach people how to do an impactful reading, and it always starts with Saturn cycles. You can imagine if someone knows, right off the top, about the birth of the business, the birth of the child, the date of the divorce, how impactful that is—they happen every seven years.

There is a second Saturn return that happens between fifty-eight and sixty. When I was fifty-eight, a client named Destinee (seriously) said to me, "Have you ever thought of opening an online school?"

"A what?" I said.

Destinee and I started the school together. Every Monday morning for the next five years, I literally had a date with Destinee. That meeting, during the entrance of my Saturn return, changed my life. Thousands of students have come through the doors. I have received so much gratitude and so many gifts in exchange for assisting people to fall in love with who they are and their fate.

Saturn cycles are the times to take risks and change direction completely, whether that means letting go and setting yourself free, or finally getting grounded and settling down. The second Saturn return is the opportunity to face mortality with wisdom, which simply means: don't assume aging has to be a bad thing. The other thing that happens is there are many people in the obituaries between fifty-eight and sixty. It makes sense—you are at the end of an era, you completed your purpose, and you're done. Or are you?

Saturn can be an arrogant dictator demanding humility. Saturn rules the knees and, at worst, insists you get down on your knees and ask for help. If your Saturn return hurts you, shocks you, or pushes you around, know it is trying to free you from a stale old story you've been living: the dated relationship, the job that had its better days, the part of you that was stuck.

Saturn will push you around. If you really want to fight with the boss, go right ahead. Good luck with that. Trying to avoid Saturn is not a good idea. Resistance is far more frequent in the second Saturn return than in the first. I've seen the cosmic temper show up when the addiction did not resolve, when the relationship overstayed its welcome, when the debt was not repaid. You listen, you succeed. You resist, you lose. There is a reason they have so many temples devoted to Saturn in India. They know Saturn must be appeased. It's really that simple.

CAN YOU PREPARE FOR YOUR SATURN RETURN?

. . . .

Here's a question everyone asks: Can I do anything to prepare for my Saturn return? I'm sorry to say that you cannot prepare for the first one. You're in your twenties, wandering through the desert, changing your mind from one thing to another. It's going to happen. You'll see.

However, if you're coming up on your second Saturn return, get ready to be healthy or to let go of old careers, old relationships, health issues, old patterns. If you know you're turning fifty-five and you've got three years before your second Saturn return, start taking care of your body now. People constantly ask why I'm so young for my age and it's 100 percent because I am so committed to honoring Saturn by staying healthy. I do cleanses, I exercise every day, I eat well. There is a decision to be made here: How do you want to age?

RISING/ASCENDANT: THE CALL OF YOUR SOUL

Another important focus of esoteric astrology is the rising sign, which characterizes your soul's path. In modern astrology, the rising sign is not described this way. It describes how you look and appear to others. It does affect your appearance. Old astrologers often listed physical characteristics that are associated with each rising sign: Leo rising has great hair, Cancer rising has large breasts, Scorpio rising has alluring eyes. In times of old, astrologers determined your rising sign by the shape of your body.

There is some truth to that. The body doesn't lie. You know that feeling when you get a gut reaction that someone's deceiving you or makes you uncomfortable because your body has registered a negative feeling? That's your body telling the truth.

Whatever constellation is on the eastern horizon at the moment of your birth—this is your rising sign, also called your ascendant. I've often said, the simplest version of astrology is to throw away your chart, identify your rising sign, and follow that path at the high road. Study your rising sign, and devote your life to understanding the full expression of that sign. The soul is the focus of esoteric astrology. The soul is concerned with evolution, your relationship with God (whatever that means to you), and your ability to find peace.

This is a sacred path. The soul draws you to books like this, to taking meditation classes, to studying metaphysical principles. The soul loves love—believe it or not, your soul is in love with you.

All animals are soulful. They have no ego. Think of your favorite pet, wagging its tail in pure excitement whenever you appear. It has few needs: food, snuggles, and play. This is not unlike your soul. Your soul is committed to you like a mother is to her child, or like a lover is to his beloved. Now, let's see . . . where did you put your soul's impulse? It has to be around here somewhere. It's common to feel far away from such a perfect love.

In a perfect world your soul would say to your ego, "Can I drive?"

"No!" the ego argues, accusing the soul: "You never take me to the right stores."

"Stores?" the soul says. "I was going to drive to the temple so we can meditate."

When the ego drives without the soul's influence, you will eventually have a crisis—a spiritual fender bender. You'll bump into your neediness and your ravenous appetite for approval. Don't worry. The soul is patient and watches. It won't impose itself on you.

In my school, when we reach level three, I always begin by introducing through meditation a prayer that directly addresses the soul: "Let my life be in service to you. Take over. I want nothing more than to fulfill my soul's mission here. I'm all in." Please feel free to use any of these prayers and put them in your own words. I suggest you make a practice at the entrance of your meditation to invite in your soul, beckon to it, and give it the keys to the car.

My soul and I are now in a soul-mate contract. It wasn't always this way. I was so disappointed when I found out Libra was my rising sign. (Most people don't like their rising sign.) I remember in my twenties, my Libra soul was so codependent, I was fully embodying the low road of Libra. I fell in love with everybody who needed help, and not in a healthy way—in a purely needy way. I realized I didn't have to be in a relationship to feel normal.

Maybe this book will help fast-track you without the hard lessons I had to go through.

From the moment you let the soul drive, you will be leading a soul-filled life, and the New Age will have a much better chance of changing planet Earth. As the New Age takes hold, fulfill your soul's purpose and understand the giant distraction of your gremlins, your ego, and your story as grist for the mill.

The ultimate role of challenges and crises in this life, said esoteric psychology, is to create enough angst and enough pain for you to finally stop the bus, put your attention on your rising sign, take it to the high road, and find peace with exactly what is. Your ego will never be at peace with what is. Look to your rising sign. This is simple advice that you won't read in modern astrology books. If someone is showing up with their rising sign qualities more than their sun sign, I know this person is trying to fulfill their purpose.

Once you've identified your rising sign, the most important question is: Are you operating with your rising sign from the low road or the high road? A Virgo rising must resist the critic of themselves. A Capricorn rising may be plagued with laziness at first, and only later, in order to succeed, discover ambition and drive to achieve. A Pisces rising may resist allowing themselves to float free and ungrounded, until they realize that this is their artistic access to other worlds. A Leo rising does not want to be in the spotlight until they become conscious and mature enough to recognize their talents and their promise.

I am telling you straight up, you are going to resist your rising sign. I have never met anyone who doesn't have to struggle a little or a lot to get to the high road of their rising sign because it's so foreign and unnatural. Once again, astrology is about meeting your resistance with the awareness of the sign you're aiming at, and disciplining yourself to seek it.

If you are reading this book, some part of you values the pursuit of wisdom. Here's the deal: we all learn the hard way. In order to let the soul drive and put the ego in the back seat, there has to be a crisis or a decision that emerges from pain. During pain, we resort to prayers and spirituality. It is not our first instinct—a design fault for sure.

One half of you will want to take the low road. The other half of you will stretch toward the high road. Alice Bailey said, "The initiation process is abnormal. The ego will not willingly move to the soul without conscious direction from your higher self." If you cannot activate a conscious higher self to take over your life, it will not show up. Why? Because the soul is gentle and waits for an invitation. The ego is obnoxious and pushes you around. Another design fault!

Just imagine what could happen if you let the soul drive, with the ego in the back seat.

"Okay, ego. We're going to the temple to pray."

"Okay," the ego says, "I'll make a deal with you. Let's do some chores, go shopping, then go to the temple to pray and do our Saturn chores."

"You come with me to pray first," the soul says, "and then we'll do some chores Saturn wants us to do, and then we can go shopping."

"Oh, all right," the ego says.

First things first, identify your life lesson by your Saturn.

Next, figure out the high road of your rising sign.

Finally, give your life over to your soul and be prepared for miracles.

As soon as you surrender your ego in service to your soul, you will be fulfilling your purpose here. Einstein said, "The intuitive mind is a sacred gift. The rational mind is a faithful servant. We've created a society that honors the servant and has forgotten the gift." With astrology, you can rewrite that script.

THE NORTH NODE: YOUR SHORTCUT TO ENLIGHTENMENT

. . . .

Although it's not a part of Alice Bailey's system, I consider the north node to be a secret in your back pocket—your shortcut to enlightenment. The north node isn't a planet. It's a coordinate based on the exact place where the moon's orbit intersects the Earth's orbit as the moon is moving toward the Northern Hemisphere. (The coordinate where the moon's orbit intersects the Earth's orbit while moving toward the Southern Hemisphere is called the south node.) This is a lot of astrology jargon—no need to remember a thing I just said. Just apply its meaning to your life. On your chart, it is written as the "true node" and it is in a sign. The south node isn't written in. It is implied by being the opposite of the true node.

If you want to evolve on the fast track spiritually and you need permission to do something completely contrary to the rest of your chart, this is your permission. It's the secret sauce that few know about.

The north node is not an overt personality trait. It is something to aspire to. It's your true north, your North Star. You can head toward it and it takes you into your future. It's always in front of you. It's a permission slip given to you by your higher self that says: "If you follow this path, you can skip a lot of hardship and get right to the answer."

The south node, which is exactly 180 degrees opposite, is where you've come from. It's far more comfortable, like wearing an old pair of slippers or returning to the house you lived in as a child. The south node is the default. If ever you're upset, you're not going to want to go toward the new. You're looking for comfort, and that's the south node.

It also describes past lives, repetitive patterns, where you've been successful, or even where you've failed (your failures feel familiar). The north node is what you aim for to find growth. It takes you straight to enlightenment. Once you know the north node is where you're aiming, you'll find out your shadow is in your south node—distracting you as you revert or go backward to take the path of least resistance.

It's not a bad thing to seek comfort. It's a good thing to know where your comfort is, in order to find calm. Then, study your north node and get a running start to the fulfillment of your real purpose. Too many people make the south node bad. There is nothing wrong with going back to your favorite source of ease as long as you have in mind your ultimate goal, which is to head for the future.

PART II

Understanding Yourself and Others

By now, I bet you're really curious about your own chart. (Or maybe you've already skipped ahead and just read your sun sign. Did you? As a Gemini, I would!) Don't just check out your sun sign chapter and stop. Remember, you have within you not just your sun sign, you also contain the opposite of your sun sign. You have your moon, Mercury, Saturn, your rising sign, your north node, and you might have a stellium (three or more planets in one sign or in one house). There is so much to study. You may relate to the dilemma of a completely different sign for reasons only a professional astrologer can see.

On my website (www.IDontBelieveinAstrologyBook.com), you can find a form to record your own signs in each of the planets, as well as the signs of other important people in your life. You can also keep track of your own signs here, in terms of what we are focusing on for this book, for each reference:

MY SUN SIGN IS:

_____

MY SUN SIGN IS IN THE ELEMENT OF (CIRCLE ONE):

WATER   EARTH   AIR   FIRE

MY SUN SIGN IS (CIRCLE ONE):

FIXED   CARDINAL   MUTABLE

MY SUN SIGN IS IN THE _____ HOUSE

THE OPPOSITE OF MY SUN SIGN IS:

_____

MY MOON SIGN IS:

_____

MY MERCURY IS:

_____

MY RISING SIGN IS:

_____

MY SATURN IS:

_____

MY NORTH NODE IS:

_____

PARTICULAR THINGS I WANT TO
REMEMBER ABOUT MY CHART:

_____

_____

_____

_____

8

The Psychology of Aries

I AM

Element: Fire
Mode: Cardinal
House: First
Planet: Mars
Body part: Head—they are headstrong.

If only you understood I am part animal. I am an energetic, power-driven being. I push—yes, sometimes I do, when I work out and when I speak out. That's not bad. If you think about when I am born, during spring, you'd realize it requires a lot of energy to move through the cold season and pop out with bright colors. I am just that: the one who pops out, who brings life-force. I like that about myself.

I speak out. When the restaurant is slow, or traffic sluggish, or especially during a political conversation gone wrong, someone has to say: "That's not true!" or "Hurry up, the light is green, let's go!" I will not let dishonesty or injustice become acceptable. I will not sit and do nothing. Someone has to say something.

I'm happy to teach you how to do it right. I come with a clear knowing, which can turn into a slap on the back, a caring, sincere heart, or an example of leadership. Don't misinterpret my impatience. I just get riled up. Don't tell me to calm down. That just makes me angry, and you won't like that.

Who said anger isn't useful? "Passion" is a better word. That's what I am: passionate. I get excited about a lot of topics. If you can appreciate the heat, we are going to get along just fine. If you don't do what you said you would do, or you handle the less fortunate with disrespect, you bet I'll say something. That's who I am.

Listen: if you aren't a fire sign like me, I don't mind, but don't mind me. Fire does not run lukewarm. I personally have no patience for lukewarm. I run hot. I seek excellence. Competition inspires me to do even better. From my point of view, there is no medium. I am in to what I do with all I have.

Aries disagrees, competes, and actually enjoys a good argument. You will recognize them as the loud voice in the room that stands out as the leader. They ask the questions others are too afraid to ask. They are active listeners who think on their feet. They have an insatiable open mind and a voracious appetite for new knowledge. You'll find them reading books about new ideas for hours.

They refuse to follow blindly. The first sign of the zodiac, Aries is happy to initiate—in the conversation, in line at the movies, in the front row in a workout class. They are quick, sometimes rash, and live by the words "I am."

What an alive mind you carry, Aries. You so willingly give your two cents worth. Known for passion, you won't meet an Aries who doesn't care a lot about something, especially injustice or the less fortunate. Maybe it's business, or their hobby, or their favorite person. Whatever it is, they are enthusiastic. They get obsessed. When working on something, they won't stop until the job is done.

The Aries stereotype of being argumentative fighters who are pushy and in charge is often accurate. However, there are introverted Aries whose qualities aren't as obvious. Even if they are quiet, you can be sure they are questioning inside their head, and it's only a matter of time before they say something. They are not afraid to confront, argue, and take the lead. It's instinctive. Fire signs use drama to wake themselves (and us) up. Nothing is subtle about Aries.

Aries children have excessive energy. They are often labeled as outstanding and/or troublemakers. A daredevil lives inside them. My best friend in high school was an Aries. Early on, as all Aries do, she displayed a talent for sports, tennis being one of them. It was no surprise she threw her racquet and made angry noises whenever things went wrong. In preschool, when it was time for a nap, she asked, "Is my mom paying you? Because I don't think we need a nap." So sassy. They don't want to miss anything. They are unable to rest and relax until life teaches them (too often the hard way with an accident of some sort) how to slow down.

Many Aries children grow up learning to hold back. If you constantly heard, "Tone it down. Don't be so pushy. Why are you talking so loudly? You're too much," you would, too. When they are accused of being too *something*, it hurts their feelings, although they won't show it. They have no idea they are being loud or selfish until someone criticizes them. They just thought they were helping. Sadly, this explains why an Aries adult can suppress their authentic self.

The good news is, Aries learns quickly from the mistakes they make even more quickly. They accumulate wisdom in the school of hard knocks, and they have a front-row seat. Eventually, Aries matures into a calm, focused adult, leaving behind the label of the wild, bright kid. Aries can age well, though they never fully leave their youthfulness behind.

Their athletic capacity follows them around. Remember as a kid when we all had so much energy to play ball, be the cheerleader, jump in the lake? It dwindles with age in most of us. Not in Aries, whose childlike joy endures.

Exercise keeps Aries from aging. I always encourage them to get outside or go back to the gym. They need to keep energy moving. Even without working out, they look strong. It's amazing how fast an Aries can build muscles and get back in shape after stopping. They are just built that way.

Aries, your presence affects energy, seen and unseen. You are not boring or ambivalent. Because you have a strong character—everyone notices it—you aren't easily stopped, at any age. However, here's the secret: you suffer from insecurity. No one knows because you have too much pride to talk about it. You assume once the project begins and you jump in with all that enthusiasm, it's only a matter of time before people think you are too much. You long for positive feedback, but won't ask for it, and people may not give it because you seem so confident. Still, you think any minute now, you're going to get in trouble. You expect to be rejected for taking over. Because you understand criticism and rejection, you are a champion for the underdog. You can push through your own insecurity in the name of someone else's cause.

The greatest gift for Aries is to have a best friend who will cheer them on and listen to their fears without interrupting. Aries needs someone to tell them how good they are at so many things. They need someone to contradict their insecurity and comfort them. Being friends with an Aries is comforting, too. Aries is a natural protector.

My son, a double Aries (sun and moon), is a good example of this energy. He came home from school one day, at age eleven, very upset. He said, "Mom, I'm in trouble."

"What happened?" I asked.

"All the teachers in school called me into a room because I hit the bully."

The Aries in me (I have moon in Aries) quickly responded, "Good for you! Who other than a double Aries would dare to hit the bully? Nobody else was brave enough. Somebody had to do it."

"Really?" he said. "I'm not in trouble?"

"If I didn't know your chart, you'd be in trouble. You couldn't help it."

It's probably true that you will sometimes irritate people because you say what the rest of us are thinking and would never say. It's not an easy role to play, to be the one to speak the truth. Not everyone wants you to shout out in public that the emperor has no clothes on. People want you to be quiet, tuck it in. We all knew it—why did you have to say it?

When Aries wants to break ties with someone, they are good at letting go. They can cut someone loose, then snip, they're done—gone and farewell. Aries, it seems to us that it's all too easy for you to turn the corner and say, "Next!" Slow down to hear out what happened to the other person after you left. Turn back and check in to show that you actually respect that person, even if you don't want to be with them.

Can you admit that you really do want to be in a relationship? Can you remember that not everyone has your sharp edge? Relationships can be difficult for Aries. Yet like their opposite sign, Libra, Aries may not realize how much they need partnerships—as long as they come with plenty of freedom. Partners and friends can't easily interact with Aries's natural independence. Aries says things like:

"Are we going to go work out together? I'll go with *you*. I'm not going with the whole group."

"I'll go if I can take my own car."

"I'll go to the movies if we don't go to the chick flick. Oh, that's the one you want to see? Okay, I'll meet you afterward."

Aries is fine going to a movie by themselves. Easy-peasy. However, Aries's independence can make their partners and friends feel like an extra in the Aries show: "I don't think you need me at all. You're so self-sufficient." It is true. Aries doesn't need you; they want you. Isn't that better? Aries thinks so.

You may need to practice forgiveness, for others as well as yourself. You must know that your words have a strong effect on people. Especially when you are triggered, all caution goes out the window. You're stronger and louder than the rest of us. If someone asks you to tone it down, it just means that person is more sensitive to sound. You can adjust. Don't take it personally. You are a good listener and you can learn to be more sensitive to what other people are feeling.

Thank you, Aries, for your valor and constant impulse to do the next right thing. You were born to argue for all the right reasons. You push against reality in order to create a new version. Too often, people misunderstand your enthusiasm. You are a fiery character who gets excited, all in a moment. We need your passion so we don't lose ours. We are glad someone hit the bully and spoke up for the less able. We are glad you tell the truth so everyone can hear. You are here to change the old order. Keep going.

PROFILE OF AN ARIES

One of my best friends—I'll call him Carl—has seven planets in fire, and five of those planets are in Aries. He grew up on a pig farm in Canada. By the age of five, according to the family lore, he was in the tractor with his dad, and he was driving. He put his hand on his dad's knee and said, "Don't worry. I know what I'm doing."

Carl has been married several times, and with each divorce, he gave the wife the house and financial support for the rest of their lives. As a natural leader, protector, and provider, he appeared invincible, even when he was experiencing financial difficulty. He never let it show.

When he met a spiritual teacher, he learned to meditate. The teacher told Carl to put on a suit and follow him into the bathroom. The teacher sat him in front of the toilet and said, "You're going to meditate here every morning."

Carl asked, "Why here?"

The teacher said, "Because you're full of shit. Your life is shit."

Only a spiritual teacher could get someone like Carl to even consider that conversation.

ARIES LOW ROAD

On the low road, Aries doesn't know they hurt others. They are self-consumed. At worst, they generalize and exaggerate, announcing their position loudly in a way that makes their truth *the truth*:

"The rich people of the world have ruined everything!"
"If someone did that to me, they'd hear about it."
"There's something wrong with you."

They don't make room for other points of view or accept blame. When Aries is good, they're very good. When they're bad, they're the worst. They are all or nothing.

They think they know what you need, yet they forget to actually ask first. They take over. When an Aries learns to turn the observer on, to pay attention to what other people are saying, their awareness softens them.

ARIES OBSERVER

The observer shows you how to pause and be considerate. It's not easy because of your lack of impulse control. You probably will not be able to turn on your observer in the heat of the moment. You must practice this for a while. The observer can help you recognize when you need to say, "I'm sorry." And mean it.

The observer helps you accept that you stand out. People see your strong energy as that of a leader and want your direction, especially if it's considerate. Your observer says, "You are a delightful child who views life with enthusiasm, energy, and fresh eyes." Remind us how to love this life, Aries. We need your leadership.

ARIES HIGH ROAD

Everyone needs a cheerleader, an enthusiast by their side. People may say, especially to Aries women, that you are too harsh and blunt. If that's true, so what? On the high road, an Aries meets such a response with grace, apologizing to others: "Sorry, I didn't mean to take over."

Lots of Aries don't feel they ever need to apologize. Do you think Lady Gaga, Elton John, Celine Dion (all Aries) apologize for their big personalities? Of course not. They inspire us with their enthusiasm. If there's one thing Aries is not, it's subtle. That's not something requiring an apology.

Yet it's a beautiful person who can say "I'm sorry" and mean it without feeling shamed. It can feel nearly impossible for an Aries to say "I was wrong" or "I need you" or "please help me." When you find that soft inner place (I promise it's in there), you've found Aries on the high road.

ARIES MEDICINE

The best medicine for an Aries is physical movement. That can mean hiking, cutting the lawn, a tennis game, running—so many possibilities. If you've been told you're no good at sports, forget that story. You haven't found the exercise you really love yet (it might just be walking—long and fast, with loud music in your headset).

Sing loudly, let out your anger, and express your feelings. Sitting on your fire stifles your energy and creates depression and lethargy. Express it.

ARIES'S LIFE LESSON

You are here to learn humility. I know you don't like hearing that. You have a hard time understanding when people get mad at you. It's okay to admit you are wrong. Don't forget to ask what everybody else wants. Read the room, adjust your timing, and remember to include others. "Oh! I should have asked before I made this decision." Humility releases you from shame. Of course you got it wrong—you learn lessons the hard way. No shame in that.

ARIES MOON

You are impulsive. You have fiery feelings. An Aries moon can be a bully at worst, or an inspired leader at best. When your emotions get fired up, you have no off button. You get super angry, really fast. Just as fast, it's over. Meanwhile, the person you screamed at still feels hurt. Like any Aries, an Aries moon needs to practice those words the observer encourages: "I'm so sorry, I was wrong." One thing you do not lack is enthusiasm for those you love and energy to get the job done. This is the strength of an Aries moon.

MERCURY IN ARIES

Your mind is fast and impulsive. It's hard for people to keep up with you. You are a pioneer. You keep going when everyone else stops. You're breaking new ground. You are willing to release the attachments the rest of us have to maintain the status quo. You are not afraid to bring us into the new in service of the collective.

It would be good to learn to say: "Don't argue with me right now, I'm all riled up." There is nothing worse to a Mercury in Aries than when someone says, "Calm down," right in the middle of a fight. It's okay to respond, "I have to get this out. I'm sorry it's so strong." It's virtually impossible to shut a Mercury in Aries down—nor should we. They need to vent their fire. Nobody wants to argue with a Mercury in Aries when they are upset.

Mercury in Aries is a sprinter, not a long-distance runner. When their enthusiasm dies down, they move on to the next thing. In the moment, though, they get super excited and go down the rabbit hole. Don't judge yourself for this, Mercury in Aries. It's your nature. "I'm going to start a business!" "I'm going to be an astrologer!" You're all in, and just as quickly, you're out. I've had people with Mercury in Aries sign up for my astrology school. They come for a few classes, and then they'll disappear. When I follow up, they tell me they are already on to something else. "Oh, no, I changed my mind, I'm into Reiki now." The fire burns hot and then snuffs out, and the whole story has changed.

ARIES RISING

You are a fighter. Why would a soul fight? You fight for us to remember the privilege of living this life, to instill love and honor. If you are pushy, that is as it should be. You are simply trying to make contact, to get closer to us. Most of all, your desire is to help us stay awake and not miss our life. You, Aries rising, shout out with your very presence, "Wake up! Be alert! Be real!"

You are born with a naturally strong body. Therefore, you are physical. If you are being your real self, you won't be comfortable sitting still. You need to move. "Come on! Let's go already!"

You're the personality who says, "Don't tell me what to do!" You are too much of a rebel to just follow unknowingly. Watching you can be exhausting. That doesn't mean you're always imposing; you are just being yourself.

Yet, because people resist their rising signs, Aries rising can resist this urge to interrupt and run high voltage. You may tone down the straight shooting because it feels awkward. The soul does not want to impose. "Am I taking up too much space?" "Do I take the lead again?" "Does it look like I'm bossing people around?" "Should I be gentler?" Aries rising, remember you are supposed to inspire us into action. Your soul promised to take on leadership. That was the agreement.

If your rising sign is Aries and the rest of your chart is more docile, I'm so sorry. Your soul came here to be in charge and to push. That might feel shocking. The dynamic between fire in your rising sign and another element in your sun sign can create an inner conflict. It feels like one foot on the gas, and one foot on the brakes.

Truth be told, you are intense. If you feel far away from your get-up-and-go, I'd like to challenge that. If you don't express your fire the way your soul wants, it's going to create depression and self-esteem issues. You may become accident-prone or lethargic. You are not built to sit idle. Get up, move!

At the highest level, you will have the courage to ask for help from someone who understands fire and shoots from the hip with no inhibition—this is a quick way for Aries rising to get comfortable in their true expression. Fire is there waiting for you. It's your divine inheritance.

SATURN IN ARIES

Be a kind warrior. Stand up for yourself.

Can you admit you're bossy, feisty, or pushy? You have to move energy through your body. You have to realize your aggressive behavior is your funny way of trying to make contact. If you are passive, you need to go exercise. If you are too aggressive, you can learn when to stop.

Saturn in Aries is here to learn how to do healthy independence. Think for yourself. Find your natural sense of autonomy, confidence, and agency while being kind to others.

Life lesson: Be independent and spontaneous. Fight for love, while staying true to yourself. If you're scared of your power, increase it. If you throw it around, tone it down.

MEDITATION FOR ARIES

I am learning how to notice my effect on people. I am cultivating compassion so that I understand that truth can hurt. May I learn the peaceful state that lives on the inside and rest there without distraction. When people find me offensive or reject me or react, may I learn how to take a deep breath, say I'm sorry, and inquire, "What just happened?" May I never assume I am the one with all the answers. I can find humility within myself. Humility is my strength.

THE ESSENCE OF ARIES

Do you know that part of you that gets so excited when you see your favorite person, like the dog jumping up and down as you walk in the door, its tail wagging, all wrapped up in joy that you are home? Think Aries. It's the impulse in all of us to go, do, act, move, work out, sing, dance. It's the kid in all of us that needs to be civilized and taught how to exchange their outside voice for their inside voice. Don't ask an Aries what they think if you don't want the straight goods. Don't tell this part to cool off and tone down their anger. When they're mad, they're mad!

Aries has a voice that speaks so clearly, you don't have to wonder if they mean what they say, or what their opinion is. You will know very quickly if they like you or not—and so will they. Crystal clear, this person has likes and dislikes. They are black and white. When they've had enough of you, you will be dismissed—not without good reason. We all wish we could be that clear, to know our preferences and then stay true to them. To some, that comes across as heartless, although that is not what Aries intends.

The evolved version of Aries is willing to communicate. They are aware enough to know their effect on people, like when they have a change of heart, and they communicate with kindness and wisdom. Everything changes, and Aries is not going to pretend something is true when it no longer is true. If Aries can love that about themselves and add large doses of love for others, their truth will set us all free.

9

The Psychology of Taurus

I HAVE

Element: Earth
Mode: Fixed
House: Second
Planet: Venus
Body part: Throat—they have the gift
of a resonant voice.

If you only understood how self-conscious I get when someone is watching me, or there is some kind of pressure to perform. It's so uncomfortable that I freeze. I enjoy taking my time so I can accomplish my task and do it well. Please don't rush me.

I am at my best when I know what is expected. Give me clear instructions and I can learn the task, over time, on my schedule. I will get there and then eventually, get really good at what we're doing. I need structure, a defined role, and a contract written out that will not change. No question about it—I love to work. One of my challenges is that I often say yes when I mean no, which has me working too much. Once I start, I won't leave any project untended. I have to finish what I start.

You know how in nature (my favorite place), everything goes in seasons? It's the same for me. There are times I get all excited to work out, for example. That lasts awhile—until I run out of steam. Truth be told, I wish I had more get-up-and-go—however, it's okay. I like how my seasons flow.

I love feeling safe and secure. When I trust that I have resources in the bank, my home is clean, and I am with my favorite animals and people just hanging out, I am in heaven. You might think I'm a simpleton. I am. I know what I like. So I stay with my favorites over and over again. It doesn't bother me. I like hanging out at home, and I don't want to explain myself. If you are invited over, know that I must feel close to you (there are so few I can say that about). If you are in my close circle, you can count on me to be there for you when you are in need.

I am so loyal; over time you will see that. Our bond will last a lifetime. I'll see to it. Just tell me what you need from me. I'm happy to help you out. With enough lead time, I will fit you into my schedule. Just don't push me or expect too much. I'll always do my best and have your back. Trust me: when I give you my word, it's real. I embody simple values, music of the past, jewelry and antiques passed down through generations, my favorite family photos. I love history and the stuff of life that outlasts us.

Call me old-fashioned. I will take that as a compliment.

Taurus longs for safety, security, financial stability, and comfort. Taurus watches their favorite movies again and again and plays their favorite songs on repeat, even if it's driving everyone around them crazy. That's Taurus energy. It's the part in us that is simple and consistent. You could compare Taurus to Winnie the Pooh—a slow talker, even a slower walker, sauntering through the woods looking forward to the end of the walk, the honey, and the sweet friend to share it with.

The stereotype of Taurus as slow, lazy, boring, or stubborn is unfair. Not every Taurus is turtle-slow. They can move with efficiency. They are certainly not lazy—even if they think they are. Quite the opposite. Hard workers, they never give up. They stay the course. When it's time to relax, Taurus will seek comfort at home. Yes, Taurus is slow in changing their mind, that's true. Often, they stay in the same job for many years. They may complain. Still, they won't quickly change unless they have to.

Taurus has the gift of patience. If you repeat something enough times, slowly at first and then with greater efficiency, you get really good at it. Taurus believes repetition creates success, even mastery. They are brilliant, in their quiet way.

"Stop to smell the flowers" is a Taurus quote. They like to savor a warm buttered croissant while slowly sipping their coffee or tea in their favorite mug, in the comfy chair with those old slippers on. Food excites Taurus. Have you noticed that you order the exact same dish at your favorite restaurant over and over again, and hate it when the menu changes? You wonder why anyone would change something that works. It's not unusual for you to wake up thinking about your meals. You have a funny relationship with the D-word (diet!), thinking you *should* be losing weight. It's okay for you to love your body the way it is. It makes you, you.

Taurus brings elements of their home with them wherever they go, not unlike a turtle. One of my best friends, all the way back from kindergarten (who was a Taurus, so we never lost contact), had a mother who was also a Taurus. I used to go to her house before school. Her mom was always baking something, and boy, did the house smell good! My mom never baked. There was something so comforting about my friend's mom. Here is a Taurus trait: they instinctively know how to make a house homey, filled with old relics, photos, and lots of plants. It feels good to be in the home of a Taurus. They love to collect stuff and label the collections. They can save things for years, just like they save those old comfortable sweaters and slippers that they just keep putting on—holes and all. Obviously, they know what they like and what they don't like— and they don't like surprises. Predictability is their preference. You could call in a Gemini or a Sagittarius to shake up a Taurus, just for fun.

Taurus is a natural gardener, nurturing food and flowers with their own hands, directly out of the earth. They are, after all, an earth sign, ultimately grounded. Taurus doesn't understand people who are flighty, flaky, or lack follow-through. Their mottos are: "Do things right the first time" and "If it ain't broke, don't fix it." No rushing around required. No change just for the sake of change. That is so Taurus.

They are excellent with their hands, fixing things, giving the best hugs, putting the flowers into a beautiful arrangement. Massage and bodywork are often their specialties. Computers and technology are not Taurus's favorite things, especially at first. They feel so distant and cut off. Taurus prefers face-to-face contact. Social media is distracting. And yet, to see old friends there is a thrill. First Taurus complains, then over time, new technology (any change, really) becomes acceptable.

They just might be the sweetest of all the signs—that is until they get angry, which takes a lot. They would prefer to be outdoors or watching their favorite TV show or listening to the songs they love than get into an argument. If you've seen an angry Taurus, consider it a rare sight.

Sadly, they live with an insecurity that they aren't good enough. They can't avoid hearing the noisy gremlins putting them down. Because the Taurus gremlins compare themselves to others, Taurus often feels they are falling short. They simply can't see themselves objectively. It's hard for a Taurus to accept a compliment, especially about their appearance or talents. Barbra Streisand is a Taurus. She gets such a bad case of stage fright every time she performs that we have been told she can get sick. You're the best singer in the whole world, and you don't know it? They often have outstanding voices for singing and for talking. Barbra Streisand, Cher, and Adele: all Tauruses. Even if you can't sing, I bet you have your go-to music you've listened to over the years. You may be better at singing than you think, though. Taurus is the last one to command the spotlight or proclaim themselves talented. "I'm not that good," says every Taurus.

My suggestion, Taurus, is to listen to a friend or family member to hear how much we adore you and believe in you. We see your talents and beautiful qualities. You are a rock. It's exactly your quiet fortitude that allows us to rely on you. By the way, we don't think you're boring at all—that's all in your head. If you only knew how reassuring your stability is, you might feel better about yourself.

You can see why Taurus might seem old-fashioned and hard to get along with at times, especially for those who like change and excitement. Don't try to persuade a Taurus to change for no good reason. This is where Taurus's stubbornness comes out. Modernization is not a good reason to change for Taurus. What's wrong with the old way? If your grandmother or grandfather did it this way, and your mother or father did it this way, then you're going to do it this way, too, no questions asked. That may come across as stubborn. In truth, you just know what you like.

Wearing a gold family heirloom or a friendship ring feels like you are connected with your past and the people you love. There is something about gold that Taurus appreciates. Just think of the old prospector who would bite the gold to be sure it's real. Taurus only wants what is genuine and authentic.

I know a Taurus who accrued great wealth. He no longer lived with financial insecurity. So, when he liked something, in fear of it being discontinued, he would buy it in bulk. I laughed when I saw he bought three pairs of his favorite running shoes—all in the same color. In his closet, he had multiples of the same shirts he liked, all in order and wrapped up to keep them safe.

Because each sign has a spark of its opposite, there is a little bit of Scorpio in every Taurus, which explains why Taurus trusts slowly. Taurus, like Scorpio, needs to be in control. They can appear guarded, a little cautious, and definitely suspicious about new people. Once they love someone, Taurus is loyal to a fault, so breakups, fights, and divorces are especially hard on them. When their sense of security is challenged, they freeze. Once they've bonded to someone, losing that person is like losing a limb. It takes a very long time to heal.

It's ironic that Taurus makes other people feel secure, yet they are plagued with insecurity. They worry their hips are not proportionate, or they have the wrong nose for their face. They judge themselves harshly. We see someone we love—they see faults. I recently worked with a photographer who is a Taurus. I've never seen a more beautiful woman, yet when I told her that, she said, "Eh . . . not really. Thanks anyway."

It's okay to be slow, deliberate, careful. You still aren't sure. Yes, Taurus, it is okay! If you hear it enough, will you finally believe it? If you understand that the negative broken record, which sounds so convincing, isn't telling you the truth and is just a bad habitual thought, you can change the tune. Taurus, I am sure you have broken many habits in this life. You can break this one. Start saying nice things about yourself. You are the provider—what a gift you give to all of us that you call your family. You are often the glue that keeps us together. We love to come to your house for that same yummy dinner you make so well and for all of your sweet four-legged loves. Food imbued with love. That is the truth.

Thank you for your deep ability to love and not demand. I wish for you that you could receive the way you give. Your stability is so comforting to us, even while you may feel as if you are slow. Your pace allows your life to get better as you age. Stay tuned—things will end up going your way.

PROFILE OF A TAURUS

Everett is a classic Taurus. He loves food and indulges in sweets. He is obsessed with the show *The Office* and has watched all the seasons well over fifteen times and loves to quote the characters, who feel like family to him. He plays the same songs over and over and is a talented singer with a beautiful voice who majored in vocal music in college. He never stepped into the spotlight for long. He has struggled with lethargy and the lure of a sedentary life. He has only been able to exercise when he makes it into a routine that feels comfortable. Then he gets a down day and he gets back out of the habit of moving his energy. Sometimes it just seems so difficult to move.

His family used to tease him that he had a special relationship with gravity because he seemed glued to the ground. Everett could never skateboard or jump very high, like his athletic brother. He always loved swimming because it was the only time when he could get a break from that feeling of being bound to the ground. In the water, he was quick and graceful. On land, he was always slow. His mother used to call him the slowest boy in the world. He sometimes wonders if he isn't accomplishing enough in his life working in sales, yet his gentle charisma makes him a successful salesperson, and he is good at helping people who have a problem.

He likes his job and works hard, yet we all know that his happy place is to cuddle on the couch with his young son, watching the same movie they've both seen many times. He loves to make his anxious Virgo son feel safe that way. He makes their house a home.

TAURUS LOW ROAD

The low road of Taurus is a result of believing what the gremlins say, which increases fear and insecurity. The sky is falling, it's a worst-case scenario, so you'd better go pack up everything in the house. Do we have that spare change we hid in that little bag? Because we might need it now! They catastrophize at the thought of an unexpected event because inherently they do not feel safe. They love comfort so much—they would love it if they didn't have to move from the couch, ever.

It's hard for a Taurus to ask for a raise or a promotion. They devalue themselves and charge less than what they deserve, especially on the low road. This can invite depression in, leading to giving up because of past memories they just can't shake—one way Taurus gets stuck.

A low-road Taurus is hard to spot. They act like everything is okay, they are stable, and everybody is happy. Secretly, however, they feel unappreciated and grumpy, regretting that they never achieved their goals. This is a Taurus fear: "I'm going to spend the rest of my life wishing I dreamt bigger, dated more, exercised more, had more friends. I can't find my energy, so I'll just sit here without moving, knowing I'm not fulfilling my purpose in life."

THE TAURUS OBSERVER

All you need to start channeling the observer is a big dose of compassion for what you really are: kind and gentle. You deal with insecurity, it's true. So, you aren't always highly motivated? You'll do the things when you're ready. You work hard. You have permission to relax afterward and give yourself that little reward. Stability is your gift. The observer says so.

I know you have money stashed away. It's okay to be a saver, not a spender. It's okay to delight in sensual pleasures, and to do things over and over. The observer can help you see this. So you've already seen that movie ten times? So what? Let's see it again! You loved it the first time and you will love it even more the eleventh time.

TAURUS HIGH ROAD

To understand the high road of Taurus, think of Buddha. Buddha was born under the full moon in Taurus. He came from great wealth, snuck out of his compound, saw people starving in the streets, and was so distraught that he left his world of privilege and ended up under a tree where he took to meditation. That's so Taurus: "I have an idea—let's just sit here for as long as possible, seeking peace!"

Think about the Buddhists who wear those orange robes. They eat dal and rice every day. They chant the same chants for years. They've been reading the same books for millennia. You could also think of the Jewish faith as very Taurus—they read the Torah over and over again, the same book, every Shabbos. They read the same chapter and review it again. In fact, Taurus rules all religion—the rosary chants, the parables, the familiar rules for living a good life, the repeated prayers, the faith without questioning, the traditions. Religion thrives on ritual and repetition, and so does Taurus.

However, Buddha evolved. He realized and famously said that all suffering comes from attachment. It's no coincidence that attachment is one of Taurus's design faults. This is the Taurean struggle: to let go, throw away old things, and ask yourself, "Why do I keep all this stuff?" Releasing is the path to enlightenment for Taurus (and for all of us).

Taurus on the high road is a giver, not a hoarder. They idealize their partners and children and then cater to them. How a Taurus loves to have grandchildren to dote on and pour love over! People may say, "Why do you go to so much trouble for people? What makes you do that?" It's your Venusian nature (Venus rules Taurus) to be devoted to those you love. Your promise of loyalty to family, pets, and those you care about is unlike any others.

Over time, Taurus can try to give with no attachment and to let go lightly, without holding on too tightly. The more life they experience, the more they can cultivate a "calm down, this too shall pass" mentality. This is the mature Taurus—so relaxed and easy. The real challenge is to receive and acknowledge how much you are loved, take it in, and let it melt your heart. You softie!

TAURUS MEDICINE

Taurus, sometimes the best medicine for you is to just stay home, guilt-free. You love being at home, so why force yourself to go out, especially when you need to decompress after a stressful time?

Baking, cooking, and a full refrigerator are medicine for you. You feel good being the helper, and you are a very thoughtful person.

Remember that you are an earth sign. Go outside and garden. I shouldn't have to tell you that because it's instinctual.

Exercising is greatly satisfying for you. However, you tend to resist exercise. Working out, on your terms, with your rhythm, in your home or out in nature, is good medicine.

You also respond well to structured exercise or cleansing food plans (let's not say "diet"!). Natural foods, the way the earth made them, make you feel amazing.

Get your car detailed. Buy new pillows. Get a new comforter. You don't like to waste money, yet changing things up a bit might be just what you need. It's good to move your things around and let go of what has collected dust for too long. This isn't easy for you and it's just a suggestion. I would never demand that you do anything you don't want to do. That's how to get that bull riled up. I wouldn't want to do that.

TAURUS'S LIFE LESSON

Your life lesson is to embrace self-esteem and recognize your physical beauty, Taurus! You really are beautiful like the earth is beautiful—even when the earth is a mess, dropping leaves or after a storm, we still see her bounty and glory.

You don't have a big ego, and that's a good thing. Don't forget, though, that ego is part of who you are. It's in there, and you deserve to celebrate how much magic you bring to others. Feel free to increase your rates or ask for a raise, even though I know this isn't easy for you.

TAURUS MOON

This is the most exalted position. Why does the moon love to be in Taurus? Because of its stability. Emotions are so disorienting when they come and go. Taurus moon is stable and far less moody. They will never break up with someone unless the situation becomes extreme. On the rare occasion that they do get upset, be prepared for strong emotions that demand to be heard. That's when the bull comes out. Loyal and solid, their psychological wisdom is their strength.

MERCURY IN TAURUS

Here we have a dependable, responsible person who might have been told somewhere in the past that they had a learning disability, or perhaps they were "slow." Your mind works at a slower pace. That has nothing to do with intelligence. If your Mercury is in Taurus, you are a careful, deliberate thinker who doesn't speak rashly and considers what you say and write before expressing it.

You are a hands-on, experiential learner. It's not your fault that traditional education didn't value that. You don't want to hear the theory—you want to do it yourself. Don't be self-conscious if it takes you a few tries. Once you've got it, you've got it. You have a mind like an elephant, and an elephant never forgets. However, as a consequence of that early insecurity, you double-check yourself a lot. What a great teacher you can be because you organize systematically and explain big concepts in bite-sized bits.

When you talk to someone with Mercury in Taurus, it helps if you touch them. Take their hands and say, "I need you to hear this." Then they can shift their attention in the right direction.

TAURUS RISING

You have Buddha-like energy. You bring calm wherever you go, and yet you are strong. Half of you longs for normality, while at the same time, not unlike Buddha, you are seeking detachment and ease. That is a funny combo. Strong and gentle. Free and longing for security. That is what your soul seeks.

Safety is what you bring, and yet you suffer from the longing to feel safe. You *are* safe. Think about it: Has there ever been a time when you really didn't have what you needed? Even if your dreams have not been fulfilled as you thought they would be, other plans arrive that are beyond your expectation. Your motto when you are at your best is: "Life takes care of me." You know this in your bones. Taurus rising has the potential to be trusting, calm, and patient.

Your body loves comfort food so it's not a surprise if, over the years, you become a little bit soft in the middle—all the nicer for hugging. You might have a thick neck and most probably a healing voice and good looks. You have broad shoulders because you provide stability and carry a sense of responsibility.

The soul invites Taurus into a life of gentleness. It's interesting how you hold your cards close to the chest. You watch people while feeling neglected, or misunderstood—you probably won't say anything, though you don't really need much. Not everyone is so concerned with others the way you are.

What does a mountain need? What does a tree need? Water and nature. It is essential that you find a connection with the outdoors and those very few who you consider true family. When Taurus rising achieves a simple life of nature, beauty, and comfort, they are living a soulful life.

SATURN IN TAURUS

It's okay to go slow.

You have a need to keep things comfortable in your own way and on your own terms. The key is to realize that you are susceptible to getting stuck in comfort, or having it your own way.

Ask yourself the question: "Are there repetitive behaviors in my life that I could change with a small shift?" Just know that you need consistency and simplicity to be happy. There is no need to complicate things. Your lesson in this life is to find the beauty in simplicity. Be like the turtle, moving slowly and steadily. Remember, the turtle won the race.

Life lesson: Do not rush. Pleasure is your birthright. Enjoy life through your senses.

MEDITATION FOR TAURUS

I am comfortable in my skin. I'm finding my worth. I'm willing to acknowledge my hard work. It yields fruit, even if my mind disagrees. I see the value in loyalty. I relish the opportunity to be an example of simplicity and stability. I have everything I need.

THE ESSENCE OF TAURUS

Who said peace and quiet are boring? Taurus keeps the old photo of their parents on a shelf because it elicits memories that make them happy. They think about those times back when their whole family lived together under one roof. They think about the young part of themselves that loved *Mary Poppins* so much and listened to "Supercalifragilisticexpialidocious" so often that they memorized all the words (and still know them).

Taurus loves the consistency that celebrates the same thing over and over again. Modern-day life is complicated. The social media assault means we are exposed to endless data. Computers have replaced the good old-fashioned Etch A Sketch, the walk in the park, the push-button phone. Now we all have a minicomputer in our hands. Isn't the modern world exhausting? So much so that Taurus may lose their get-up-and-go and feel stuck in a world of fatigue. Isn't "tired" supposed to be associated with old age, when energy has waned and gravity is taking over? Taurus wonders about that.

"Don't get stuck!" Taurus wrongly accuses themselves of this, wishing they were more mobile or successful. That thought can ruin a Taurus's whole life. Instead, when they turn to nature for examples of how to keep evolving and accepting what is, they feel better: the trees, the sea, the mountains all keep endlessly growing and changing without judging the seasons they go through.

Taurus has a favorite room in the house, or a favorite chair. They love nothing more than to cuddle up with the dog and the cat and hope no one calls. People may call that lazy. It's just the part of Taurus that wants quiet. Taurus works hard! They save their peace and quiet for the end of the day, the weekend, or the days off, when they can veg. There is nothing wrong with vegging. If only we all knew how to relax and just be. This would change the planet, all in a moment.

10

The Psychology of Gemini

I THINK

Element: Air
Mode: Mutable
House: Third
Planet: Mercury
Body part: Lungs, arms, and fingers—they are always breathlessly excited and talking with their hands.

If only you understood what it feels like to have ants in your pants—to be able to make something fun with the slightest effort. I'm willing to go shopping at the last minute to get what we need, read that magazine about the shiny ones who made it on the front page, watch that show out of sequence, and then watch it again in order. I have so many books to read, podcasts to listen to, and so little time to get lost in the magic of new information. How will I do it all? I surely will try.

I love to listen and learn and engage with so many topics, it's hard to stay on just one. I'm always happy to move my body around. I'll jump in the car willingly, without knowing where we're going. I'll spontaneously run to the store to get something I lost, or get the new book I didn't even know was there until I saw it. If I bump into someone who needs a ride home, I'm there. What do you want me to do? Hold your phone while you load the groceries? Load the groceries while you talk on your phone? I can do it all, and then some.

Part of me thinks you'll never understand me or know what it's like to be me. Can anyone be as interested in new thoughts and ideas as I am? I'm constantly multitasking. I have the energy to jump up and do things, to change plans in an instant. I know how to pivot.

I dance through life, problem-solving all the way. Can you put on makeup in the rear-view mirror while stopped at a red light while singing loudly to the newest Adele song (making up the words you don't know) while planning your workday while talking to your friend on the speaker phone, all at the same time? I can. So what if I'm late, or forgot the ingredients for the cake I'm going to bake tonight while finishing my work, loading the dishwasher, feeding the dog, and helping my kids with their math homework. I can fix all that in just a minute with a quick text—wait, where did I put my phone?

If you had all the thoughts zooming around the roller coaster of a mind I have, you too would be laughing at inappropriate times. I just made up the best poem—and I forgot to write it down. Oh, look, there's my phone! Hold on, I'm going to stop the car to record a voice memo. There is nothing I can't do in an instant. If constant whiplash and change irritate you, stay far away from me. Truth be told, I am a party waiting to happen. Try having fun without me, and good luck. You need me to bring fun into your life. I'm always looking for a dance partner who can keep up with me. Is it you?

Gemini is curious and interested in everything, and has a ravenous appetite for learning new information. They love to talk, to know what's going on, and they have the attention span of a gnat. Who is more fascinated with people? No one. There they go, down the rabbit hole of social media and the endless videos, stories, history; the internet is made for Gemini.

Look up anything in an instant, no need to remember all the details. You can always look it up again. Social media is like a coffee shop for a Gemini to hang out in.

Gemini is stereotyped for talking more than listening. That is often true, although Gemini can learn how to listen. Geminis who don't relate to the classical stereotype may be quiet, even shy. Some Geminis are introverted. When no one is looking, they talk out loud to themselves. And why not? You are fascinating company. The way a Gemini texts is cryptic and fast. You may need an interpreter. Or just let it slide. The Gemini will call in a minute and fill you in, anyway.

Gemini has a reputation for being ditsy or fickle. Actually, they are intellectual, even if they don't always show it. This is the kid that just loved school. In high school, they figured out how to skip class and still did really well. They are the charming bookworms, flirty professors, or slippery politicians whose language never answers the question straight. Being ten steps ahead of everyone else can appear as ADHD or distractibility.

While the sign of Gemini is the twins, there are way more than two variations of Gemini. They have many sides. Nonbinary is easy for them. Gemini can be ambidextrous and operate using both their male and female sides, or neither, or they can change from one to the other, just like that. As soon as you think you've pigeonholed them, they change. Mutability and changeability are Gemini's natural gifts.

If you could hear their internal dialogue, you would hear *Romper Room,* a circus, a kindergarten classroom with books everywhere, colored pens, and a messy desk. Gemini, your nature is that of a six-year-old. Not that you are immature (although sometimes you are, let's be honest). You have a joyful, childlike spirit that charms even the most jaded.

Should you grow up? Nah, that feels like someone else's idea. You get in trouble for not showing up and not even calling when you said you would. Oops, you double-booked. You feel bad. Were you being duplicitous? Not on purpose. Who could possibly wrangle all your thoughts and goals and coordinate all the people in your world? If anyone heard your inner voice (the gremlins), they would know that a "bad kid" lives in your head, or at least, a kid who thinks they must be bad because they always get in trouble.

If being spontaneous is bad, then you are! You thrive on constant stimulation, grabbing the magazine, reading the back of the book first, wondering about how the toilet paper package was made—your mind is so curious that you can't self-soothe. You can't turn it off. You just can't.

They seem confident, yet Geminis secretly wonder if they really know enough to pretend they know enough. "I know I'm not really an expert at what I'm doing. Did I remember the correct details . . . I think I did? Are they accurate? No one will know. Or will they? I'm getting bored and moving on . . . oh no, not again. Can't I stick with anything?"

Then there is the Gemini that is *very* good at a lot of things. You know who you are. You might even feel self-conscious or guilty that you're smarter and faster. You stand apart because you did fifty things without trying and, by the way, you did them so well that now people are imitating you. This happens to Geminis a lot—people imitate them. How do they manage to be so smart and funny, making up nicknames for everyone? They are light-hearted, quick-thinking, and charismatic all at the same time.

A classic Gemini problem is sleeping, what with that very noisy internal dialogue. This explains why your nervous system works overtime. You run on a higher frequency than the rest of us. This is why meditation feels elusive for you. I'll tell you why: you wiggle too much. You become impatient without immediate results.

You've got this motor going vroom-vroom, which has you moving too fast. It feels like you're going to be late, even though you don't really care if you get in trouble. Lucky for you, you are endearing, so you get away with it. Your charisma is evident in that smile and your humor—you tickle us. You spark interesting thoughts. You are the quintessential storyteller. We laugh at your stories. You lighten the energy, and we all feel better when you are around.

So what if you are inconsistent? As an astrologer, I give you permission to be so. Sometimes you'll be late. Sometimes you'll be on time. Sometimes you'll forget things, and sometimes you'll remember the most ridiculous details. Yes, you can be flaky, yet look what you do for the room, for your family, for your friends. You are so much fun!

Your promise this lifetime is to show us curiosity and the innocence of the fresh mind that never takes for granted the simple pleasures in life. Even if it requires you to get a little more excited than the rest of us, it's simply you being you, and that is the promise of every good Gemini.

Thank you for your sweet, light spirit. You sure know how to laugh when you finally get out of your head, inquire about this life, and bring levity to what you do. It's okay to be a perpetual student—it just means you never want to stop learning. The world is better for having you in it.

PROFILE OF A GEMINI

Jennifer grew up in the Southern states, on a farm. She was still quite young when her parents recognized that she simply could not be stopped. She was playing tennis, singing in the choir, playing in the band—she wanted to do it all. Her parents thought of her as a bit out of control because of her constant busyness and interest in absolutely everything.

As soon as she could leave home, she moved to California and got a degree in marketing. She ended up at Esalen Institute, a holistic center famous for the part it played in the Human Potential Movement in the 1970s, that still serves as a center for creative thinkers—which is 100 percent Gemini. They call themselves "a community of seekers," and Jennifer thrived there.

While she was there, she had sex with everyone—boys, girls, it didn't matter. She was so full of love. Finally, she met a man who took one look at her and said, "I'm going to marry you," and sure enough, they got married. Now they have three children, and she homeschools them in her Colorado neighborhood.

Every Saturday morning, Jennifer invites a group of women to her house to sing. They play drums and she makes up the songs. She thrives on the action, the attention, and the presence of lots of people she loves. Jennifer sings every chance she gets, including at the dinner table. Like a true Gemini, she is always multitasking, making fresh banana bread while she's working with her child on a phonics lesson while her computer is scrolling through unbelievable photos of her adventures while she's getting dressed to go to dance class. She is like those goddesses with the many arms. She can do it all at the same time.

To this day, Jennifer is so pretty and has the sexiest energy. She is a little entertainment unit, and she wakes up smiling every day. Wherever she goes, she lights up the room. That's the archetype of the classical Gemini—you can't stop looking at them and listening to them. They wiggle and giggle and talk and jump up and down and make you happy to be alive. Their joy is contagious.

GEMINI LOW ROAD

Gemini's low road is to be scattered, forgetful, anxious, and to overthink everything. They can't get a full night's sleep, which makes them seem a bit out of it. They keep their distance and, at worst, miss out on intimacy. Even though they present as social butterflies, they remain detached. Geminis can become irritating (even to themselves), never realizing it's their speed and constant chatter. Who wants to hang around with somebody who is always three steps ahead and won't stop talking? At the low level, Geminis just go on and on without reading the room. I dated a Gemini and I finally had to say to him, "Okay, Mr. Gemini. You have to ask *me* some questions about *myself* now. Just pretend you're interested."

People can get hurt by you, Gemini. Maybe you left a job and didn't say good-bye. You made new friends and carelessly abandoned your previous friends. You aren't around to notice who was hurt by your swift departure. You're already on to the next thing. Did you take time to listen?

Bottom line, when Gemini is on the low road, they live in their own little reality. They can be inaccurate and sloppy. They play with people for their own amusement, then leave them without warning, which can break hearts. This is a Gemini's greatest fear: "No one ever really knows me. I am just playing this role that is not really true. I can't get to my real self. I am faking it and no one knows."

THE GEMINI OBSERVER

The observer says: "Yes, you talk a lot. You are always changing. You multitask like the Tasmanian devil. Can't you see the humor in this?" When Gemini's observer steps in, you see your interactions with kindness and realize that you are on automatic. "You know what?" you can say to yourself, "I have a short attention span and it's okay. This isn't going away. I need to slow down just a bit." The observer has you smiling at your endearing behavior and asking, "Why do I make a joke out of everything? Can I try to be patient? Can I let go of my inner kid when the situation calls for it?"

Remember that talking is your gift. Just don't forget to listen. Practice listening. The observer can help you stop filling in people's sentences or talking over your friends. If you can consciously watch yourself without judgment, it will shift that fast-moving nervous system you have. If you do five-minute meditations, that will change your life.

Your observer tickles you. This is where your humor system can really support your ability to not take things personally, or to walk away too quickly. Gemini loves to laugh, even at themselves.

GEMINI HIGH ROAD

At best, Gemini takes life lightly, especially when their ego is in check. They quickly free themselves of toxic situations because they are so willing to change or let go. "The reason angels can fly is because they take life so lightly." That's so Gemini. You change your point of view, with humor, all in a minute. High-road Gemini is still inconsistent or can run on the late side or forget things, though they carry self-awareness and can adjust when needed. They have learned how to listen and be as attentive to the other as they are to themselves.

On the high road, Gemini is a teacher, writer, or researcher. Once you realize you are a brilliant speaker and wordsmith, you will find your calling. Learn to own your brilliance, rather than giving in to the slippery slope of the mind. We will all benefit from your discoveries.

GEMINI MEDICINE

Whether they think they should or think they shouldn't, the fact is that Geminis need to talk. Write in a journal if you don't have good listeners. Just don't forget to read it out loud. The challenge for Gemini is that they will write and write and write, and never really listen to their own voice. They just stash the notebooks away. For reality to sink in, reread it to hear your busy mind. Then you can smile and accept it, or choose to change. If the same issues come up sixty thousand times, it becomes obvious you are avoiding something. Recognizing this will help you to actually understand what your mind is doing.

Geminis benefit from meditation, even though it's not natural for them. They start and stop and pretend they do it all the time. *Busted!* Moving meditation is a good option for Gemini. Try walking or dancing or doing yoga. You don't need to meditate for very long to get the benefits. As a Gemini, I know I can only meditate comfortably for fifteen minutes. I have a friend who did ten days of totally silent meditation, and she's done it countless times. That's a Gemini's worst nightmare. Doing nothing on purpose? Not talking for how long? If you can learn how to get the ego mind/gremlins to sit down, even for a few minutes, you will free the nervous system from being overworked.

Exercise is good for you. You will notice that once you finish your workout, you get creative downloads. It's important to exhaust your mind every so often.

Here's a suggestion: put on music to quiet the noises in your head.

A strong source of medicine for Gemini is friendship. There is no question that you need someone to talk to! I have had my best friend for over thirty years. I talk to her almost every night. It's been my saving grace. If I don't talk to her, I don't feel grounded, and she says it helps her, too (she is also a Gemini).

To feel less scattered and airy, practice grounding. Walk barefoot. Collect crystals and carry them. Cook food. Make a schedule and stick to it, at least occasionally.

GEMINI'S LIFE LESSON

You are here to learn how to quiet your mind. That sounds impossible at first, until you start the practice of listening. Notice that the words "listen" and "silent" have the same letters, at least in English. Think about that, Gemini: in order to listen, you have to be silent. To turn off the inner dialogue means that you listen to the other without imposing your story on top of it: "Oh, that reminds me of . . ." or "I know all about that." When you become silent on the inside, your communication skills become profound. I've learned to spend a lot of time listening. I even tattooed it on my arm.

You cannot get to the soul when the ego is in charge. All the chatter that runs around inside a Gemini's head is the ego mind showing up. It may feel like a Herculean feat to get your ego under the influence of the soul. That is your lesson and learning it will grant you more freedom than you have ever known. And by the way, talk about design faults—every human on this planet has a noise factory that, without wisdom or awareness, will become the ruin of them. That is what destroys people. When the mind can take a seat and be obedient to the soul's calling, we can operate with kindness, compassion, and love. Try it—you'll like it!

GEMINI MOON

You don't cry easily and can come across as detached. At worst, you can develop attachment disorders, dissociating as soon as it gets tender and mushy. You say, "I don't want to talk about that." What? You don't want to talk about your mother's diagnosis, or that your dog is sick? Instead, you want to change the subject, talk about the weather, tell us what you had for lunch, give us seemingly unimportant details, just to discharge the internal tension. You'll talk, just not about *that*.

Speak your feelings out loud. It is good for you to do therapy—pay someone to listen to you. You need to talk about your feelings and confusion; otherwise, you will cut off your emotional body and you will become stoic, disconnected, and awkward. While you are good at intellectualizing your feelings, you aren't good at feeling them. Perhaps you can cry at movies or for others, just not for yourself. Emotional disconnection prevents healthy relationships.

People can be baffled by Gemini moon's detachment. When a Gemini moon says, "I'm scared" or "I'm sad," know that you have witnessed something rare.

MERCURY IN GEMINI

Mercury loves to be in Gemini. Mercury rules Gemini. You have the gift of gab. You are an information collector with an unbelievable memory, obsessed with minutiae, able to rattle off statistics with great accuracy, never missing a beat. You effortlessly text and communicate via technology.

Nobody has to wonder what they're thinking. You are great at networking. You have a hard time turning off your brain.

GEMINI RISING

Your soul longs to speak straight from your heart. If you learn how to empty the mind and seek peace, you become the one who can draw a map for the rest of us, with a list of ways to achieve mental calm. When your soul leads, you have the ability to become the teacher who role-models a spiritual life or a success story that we can learn from.

As a channel connecting heaven to the earth, you are a great writer, though you may take that gift for granted or resist it. You often may not want to write—it takes too much time, and you are in a hurry. If you do, there is fame for a brilliant Gemini rising who wants to share their truths. You have the ability to overstep the mind and go straight to the heart of the matter, which is why your words touch us deeply. Whether it is written or spoken, words are your magic.

You are comfortable in your body, with quick, effortless movements. You are good at hiking, yoga, dancing—anything physical at all.

Resist the soul's call and you can become indecisive, addicted to chase and change. Your work in this life is to connect to your soul's voice, rather than playing confused or indecisive. That's the low road of Gemini rising: not staying long enough with what you need to study or teach. The high road is finding something you're good at and sticking to it.

SATURN IN GEMINI

Communication is your gift and/or challenge.

You must learn to master your mind. Your mind can get the best of you. Once you realize that it is just one voice of many that live inside your head, you can find your observer. For you, the position of the observer will set you free. Put on some music in order to quiet the noises in your head.

You came to share your ideas: talking, writing, broadcasting, journaling, teaching. Be flexible with how much you change. It's your lesson. Stop judging the amount of change you require.

Life lesson: Allow yourself to have multiple ideas and to be complex and nuanced without judging yourself. You came here to experience variations and feel free about change. Who cares how many times you've changed jobs?

MEDITATION FOR GEMINI

I want nothing more than to be a child, to see the world anew. I'm here to be the sparkle that tickles people back to remembering how delightful life is. When I get resistance because others feel like I'm doing, talking, moving too fast, I can speak up and say, "I can slow down. I can understand your point of view." The more I allow myself to be childlike, the greater the comfort.

THE ESSENCE OF GEMINI

Who said being a kid has to end? There are kids dressed up in grown-up clothes in grown-up roles. That's Gemini, who can work and play at the same time. A kid in grown-up clothes could be considered dangerous, or at least find it challenging to fit into societal expectations. As long as they can remain curious and feed their appetite for joy, it doesn't matter how much time they spend pursuing answers to their many questions. The pursuit is the fun part! Gemini specializes in discovery and adventure, science and writing and reading, and doing it all so quickly. No wonder they get in trouble! No wonder their multifaceted interests range across the board! No wonder they can seem superficial. Don't be fooled. They are not.

"Be yourself," said every Gemini. "Don't accept the norms of society. Don't let them put you in a box!" Everyone knows you can't hold air in a box. It will sneak out and free itself. Hello, Gemini!

Fascination is what makes a Gemini move through their world with so much speed and delight, changing hats, changing roles, allowing the moment to determine what comes next. Plans? Who needs plans? They have the gift of spontaneity, allowing their energy to stay flexible.

Their conversations are laced with new thoughts based on the most recent book they read or podcast they listened to, or the video or documentary they just watched. Their minds remain young and curious, no matter their age. Growing up is overrated. It's never too late to have a happy childhood . . . again, or for the first time. Not if you are a Gemini.

11

The Psychology of Cancer

I FEEL

Element: Water
Mode: Cardinal
House: Fourth
Planet: Moon
Body part: Breasts and stomach—they are the sign of the mother, and they get gut reactions.

If only you understood what it's like to feel people's energy before they even talk. I am at the mercy of the human condition, which is painful. Too much negative energy and I want to go home. How I love to work in the privacy of my own space. There's nowhere else I'd rather be. I'd rather pass on invitations to arbitrary friends' homes or parties. I'm not interested. I'm happiest at home.

However, if it's professional or necessary, I will do what I need to do, regardless of where I have to go or who I'm sitting next to. I didn't always realize I was an empath (the one who can feel the pain in others). I feel everyone's pain, and always put others first, which eventually exhausts me. These days, I have more compassion for myself. It's never been hard to feel you and care. It's been my challenge to take care of me first.

You probably don't understand why I must protect my heart so carefully. Very few are allowed into my inner circle and even then, I keep my heart shielded. I have too many memories that justify this: losing my first pet, my divorce, letting go of my parents, so much more about my past that I don't want to talk about anymore. I don't want to share. All of it has the potential to hurt my heart, although as I get older, I'm learning to heal those wounds. This explains the sensitivity and attention I give to my health, like how conscious I am of what I eat. I've had to learn to watch out for my physical well-being.

I would never say this out loud: I wish someone would please touch me. I need physical contact. Invite me to a family event—even if I say no. My heart will swell. Better yet, come over to my house and ask about my children, my pets, or my past. I love to get everything done that I promised to do, and spend time with just a few of my favorite people. I wish my role as the homemaker, parent, and partner was valued the way it deserves to be.

Our society doesn't understand the pain of being human. I can help with that. Here are some simple values that seem obvious to me: Kids need stability and a consistent grown-up they can rely on. Relationships need updating so no one pretends and gets stuck. Honesty with yourself is a necessity. And don't forget the importance of good food. Any questions? I see things so simply. Self-care, honesty, and family. That's it.

I see through lies. I should have been a therapist, although I couldn't hear all those problems all day. It's too much for me to bear. People's issues are clear to me, even before they say a word. I'm getting tired of talking. I prefer to be doing, working, being quiet, creating, cooking, sewing, painting, gardening, taking care, being physical, exercising, and moving around. With my full schedule, talking is overrated. You will know if I love you by my actions, not my words. If you are lucky enough to get into my inner circle, it is unlikely you are going to get out. I am loyal.

Cancer cares so deeply it hurts. They love their family. Cancerians play the role of the glue that keeps everyone together. It doesn't have to be blood that makes you care about the elderly neighbor, or the adopted son you took on, or that stray cat walking down the street. A Cancer sees the cat, takes it home, remembers there are already seven other cats there, and gets emotional about the realization that no one else helps the strays. They say to the kid across the street who didn't get dinner again, "Come on over, we have plenty." It is the selfless part in all of us that feels compelled to give to those who are neglected or forgotten.

There are negative stereotypes about Cancer: playing the victim, the martyr, crying all the time, being overly sensitive, and worst of all, their name is associated with a disease. More often, you won't see Cancer expressing their emotional pain. As they grow older, they learn how to manage their emotions. They start off vulnerable, and at best, mature into deep emotional wisdom.

Another stereotype is that Cancers are nurturers because Cancer is the sign of the mother. However, they are not all openly nurturing. They carry a shell—think of a crab. You don't just go to their house without calling first, or they may not let you in. Some of them don't want kids, and they get upset when they read that all Cancers are maternal and nurturing. They may have raised their siblings at an early age, or they are teachers, or have pets, and that is enough. There is always an exception to the stereotype.

Let it be said: not all Cancers cry easily. With time, a Cancer learns to protect their heart, having dealt with heavy emotions in childhood. Then their water freezes over, and they learn to stop crying. This especially happens to Cancer men who were taught in our society that men shouldn't cry. They turn to ice. They hide inside their shells. Of course, it can happen to Cancer women as well, especially if they have had a bad breakup or childhood trauma.

However, truth be told, Cancers *are* sensitive, even if they hide it, and they do care, even if they don't show it. What's really going on inside? You are, or have the capacity to be, an empath and a seer. You feel things strongly. Can you find that part of yourself again? Don't be surprised if you find yourself becoming self-absorbed while managing all the feels. A crab holds on for dear life—even when it's time to let go, they are clinching. Let's be clear that it's for one reason only: because you care so much!

One of your magical traits is that you can see your inner child, which is why we all love a Cancer. It's so easy to connect with you—you see through our pretense and reach into our soft spot. This is why kids like you so much. Cancers make us feel safe. We all long to trust and know our family cares. Because you carry so much love, you worry about us. You focus on making our fears subside. You take on our concerns as if they were yours. This explains why Cancers have more gremlins than the rest of us—because they worry so much about everyone and everything.

Cancers carry the feeling of being victimized. "Why me? Why do I have to feel so much? Something feels wrong. Is something bad about to happen?" You carry that universal fear that we have no control over what's happening to us; therefore, negativity follows you around without logic or justification. You can be a sponge for other people's stuff—their feelings, their fears, their sad stories. This explains why food is such an issue for you—you use it for comfort.

You invite very few to your house. Cancers don't like being around unfamiliar people—it's overstimulating. "I'm not joining you tomorrow, and by the way, don't bring John over next time—he and I did not connect." If you are around a Cancer when they get moody, do them a favor: Without saying a thing, just let them be. Leave them alone. Don't take it personally. They require quiet time. They will be glad you understood.

You might be surprised to learn that Cancers are superb businesspeople. Cancer has that stick-to-itiveness to stay the course. It's one of their superpowers. Once a Cancer commits to something, they are built for endurance, hardship, and can work through the pain. It's that little bit of Capricorn in them—their opposite sign. Their productivity, focus, and incredible sensitivity mean they don't miss a beat. "Oh, you forgot to bring the coffee into the meeting, and by the way, Tom doesn't look like he's feeling very well today, and I just heard that your mom's not well, is she okay? Is everyone okay? Good, let's get to work." They know how to get the job done while also maintaining an unbelievable awareness of what's going on for you, often at the expense of their own needs.

Cancers are physically strong and resilient, having one of the strongest constitutions in the zodiac. They don't always feel strong. Cancer, you are so much stronger than you appear. Many body builders are Cancers. You are a tender soul with an extraordinarily strong body. Your pain threshold is higher than most—this is obvious when you think of Cancer as a mom. Imagine her carrying a baby for nine months. She goes through the profound pain of childbirth, then gets up the very next day to feed the family.

During holidays, she doesn't rest or relax. Quite the opposite: she stays up all night wrapping presents, making the holiday meal, and then she cleans it all up. She does all of it, even when nobody remembers to thank her. Even if you aren't a mom, think of this as a metaphor for the hard work and self-sacrifice Cancer is prone to taking on. Make no mistake: there is nothing weak or vulnerable about this sign when they are on a mission.

Have you ever seen a crab literally walk sideways? They don't rush in. First, they wait and observe to sense what's occurring. To some, it can appear that Cancer is avoidant—call it pickiness or discernment. They are waiting to see if it's safe. Until they get that feeling to go, they hesitate. They are like a combination lie detector/safety machine: "Beep, beep, beep, stop."

Cancer can run through emotions from joy to sorrow all in a moment. Cancer and Capricorn are the extremists—either all in or all out, either in love with you or they don't want to sit anywhere near you. They're either going to parties and are social animals or they are not going out, even with their families. The tears of a Cancer come forward with a simple thought. The laughter of a Cancer can be contagious and loud as well.

People don't realize how funny Cancers can be—they are the best mimics and comedians. Robin Williams was a Cancer with a Pisces moon and Scorpio rising—triple water! He was so empathic that he picked up on everybody's energy. Even a low-road Cancer can disguise their pain with laughter. They will notice the sounds of children giggling or the sight of a father holding a child. Because Cancer is kinesthetic, physical touch, a child's hug, or a dog's cuddle soothes them. Truth be told, every Cancer secretly wants to be held—even if they won't admit it.

Will Cancer get exhausted? Yes. Will they tell you? Probably not. "You don't have to help me. I've got this," says Cancer. They have a hard time asking for help. Admitting you need help is a sign of maturity, Cancer. As a younger person, I bet there was a special relationship with a sibling, grandparent, or a best friend who protected you, or really saw you. If nobody was there, that sours into, "No one ever cares. I'm all by myself. I'll never be supported. No worries, I can do all of this myself." That negative trapdoor instilled by their childhood can stick like flypaper.

If you store painful memories easily (and you probably do), they can create a sad personality based on a sad story you keep telling yourself and others. Oh, the long-winded stories with details that only matter to you! You will rehash those negative stories to anyone who will listen. Too many memories create real-time fear based on the past. "Oh no, I remember this. This reminds me of that other time. I'm not doing this again." It's a protective mechanism, a shield you carry unconsciously, based on old memories that prevent the here and now from being different and even happy.

Well, you've got a good case, Cancer. A lot of things did go wrong. Once you learn how to come back to the present time, right now, rather than focusing on what was before, you will find the door to real freedom and a renewed chance for joy. The observer assists you in realizing that whoops, you just got stuck in the past. It shows you how to come back into the now.

Cancer embodies the tender heart. Unlike others, who may avoid their feelings and ignore what's happened, Cancer never forgets. If your mother has died, every year on her birthday, you will cry and feel heartbroken—that's real. Once you are deeply loved by this sign, you will always be remembered. If you are lucky to be in Cancer's inner circle, you'll be able to read their mind. Just don't tell anyone else. It's a very private place in there.

Thank you for your kindness. You are such a tender soul, even if it's secret. Once you realize that emotions are a gift rather than a curse, there will be a beauty to your sweetness that answers your soul's calling.

PROFILE OF A CANCER

Linda, one of my closest friends, is a Cancer. She has finally learned, in her seventies, to process her emotions. This has had a physical effect. She is tall, strong, and gorgeous, and she plays tennis now better than she ever did when she was younger. She is thriving because she evolved into the highest Cancer qualities.

Linda grew up in a violent household with an alcoholic father. Her brother died at seventeen in a car accident, which impacted the whole family. Instinctively, to protect her mom, she absorbed the family pain. She was extremely pretty, became an international model, then got pregnant at a young age when she wasn't married. Not long after, she married a man, and they had six more children together. She became supermom. Her husband was very wealthy for a time. When he lost everything and their finances became difficult, she stepped up her game. There is nothing worse than instability when you depend on someone else, especially if you are a mother. She had grown up with this and was familiar with the story called "I will do it myself."

Everything seemed okay from the outside. Yet she confided to me that, during the harsh years of her marriage, she hid in the closet, biting her fingers to release her pain and never telling anyone how bad it really was.

At last, she realized she was hiding from the pain body. Her emotions were frozen and hidden in the closet. She had been absorbing pain her whole life. She went to therapy, then asked her husband to leave. She courageously became a single mom to all those kids and started a successful parenting magazine to become a child portrait photographer—which is so Cancer. She worked in a darkroom at night, processing photos after the children were asleep. Cancers are industrious.

She was a single mom for a very long time. Eventually she was able to open her heart again. Boy, did her new man have hoops to jump through. In true Cancer fashion, she didn't trust him at first. For many years, he remained devoted to her, until she was eventually able to let go of her ancient stories of distrust that the father of her children (and her own father) had imprinted on her. Over time, she realized he was safe.

Are her kids at her house every Sunday night having dinner parties? Yes. Are the holidays at her house a wild affair with grandkids and family? Definitely. Does she let her boyfriend of ten years live with her? No. She refuses to have him in her house all the time because she knows she needs to be alone to reboot. She is fully self-aware and no longer crossing over her boundaries. She is successful, happy, and at peace. She freely gives away her love and compassion to all the people she lets into her life. And boy, does she play a mean tennis game—who knew Cancers are so physically strong? They have that Capricorn need to be the best.

CANCER LOW ROAD

On the low road, Cancer can become a victim to the pain body. The martyr, the sacrificial lamb, the neglected one—resentment lives inside them, seeping out as quiet complaining and at worst, physical ailments. "Poor me" is the broken record of low-road Cancer.

If a Cancer cannot stand her mother-in-law and has been sitting next to her at holiday dinners for decades, tension accumulates, and then they wonder why they feel sick just before the holiday dinner. The problem is, if someone asks, "What's bothering you?" Cancer answers, "Nothing," or "I don't want to talk about it." Low-road Cancer absorbs a nonverbal negativity that, over time, turns into physical symptoms. "I'm not in the mood. I'm tired. I don't really feel like it." These are all negative ways to say: "I have lost myself. I don't want to do that. I need to be alone."

Another version of low-road Cancer is to be an endurance machine who goes to work consistently and never says a word about what's bugging them. In secret, they are indulging in something to release the tension, hiding out at home drinking wine, smoking cigarettes when no one's looking, or eating the very thing they know they shouldn't.

At their very lowest, this water sign freezes, and they go cold and numb. This personality type can get sick because they shut down their flow. What is health and vitality if not the ability to keep the body and mind mobile? All physical ailments are unprocessed emotions, and low-road Cancer is the sign least likely to process their own emotions.

THE CANCER OBSERVER

Turning on the observer can be more difficult for Cancer than for other signs. The feeling body is highly distracting, convincing you of its ailments. You care so much it hurts, and that pain causes you to go numb. The observer is all about accepting vulnerability. Turn on your observer and say: "Uh-oh, I just went numb." And then ask yourself in honor of authenticity: What am I feeling? If you practice that question repeatedly, you will recover access to your sensitivity. The observer helps to honor your capacity for love and caring as a strength, not a weakness, granting you permission to use your sensitivity as a gift rather than a curse.

You have permission to be a caretaker. It would be crazy to ask you to let go of that natural ability. Just be aware about giving to yourself the same way you so generously give to others.

CANCER HIGH ROAD

The evolved, mature Cancer brings us wisdom. You are allowed to give advice after all that you have been through. High-road Cancers are masterful manifesters. A notable example of an enlightened Cancer is the Dalai Lama. He is a double Cancer (sun and rising sign), and a role model for peace and kindness. The Dalai Lama exists against a historical backdrop of four thousand years of Buddhism. He lived in Nepal among all his relics—history that the Cancer loves so much—as well as the memories of his last twelve incarnations. It is recorded that he has reincarnated twenty-three times, culminating in this life. His community existed in a beautiful temple called the Potala Palace in Lhasa, China, on top of a mountain.

Then, one night in 1959, he was invaded. Everything was gone. The entire history of that Buddhist tradition was taken. The Dalai Lama had to leave and was never able to return. That temple filled with generations of historical artifacts, with walls embedded with centuries of Buddhist chanting, was destroyed.

What an emotional disaster for a Cancer! The Dalai Lama now lives in Dharamshala, India, in exile. He meditates for hours every day. His Holiness has every reason to distrust, after what has happened to him and his people, yet he prays for the ones who assaulted him. He prays for the Chinese. He utilized a Chinese writer to help him with his book called *Forgiveness*. The high road of Cancer: to master forgiveness even for those who have caused great pain. Such a noble act.

Cancer on the high road teaches us how to let go. They understand that carrying pain can obliterate the love that is our birthright. They learn to forgive, to release the resentment that comes from leaving pain unhealed and unforgiven. The high road of Cancer is knowing how to ask for help, receive it, and admit to their fears—preferably to do all this before a health crisis forces you to do so.

We all know this tale: when someone gets diagnosed with cancer, everything must change—diet, lifestyle, getting to the proper doctors, and learning to ask for help! No more excessive giving. Instead, it's time to receive healing. That is a Cancer lesson. Receiving is their greatest challenge.

CANCER'S LIFE LESSON

For a Cancer, being human isn't easy. You're a gift—a conduit to take on the pain, heal it, and pass that wisdom to others. You are so much stronger than you know. Healing is your highest calling.

Too often, you take on the pain of your family and ancestors. It's not an easy lesson, yet one of the most spiritually advanced callings is to take on family karma (which to some extent we all do) with the ultimate desire to uplift the trauma and heal. That is a large order, to heal the wounds of your ancestors.

Learning how to cultivate boundaries is everything. It's a healthy sign of strength to be able to release and cry and know when to stop the emotional indulgence. Over time with practice, you can become good at expressing emotions and finding their wisdom.

It takes a lot more courage to be vulnerable than to pretend. You think your weakness is that you care too much—that is not true. I bet as a younger person, you were self-conscious about your tears or sadness. Trust me, it's a gift—it is a strength to express love so easily.

Can you say these words? *I chose to incarnate into this life just the way*

it is. I love being alive. I am learning to process the pain body. I agree to pri-
oritize myself and to take care of me first. I welcome the sweet and sour sauce
of life—accepting pain and joy without avoiding either. I have learned the
hard way that when you avoid pain, the pain stays in your body and com-
pounds its effect, creating symptoms. I have stopped punishing myself. It is a
heroic journey to be real, face pain, and not turn my head from the love and
kindness. I will assume the job of making this human experience more noble,
no matter what the cost.

MEDICINE FOR CANCER

Start with prayers and ask for help. Go to therapy. In therapy, review your childhood. I guarantee that you have a lot to unpack. You came here to heal. Look at your story with this important question: What am I supposed to be learning?

If you have turned off your tenderness, if you have stopped crying, if you are unhealed—there is no judgment. The observer stands by, waiting for you to realize that you are marvelous, even with the stories you are carrying about your body, your family, or whatever it is that follows you around.

Crying and therapy are good medicines to process the pain body and let the waters flow with an intent to learn forgiveness. I really believe Cancers could let themselves cry at least once a day. Salt water is healing.

Sometimes, Cancer, you need to stop and focus on what's happening with you. If you cry too often, learn how to stop. You are extreme. Take time to feel and relax. Because of that compulsion to work, to give, to stop and pet the dog, to help the elderly and the children without even thinking, you must sometimes ask yourself: Can I pull away and do self-care, even when people need me?

Mindfulness practices are medicine for Cancer; they bring you into the present moment by encouraging you to pay attention to where your stories take you. I often give this mantra to a Cancer: *That was then, this is now. I trust that life has my back.* If they don't believe it, I tell them to lie to start with—fake it until you make it. When they do that, they have the potential to become a completely different person.

Medicine for you is letting the past go. All that clutter in your house, while it creates memories, can be dated and burdensome to your energy. Too much of the old does not allow you new, fresh water. You can get caught in dirty water that will not refresh itself. You have to let it go. We all know that stagnant water can turn to poison.

CANCER MOON

Cancer is a comfortable placement for the moon. Being the fastest planet in the heavens, the moon allows water to flow and tears to drop. Moving water is unlikely to get stuck or frozen. The difference between a Cancer sun and a Cancer moon is that when your sun is in Cancer, you can cut off the emotion. You can block it with your ego. A Cancer moon can't do that. You can't just turn it off. The moon amplifies the easy release of the emotional body. Love and cry easily, Cancer moon! In fact, it's hard for you not to cry.

You are a great cook. My friend, who has a Cancer moon, cannot come over to my house without bringing all sorts of gifts. She brings food, cards, and articles she knows I would appreciate. She's always asking, "What do you need? What do you want? What's your favorite thing? I'll bring it to you."

You are a gifted healer, especially with Reiki. You are attuned to the invisible emotional energy of other people. You lose your sense of self without having someone, or something, to care for. You live, wondering, "Am I good enough? Do I do enough for others?" Excuse me, Cancer moon, it's all you do! Your job is to nurture. You often underestimate your own worth. Realize that you *are* doing enough!

MERCURY IN CANCER

You are intuitive. You can read people. Then you second-guess yourself because your thoughts don't proceed logically. At best, you have a memory like an elephant—second only to Mercury in Aquarius. However, you can get caught up in circular thinking or get emotionally charged, and people may have trouble following your train of thought.

You are exceptionally gifted in business. Once you focus your attention, you nurture your business like it's your child. You get emotionally attached and you love to bring in the whole family. You love a family business!

It's important for you to have someone you can talk to without feeling self-conscious. It's hard for you to open up to just anyone.

CANCER RISING

Surprisingly, you have one of the strongest body types in the zodiac—you have endurance, although you can have issues with your stomach or breasts.

You have the potential to find authenticity and raw humanness—this is your soul's calling. The distraction of your ego and its sensitivity about focusing on yourself is a major barrier for you. Your sensitivity can overwhelm the healer in you. Will you become a victim to sensitivity, or a resource for emotional wisdom and the ability to feel others and carry their pain?

You feel so much—at best, you handle waves of sensitivity and don't move away from them. You process them as they happen. Crying and laughing come easily to you. You are a skilled participant in therapy and you know how to allow the emotional body to have a full turn without judgment. You may ask, "Why do I always have to be the helper? Why can't I stop myself from raising my hand to volunteer? Why is it always just me?"

Can you allow feelings to arrive without going numb or dull? Do you know how to be with what is? Can you hold your pain without being contagious to others or blaming someone else for your tears? Do you know when to stop feeling so you can let go, cleanse, and recover from all the emotions you felt that weren't even yours?

Your soul wanted to feel in this lifetime. It's a gift to be tender. You may resist the caretaker role, even if you don't have children or feel very maternal. Yet when you give yourself permission to realize the selfless delight of serving, it becomes very natural and fulfilling. As soon as you surrender to the soulful urge to nurture and give selflessly, and to use your endurance in service, you fulfill the soul's promise: to provide for others without complaint.

SATURN IN CANCER

Learn to ask for what you want.

You must take care of your emotional body. You are carrying sensitivity and vulnerability from either your childhood or the collective. Learning how to cry and allowing yourself to express sensitivity will be the key to your freedom. If you're too emotional, tone it down. If you're cut off, it's time to melt your frozen water.

Your challenge is to review your past with this question: "How do I let go and accept the karma of my family/past?" An action step would be throwing away sentimental items you no longer have use for so that your space can be clutter-free. Therapy is a must for this configuration. You can be so stuck on family dynamics that, if you don't do therapy, you will carry an imprint of your childhood. This can take a lifetime to get over and be a lifelong process. There is an unconscious, historical internalization of pain. At least do family therapy to heal that childhood wound. That is your promise in this life. You have to learn to let go of the past.

Life lesson: The ghosts of your childhood, if not healed, will haunt you. Make your purpose the quest to update your pain body for the present. You know more than any of us how important family is. You get to choose your family. Your superpower is your sensitivity.

MEDITATION FOR CANCER

I have the gift of sensitivity. The quieter and more generous I am with the part of me that has a need for simplicity, the calmer my nervous system will become. I can pull away, spend time outside, be with animals, be in silence. This renews me. I can release myself from the bondage of my family dynamics and the stories I have heard that hurt me. I can stop and pull myself out of this world into the quiet. I'm allowed to cry in order to detox and release the pain before I find the stillness. Stopping time is a necessity for me in order to maintain my open, yielded, emotional responsiveness. With too much stimulation, my gift becomes mired and pained. Too much compassion can reduce my soul's ability to give me comfort. I can manage the ability to give and to receive. I deserve stillness. It's the gift I give to others.

THE ESSENCE OF CANCER

Where did we get the idea that emotional people are weak? That if you cry you should say, "I'm sorry"? That it is not professional to cry? My guess is that this was all put in place by a Capricorn who had no time for intuition or feelings. If you can feel your instinct, if you can know in your gut what is true beyond the words or pretense, you are way ahead of the game.

What prevents the human condition from being proud of loving so much? So the Cancer cried at the wedding or the funeral or the commercial. So they can't control the unconscious ability to love their children as they do, or they get jealous, or they get angry when they get cut off when driving? These are the pillars of what makes humans human, and Cancer is the most authentically human sign in the zodiac because when those feelings arrive, if they are fluid and open, they cannot ignore them or pretend to be something different.

Authenticity is the goal of astrology: to let the human be free to feel, to cry, to laugh, to be moved, to lift the car off the struggling child. This is our human high road. Cancer truly cares, remembers their ancestors, and stands on the shoulders of those who came before with honor. Cancer is a timeless being who knows love is the universal quality that makes humans so endearing.

We all need love, even if it's from a pet. We all came from a mother, the one who gave us life. A Cancer could have written the ten commandments. They believe in loving God (or something higher than themselves), loving their neighbor, honoring their parents, cherishing their children, never stealing or hurting people, and doing the next right thing. This is a Cancer mandate: to honor those you love. What if everyone did that?

If you can master the human condition and keep your heart open, you've mastered the point of being alive on earth. Cancer's teaching is to love and to keep your heart open without letting the past, the clutter, or even the pain of the body interrupt the memory of what matters most: to love life/God/spirit with all you have. They are the student who will one day understand the meaning of kindness at all costs.

12

The Psychology of Leo

I WILL

Element: Fire
Mode: Fixed
House: Fifth
Planet: Sun
Body part: Heart, spine—they have the bravest hearts and strongest backbones.

If only you understood how much I have to move energy and express my creativity. How do you stay idle? I can't do it. They say it's all the fire in me that has me all up and in your stuff. I just want to be sure you're on it and that you get the life you deserve.

Here, use my fire! Put me on the board, hire me for the job, ask me to stand out, and I am in. I can only tolerate boring, repetitive behavior for so long, where I'm left to do something alone—I may enroll you to help me.

When I create, my art has to go from my studio to the internet. It's not just for me. I want to share what I create, and I want to be paid for it. I can't not give all my energy to whatever I do, and I surely need the feedback, too.

I wish you would appreciate all I do. It would feed me. I get an energy infusion when I'm with people who celebrate my ideas. How I got tagged as bossy or pushy seems obvious—I just have to get it done and I go for it. Why else are we alive, if not to turn on the fun factor and create? Yet don't misinterpret my eagerness to get on stage. There is a shyness within me.

Don't judge me for my strong personality, and I'll love you. If you can't keep up or you find me offensive, I don't mind. I don't need you—there are so many others who would love to have my input. Once you're on my side, my loyalty is like that of a mafioso boss. You will always have my endorsement and interest. If you're good at something, invite me to critique: I can always add my ideas to any of yours. Just don't invite my feedback unless you are actually looking for feedback.

Please understand that I have to get up and go. Stillness and mediocrity are not in my wheelhouse. Maybe I am the cheerleader you've been looking for. Let me know what you need—I am here and have way too much energy not to share all I have with those I love.

Leo is human nature at its loud and shiny best. Why do we pay so much money to actors? Because they have the gift of making life appear fun, dramatic, and fascinating. Who can stop watching the drama of a car accident? No one. It's our human nature.

Leo is the part in all of us that needs attention, wants to fall in love, be noticed, maybe even get famous. Leo is hungry to feel special, be the star, be the best football player, take center stage. It's the kid calling out, "Mom, Dad, look at me!" It's that natural impulse that says, "Aren't I special? Do you love me? Do I look good? Do you promise never to forget me? How can I make an impact on your life that will really make a difference?"

Leo is too often pigeonholed as a vain show-off. People judge them for being too loud, pushy, or self-centered. This isn't necessarily true. Leos command the spotlight, although not always overtly, and not always selfishly. Some Leos aren't even outgoing—some are introverted and shy.

Some Leos don't believe in astrology because they don't identify with the stereotype. Leo identifies with the ego, but every human expresses ego in a unique way. What you hardly ever hear is that Leo feels insecure if they are not on a steady diet of praise and applause. They really need external validation, whether they ask for it or not. Without it, Leos shut down and then they won't want to be the center of attention. "No, don't look at me, I'm not dressed, I'm not ready."

What all Leos do have in common is their flair, whether it's subtle or obvious. Everybody knows when they enter a room. If their children are around, they get passionate—boy, do they love their cubs/children. If they get angry, they like to swear. And did I mention their fantastic hair? I swear that every owner of a salon that does blowouts is a Leo.

Being seen is a big issue for Leo. It starts in childhood. "I am seen, therefore I am" is their motto. To be sure you are seen, step into the role of the performer, class clown, virtuoso, or diva, at least on some level. Maybe it's just you pretending to play the guitar in front of the mirror. Maybe it's you holding court with your friends and family gathered around you. Maybe you're actually on Broadway or in a community theater group. You like to have yourself reflected back to you, whether it's from an audience or the mirror in your own bedroom or by your best friend. Everyone has a bit of this energy. Can we just admit that we all want reinforcement and recognition? Let's not blame Leo for embodying this energy.

My Leo mother, Tillie, looked so much like Bette Midler that people would walk up to her and ask for her autograph, and she would give it to them, never telling them who she really was. She loved the attention. She used to say to me, "Debbie, you know everybody. I want you to go to LA and tell them I could be Bette Midler's stand-in. Just look at me!"

Okay, Mom.

There is a reason why the lion is the symbol of Leo—they are so regal and noticeable: in your imagination you are the king or queen of your world. You take seriously the role of the matriarch or patriarch. You want people to rely on you. I'm not sure who put you in charge of keeping everyone happy, but you do a great job. With a natural desire to brighten up other people's days, draw attention to the happy parts of life, and inspire us by the way you present yourself, you create joy.

You're so excited about life. You wake up in the morning ready to eat the day alive. Another day! "Carpe diem" is your motto. As a vivacious, embodied lover of life, you can't stop yourself from showing it. "Let's get all dressed up, even if there is no occasion"—your appetite for radiant living deserves bling. You carry a combination of reliable authority figure—the know-it-all—and the delighted child who grabs your hand and says, "Let's dance!"

If you are the friend or especially the spouse or child of a Leo, get ready—Leo will tell you what to wear, and they will take charge of how the environment looks. Don't challenge their taste. If a Leo goes shopping with her kid and the daughter says, "I don't want to wear that," the Leo will proclaim, "Oh, yes, you do! That looks great on you." This was my mother—I would say, "Mom, I don't like this! It's not my taste." She would say, "I don't care. You're wearing it." Finally, I stopped shopping with her.

Leo has conviction. They commit and follow through; they don't let themselves and others down. At worst, Leos have a temper. My mother broke our refrigerator door once because she slammed it so hard. She threw things at my dad. I grew up in a household full of high drama—hello, Leo. When I see it objectively, it fascinates me: How does someone feel so free to let their energy out to the extent that they can literally break things? Tillie was a live wire.

I've always secretly wanted to be a Leo. Their massive creativity and irresistible self-confidence is effortless. Yes, you might have a louder voice than the rest of us. Your body is more durable when it comes to working out or getting on stage. You dance longer at the party. You sing out loud, even when you don't know the words. For you, every day is a good hair day. You know how to work it. The people who avoid you are jealous of how shiny you are, or they just can't keep up with you. Don't take it personally.

Not everyone appreciates fire. If they say you're "too much," your response is to walk away. When someone says, "Can you tone it down?" you make a face and keep going. You are resilience and determination. You will not be stopped. You won't like the criticism. If, on the other hand, someone comes along and says, "You look great," it turns everything around. You'll adore that person. In fact, compliments are a great way to get on Leo's good side. It disarms them. A really good compliment can bring out Leo's best.

I have an assistant who is a Leo, so I know this works. All I have to do at the beginning of the workday is say, "You look great!" (And she always does.) She gives me a big smile and says, "Okay, let's get to work!" I'm not kidding. That's just Leo. They need positive reflections, and they earn them. It's just who they are.

People often get jealous of Leo's endless energy. Madonna is a classic case. She blew our minds when she shattered the role of what women were allowed to do, and controversy arrived. Some are excited by her, and others threatened. Throughout her entire lifetime, people have fallen in love with her, then fallen out of love with her. Madonna gets criticized every time she tries something new. That kind of acceptance followed by rejection is a repetitive song for Leo. "They love me, they love me not."

Leo, can we talk about your quiet sensitivity? Truth be told, your ego gets bruised easily. Most people don't know that Leo feels insecure if they are not on a steady diet of praise and applause. They really need external validation, whether they ask for it or not.

When you are alone, your gremlins take advantage of you. Gremlins feed on insecurity, trying to convince you that you aren't as attractive, interesting, or talented as everyone thinks. They make you believe you've fooled everyone. Many Leos have imposter syndrome, yet because they are such good performers, you can't tell. They mask their insecurity with what appears as the opposite: self-confidence that is over the top and the pretense that nothing bothers them.

If you can free yourself to live an uninhibited life, while having the strength to care for those who you adore, you will inhabit your sign in its highest manifestation. You are a being full of love and laughter and creativity. Thank you for sharing your heart with us. You give so much. You are the one who brings us together, buys the gifts, the meals, and then you don't want the applause (okay, sometimes you do). We want your contributions. You are concerned with your looks. From our point of view, your beauty is way beyond looks. We see your generosity and the loyalty of your heart. Lucky us for having you on our team.

PROFILE OF A LEO

My first love was a Leo. He was six feet four and lived in Nebraska. He was a schoolteacher with a unique, showy teaching style. His classes were loud and lively. He played classical music as the high school kids walked into class. There he was, standing on his desk, roaring like a lion: "Turn off the television and let your mind be open!" He was devoted to direct learning experiences rather than theoretical ones. He wanted his students to think for themselves, figure out their dreams, and make them happen. He inspired them to prevent the numbness he often witnessed. He told them to never blindly follow. His motto was: "Think for yourself."

A classic Leo, he was extreme. When we met in 1975, he had just learned about open marriages. This was just a few years after there was a best-selling book about new models of marriage. A lot of people were trying out this lifestyle. I met him at Stanford while I was studying dance therapy. He was studying morality (ironically). We fell completely in love.

My individuality was strong even as a teenager, so much so that I was a virgin when we met, and I stayed that way throughout our relationship. I told him I was too young (eighteen) and didn't know enough about love, so we weren't going to do *that*. Instead, we had endless intense conversations about life, visited museums in the city, and went to plays. We kissed, we cuddled, we moved energy all right—he was a passionate man.

He fascinated me. He was a musician, of course—Leos usually have some creative outlet. His was being a classical guitarist. Everything about him was intense. I learned to leave behind the beige life. That was a gift that has stayed with me.

He ignited confidence in me. There is no cheerleader like a Leo who adores you. He said, "Silverman, you ask the damnedest questions." When you have a Leo in your corner who thinks you are a gift to the universe, it's inspiring. It's that Leo energy that secretly longs to have all they give reciprocated. He was the first person to pierce my young façade and see deeply into my soul. We all remember that first love—such a Leo topic. He opened my eyes to who I was, and what I would become. Nobody sweeps you off your feet like a Leo. Even to this day, I can close my eyes and remember that kiss.

LEO LOW ROAD

On the low road, Leo becomes self-centered, grumpy, depressed, and self-indulgent because love has eluded them. They get crispy and dulled when they lack cheerleaders. They take up the air in the room and forget to consider the others. Oh my, don't get them going on politics. You'll soon notice they are good at lecturing and not so good at listening. They can come across as self-righteous.

Leo is dramatic by default, which isn't a bad thing, although until their observer is on, they honestly don't realize it. They just think it's their right to speak their mind. If you call them a drama queen, they get offended. Low-road Leo can be superficial and indiscriminate in the worst way, subscribing to strong opinions that become hardened and stale, eventually turning into arrogance.

Low-road Leo can go toward depression. If they don't have an audience, or someone special is not around, or they are missing a family member/friend to make them feel special, they get low. Madonna, a Leo, told me that she has to work out in order to not get depressed. That makes sense—fire signs have to move energy to feel alive.

Rejection creates a negative, self-involved Leo. They don't want to listen to your story—they want to tell their story. Like royalty who thinks of everyone as their servant, you disagree and it's off with your head!

THE LEO OBSERVER

The observer can help you step out of yourself and see that your ego is in charge. For you, that's natural. So you have an ego. You get hurt easily. Just admit it. The observer can help you say it out loud: "I have a large ego and an appetite for being in control." Admitting this can set you free. You need that ego because you came here to be big and bright, to inspire people and provide life-force energy so nothing gets dull when you are around. Your observer will keep you grounded by saying, "You're looking in the mirror again. That is so you," or "You just got triggered. The heat is on, get ready." It's okay, Leo. You're going to get triggered. And you're going to trigger others. It's in your nature. The observer can help you accept this about yourself and see it as endearing.

LEO HIGH ROAD

Leo has a way of winning hearts because they do so much with full conviction and are in love with the world. It's contagious. High-road Leo is a role model in the best way. You can stand on the stage without fear or embarrassment—and make us laugh.

What a great parent; you work so hard taking care of the family. You genuinely care about your offspring. Let your kids make mistakes. That's not easy for you. It can be done. When you acknowledge your soul and your ego takes a back seat, your soul shines through with power and results. When Leo is the caretaker of the powerless, the disenfranchised, those less fortunate, they fulfill a higher purpose. Once you are under a Leo's protection, it is hard to lose their favor.

Loyalty is your specialty. You would take a bullet for someone you love. Being part of a healthy Leo's entourage is an honor. Their motives are to provide and protect. Rather than imposing their ideas, high-road Leo asks, "What do you think of my idea?" They learn to read the room and to be in love with life, no matter what they are handed. Even after experiencing painful drama and loss, their heart just keeps loving. That takes strength and fortitude, which are the qualities high-road Leo embodies.

LEO MEDICINE

Like other fire signs, being physical is so important. You get energy from spending energy; therefore exercise is your friend. You thrive on movement, music, and activity. If Leos stop moving their energy, they become like a pressure cooker about to pop, or they get depressed. You must exercise, or be on the move, or entertain—otherwise, you go flat.

Take the opportunity to perform regularly, even if it's not on an actual stage. Maybe you are an actor or a musician. You might also get metaphorical applause as a teacher, a trial lawyer, a motivational speaker, a spokesperson, or the leader of an organization or company. Or how about just telling stories to the kids? Watching your favorite shows and screaming at the boob tube with your uninhibited opinions feels therapeutic. Watching football or baseball and having loyalty to the team will elicit your passion.

You feel best taking care of the underdog. You need a cause. It might be a nonprofit or child welfare or climate activism. You love to fight for what's right.

It might sound trivial, yet it's good medicine for you to wear bright clothes. Put lipstick on, or a snappy suit. Look in the mirror and preen a little. There's no harm in it. Enjoy it! Then, step away from the mirror and stand in front of the room. Take the lead with confidence. You look amazing!

If you have a trusted friend, it's okay to ask for some ego-boosting praise when you are feeling insecure. "Just tell me how great I look!" You don't really even care if it's 100 percent true. "Tell me sweet little lies." You just need to hear it.

LEO'S LIFE LESSON

You are here to learn to find confidence from within. You can gain a lot by understanding that vulnerability is a strength. To expose your human frailty is nothing to be ashamed of, despite what the gremlins say.

A lesson for Leo is embracing your ego while making room for the soul. In esoteric astrology, the ego clashes with the soul because they are opposite energies. Spirituality, especially organized religion, can be challenging for a Leo. They don't want God telling them what to do because they already know what to do. They are the leaders of their lives and the lives of their families.

Leo loves the real world and lives in the now. Not every sign is meant to reach some spiritual pinnacle in this life. Some are simply meant to love this life and embrace it with their whole heart. That's why you are here, Leo. It's good to be in love with our world. You are here to bring animation, character, and excitement. We need someone to inspire us. This is the rightful role of Leo.

LEO MOON

You have a hidden emotional vitality. You are happier than most people with dramatic, enthusiastic emotions. You have an upbeat, cheerful personality. You thrive on drama in the best way.

The downside is when you get emotional, you try to take over. That Leo energy bursts out—"It's my way or the highway"—without fully assessing the situation.

Compared to sun sign Leo, which is the most externalized, overt personality of all the signs, you are more likely to display shyness. You are also the most creative manifestation of Leo. Creativity isn't optional. You need to create. You create without trying. You can use your creativity to help others grow their ideas into something wonderful. You don't need to take all the credit.

If you love someone, you will think about them a lot and be their support system. They will never have to wonder if you love them. This is why so many adore you.

MERCURY IN LEO

You have a forceful mind—you are not here to be vague. You are decisive and able to share what you know without inhibition. Boredom evaporates when you are around because you are an idea factory. If you learn how to listen and share with interest in other points of view, it will make it so much easier for us to get along.

You are prone to being so opinionated that it scares us to share an idea contrary to yours. Can you learn how to ask questions? You like to take the lead yourself and become the one who knows. That is what your mind is suited for: to be the know-it-all, fully enabled with confidence and so much experience, we may as well listen.

LEO RISING

From the soul's perspective, Leo rising isn't easy. It's confusing because Leo sun effortlessly shines on center stage. Leo rising resists being big and showy, even though that's your assignment. You came here to stand front and center, step into the spotlight, and embrace the beauty of life. You came here to shine for us, inspiring us to do the same. If that feels uncomfortable or feels egocentric, or you don't think you are good enough, think again. Your soul calls you to show up in a big way. Don't keep your creativity all to yourself. Ease in. Play music for your family or trusted friends. Share your writing. You are more talented than you realize. It's okay to struggle a little with your soulful urge, especially if your sun sign is in a water or earth sign.

SATURN IN LEO

Be playful and have fun. Learn to be okay with your need for attention.

You are allowed to take up space. You need to admit you have an ego. Your lesson is to either be celebrated for that fact and feed your ego or to be comfortable with your shyness and reluctance to take center stage. In either case, the more awareness you have that you need attention, the more authentic you will become.

Not every sign is meant to reach some spiritual pinnacle in this life, or be on stage. Some are simply meant to love this life and embrace it with their whole heart. That's you, Leo.

Life lesson: Permission to value joy and childlikeness, even as an adult. Your loyalty provides devotion to anyone you care about. Lucky those who are loved by you. This is both your gift to them and to yourself. You live for love (which is not exclusive to romantic love).

MEDITATION FOR LEO

I've come to be the shining star. I love that about myself. I share my life-force with the world. I want nothing more than for those I love to be celebrated, blessed, and encouraged. I'm here to be the fire that gives myself and others permission to shine and be bright. I offer encouragement to all who come around my hearth. I will give warmth and express my love to others. I am devoted. I will not tone it down because the world needs my exuberance.

THE ESSENCE OF LEO

Leo is here to amplify the energies of this life without inhibition. They are not going to tone it down, nor make excuses for their behavior—they just let 'er rip. So what if they swear or get loud? That's the right of the human who is willing to stand out and show up. They are okay with the "Hell, yes!" and then the "Oh, shit!" They are good students of life and do life with all the energy they can muster, which is a lot. They will get to the higher version of themselves when they study. Just do not misinterpret them as someone who has thick skin. They don't want to hurt you, nor do they want to be hurt.

Astrology always talks about Leo wanting to be special and having a big ego, aka EGO, aka Evading God's Oneness. Well, it's true. Avoiding the idea that we are all one is a Leo specialty because they know they are special in their own ways. They have more energy than most and no off button. Who tells a lion to be quiet? How do you stop the actress from taking up space? Who would dare tell Madonna to tone it down? No, we need the bold ones to stick their necks out, to dress up in bling, to shatter the ceiling of what we are allowed to do.

Some of you may not like the personality of a Leo. Others will follow a Leo anywhere. It doesn't matter either way to the Leo. Get them riled up, spark their passion, get them to shout what you were thinking and didn't want to say. They will say it. They do elicit reactivity wherever they go. First, you are attracted to the fire, then it gets hot and you move away. Then you come back to get warm again. People can't stay away from a Leo for long. They are absolutely not beige. They don't believe we came into this life for mediocrity.

Put them on stage, give them a microphone, and they will stand up and shine. Once off the stage, they are surprisingly shy and want quiet. They are here to be themselves without apology. On the other hand, they are learning about the softer side. They can learn to say sorry and ask the question "Are you with me?" when they are treated with kindness.

Can't we all admit we have an ego and need comfort and confirmation so that the soul will be safe to take over? That is the path Leo is on. If they have learned from astrology how to hold their egos intact with the help of their souls, they honor the lessons they are here to learn and they can become teachers.

13

The Psychology of Virgo

I ANALYZE

Element: Earth
Mode: Mutable
House: Sixth
Planet: Mercury
Body part: Colon, intestines—because they love analyzing all the shit! (They also tend to have digestive issues related to nerves.)

If only you understood how much I try. Maybe then you would have more compassion and be more deliberate about your critiques of my work or my looks. For me, critiques just make things worse. I already do that to myself. It's hard for me to take compliments well—it's too much attention and I get nervous. I am my own worst enemy—I do not like feeling half done, or dirty, or confused. I can make you a list of what bugs me about myself, and it will be long.

Yes, I endlessly seek answers, revisiting sources to be sure I am accurate as I look at data from the highest level. I love to collect information. I have to do it. I cannot accept face-value data without hard evidence. I don't trust others are as thorough as I am. Every scientist requires proof: show me the research, the charts, the results.

Health topics fascinate me. I learn and then I share. Don't be offended if I suggest the newest intervention for how you could feel better, be happier, or make more money. I might tell you about a superfood that could help you live longer. I do it because I want to help you.

The hardest part of being me is that my job is never done. There is no rest for the weary. I never stop trying to perfect and improve using natural cures or modern technologies.

Will I ever accomplish my ultimate goals for my health, looks, relationships? I have so much to do all the time that the list of things that need improvement becomes endless. I'll never feel completely good about what I'm doing. It's not enough. I will never be done.

Please don't suggest that I am always on time, or neat, or organized, or hold me to some Virgo standard of perfection. I don't do any of it well enough. What a life I have. It's not bad, it's just not easy. I don't mean to complain. When you realize how imperfectly human we all are, you won't be surprised that we all need feedback and change.

I wish I had the answer about how to help humans get better, and maybe someday, we will find a formula for good living that is healthy, organic, and reasonably priced so we can all get back to the earth, to basics, to kindness. Don't think I don't know this is the long view. I hope we make it; I find myself worried about our future. We are on the threshold. So much has to change; there is still so much to do and from what the scientists say, we do not have a lot of time. I'm worried.

Virgo is the part in all of us that requires order, never feels like they've done quite enough, and is constantly trying to improve. Health fascinates Virgo. Effortlessly, advice comes pouring out. Instinctively a fixer, Virgo takes on the problem, whether it's knowing how to tighten the screws or repair the car or treat the common cold—just say what's wrong and a happy Virgo would love to make it right. They make good nurses, accountants, doctors, and counselors. They fix what is broken, especially if it involves numbers, spreadsheets, medical tests, records, charts, or has to do with healing. They walk into your house and oh boy, if there is a burnt-out bulb, a broken sink, a leaking toilet, and you have the flu—no worries, they know just what to do.

Don't be fooled into thinking Virgos are always neat, on time, and love to clean. Actually, they are so busy that most Virgos are not on time. Yes, Virgos are good at organizing and solving people's problems, though they don't always have time to do that for themselves. Their drawers are cluttered, their car isn't all that clean, and yet they don't like the way you put the dishes in the dishwasher because it isn't just right and they push you aside: "Here, let me do it."

Virgos have a high-strung nervous system, which lends itself to anxiety. It's nerve-racking to want life to be different from what it is, and to have a list that doesn't end. They make lists about their lists. Of course, they won't be able to get to everything on time or won't have a big enough bandwidth to figure out how to finish their list. It feels sexy for a Virgo to check all items off their list. They just love that feeling. Sometimes they make a list of what they left off the other list, to remember what they didn't do.

Virgo is the caregiver, and can quickly turn into the martyr. That's not fun. Then again, you aren't in this life for the fun. You're here to get things done, to fulfill a function. I am so sorry that you slide so quickly into worry. Actually, when you are in your observer, you would see this is a false narrative. Your default is: "Uh-oh!" or "Oh, shit!" or "Oh no, I forgot that thing!" Every mistake to you is giant—even the ones nobody noticed. Good enough is never good enough for Virgo—think about that burden. Don't bother telling them we don't need the thing they forgot. Their internal critic is way too loud. "How could I have forgotten to bring my favorite pen? I knew I should have brought that sweater. I thought about it, and then I left it behind—stupid me!"

As an astrologer, I can tell you that your heart is so pure that your deep desire to serve makes a huge difference for all who know you. Without saying a word, you argue with me. You think, "I'm not that good." Okay, write this down: *I have done enough. I always get things done and my heart is in the right place.* Then say it out loud to someone who knows you so they can remind you of these truths when you get all stressed out.

Virgo's parenting is contagious. Don't be surprised if the child of a Virgo inherits the parent's gremlins, then becomes the new president of the Worrywart Club. Virgo, it's okay to question all that worry. Does it serve you? How about the collection of self-help books, the products for that new cleanse, and the appointments for the therapy you endorse?

As an earth sign, Virgo is grounded and practical. They have a relationship with plants, herbal medicine, and essential oils, so don't be surprised if they assign you a whole supplement regimen. They have educated themselves all about how to stay healthy. Organic food is a must. Getting a colonic (Virgo rules the colon) or trying extreme diets, like going vegan or keto, is right up their alley. They are happy to share more than you ever wanted to know about their elimination process. So you want to talk about the colon and digestive tract and its workings in detail, especially the gross stuff? They are in.

Ironically, they deal with health issues on a regular basis. They may have exotic digestive issues they try to fix with some fad diet, or by eliminating carbs or becoming a vegetarian. When you aren't looking, they sneak a piece of bacon, or a sugary piece of cake. Virgo's greatest self-criticism when it comes to each new regimen: "I wish I could just follow through." They are so good at change, yet it is frustrating that they don't stick with the program for long enough, at least in their eyes.

Virgo's insecurities haunt them. Their gremlins impose impossibly high standards. Virgo manufactures gremlins. Gremlins live just down the street from perfectionism and obsessive-compulsive tendencies. They take over the neighborhood by sneaking up when no one is looking and whispering, "You aren't doing a good job. You could have done so much better." It's a niggling, nasty chorus, with the intention of undermining, not helping. The gremlins show up at night and cause Virgo to make long lists instead of sleeping. If you don't listen to your gremlins, Virgo is happy to provide some things for you to worry about.

Being a Virgo is hard—in fact, it's one of the most difficult signs in the zodiac—for the Virgo, not for those of us lucky enough to have them in our life. Instead of focusing on the good they do, they focus on the one part that didn't go right. They conjure up worst-case scenarios, like assuming the car will be stolen, the house will be robbed, the children will get sick if they don't eat properly.

Yet Virgos laugh at all the right times and have a lighthearted love of wit. Great conversationalists, they talk almost as much as a Gemini because, no surprise, they are both ruled by Mercury, the communicator. They have endless opinions and at worst, can get gossipy. Virgo's smile is noteworthy—they have a surprisingly good sense of humor and know how to keep their teeth clean.

Virgos mellow as they get older. They demonstrate gratitude in a very polite way. "Thank you. How are you? Can I help you? Thank you so much." They repeat those words more than any other sign.

In true Virgo fashion, I am going to offer a suggestion: study forgiveness, and not just for other people. Forgive yourself! Perfectionism is a heavy burden to carry. Truth be told, we live in a perfectly imperfect world. Why not just accept this truth and make allowances for those who have missed the mark, done you wrong, ruined something, and just forgive? Once you turn on your observer and realize nothing is perfect here, you can find acceptance. We are all just walking each other home. No one is going to always get it right.

I wouldn't want to live in a world without Virgo. It's their humor, rock-steady dependability, and their sincere care about making things better. Not everyone can say that. Thank you for your constant consideration, your offers of help, your ability to instruct, and your compulsion to serve. This is why you do so much more than you think: your soul is in service all the time!

PROFILE OF A VIRGO

A very close friend of mine, I'll call her Charlene, lives under the influence of a reoccurring thought: that she isn't enough, hasn't done enough, isn't in the right job, and can't ever quite get it right. That's Virgo's repetitive song: "I never get it right!" She can't figure out why she suffers from a feeling of not really being "successful."

Charlene organizes in her sleep because she is deeply committed to the well-being of her family (which includes a lot more people than just her bloodline). She provides supplements or herbs from her garden, freshly squeezed juice from the farmers market, all in an attempt to help keep them all healthy. She has a flourishing garden and uses gardening gloves, cleaning her perfect nails with a nailbrush as soon as she comes inside. She makes the best meals from her abundant garden produce.

I love traveling with her. Her purse is fully stocked with Band-Aids, Q-tips, safety pins, the extra pair of socks you never knew you were going to need. She has a great sense of humor. She instantly analyzes people when they leave the room. She checks people out, watches their facial expressions, and quickly figures out and assesses anybody else she's just met—without being asked. I've often been the recipient of her assessments. At worst it gets a little bit snarky.

She definitely can't keep a secret—though she says she can. She talks too much without even realizing it. And yet she manages to get all the things done, even if she suffers from thinking she didn't do enough.

Charlene quietly fears that she hasn't dressed the right way, or she said the wrong thing. She wants to get fit, try a new health regimen; however, her constant busyness overwhelms her, preventing her from following through.

Make no mistake, she is always well prepared. "Bring everything just in case!" She would never, ever leave her doors unlocked. She has us all feeling safe. Every Virgo has a little Pisces inside that is spiritual, who really wants to "let go and let God." That loud Virgo impulse kicks in, and they say, "Don't forget to lock the doors! People are not to be trusted." That's Charlene—her trust evaporates with just a thought. She even makes me feel nervous!

VIRGO LOW ROAD

On the low road, Virgo's nervous system causes subtle ailments—everything from bad skin to high blood pressure and then all the way to chronic problems that seem like hypochondria. Virgo can be the king or queen of anxiety, easily lapsing into obsessive-compulsive disorder. They complain, judge, and worry, taking out their anxiety on others. At worst, they are tyrannical perfectionists, cold-hearted because they cannot get out of their heads and into their hearts. They judge others and gossip. They are the therapist who has no degree yet all the answers, even when nobody asked a question.

THE VIRGO OBSERVER

When Virgo turns on their observer, it's a powerful shift. A Virgo could judge a rainbow: "There was not enough yellow." Or get mad for no reason: "You left too soon, not everybody got to see you. Next time, stay around longer, and could you tuck your shirt in?" The observer reduces that tendency to criticize. You catch yourself before you even say it, or you say it and softly forgive yourself and explain, "I'm a Virgo, forgive me."

Imagine if you assessed your contribution by effort, not results. Since you are always giving your best—your desire to do the right thing is so sincere—that's called perfection. It's okay not to complete your to-do list. You can do it tomorrow. I promise you'll remember. That's why you have all those lists.

They work. You always do what you write down, eventually. In the process, maybe it's a little messy or you got to it late. You can't help it. You will not forget to communicate it with a huge apology and a dose of shame.

If you are consistent with your health regimen, in the end you will see results. Permission to give yourself a break. Really, Virgo, you must realize by now that you are so hard on yourself! It's okay to ease up. Nobody is ever going to judge you like you judge yourself. The observer will help you see it.

VIRGO HIGH ROAD

Virgo's gift is selfless service. Think Mother Teresa, a Virgo. Practicing service with no agenda, she helped the orphans and people with leprosy, neither of whom she could fix, although she never gave up. She was considerate and attentive.

It's difficult to be on the high road for Virgo—the human operating system cannot turn off those voices completely. It really is a challenge for all of us. Virgo, you have a particularly loud inner critic. Could you realize how hard you try and let that be enough—or at least try to? Can you imagine accepting imperfection as beauty?

Just look at nature. Leaves fall off the trees, flowers die. It looks messy out there and yet it is beautiful. Nature is full of imperfection, yet we marvel at what we see. On the high road, you can release the notion of perfect in exchange for acceptance. That may sound like theory to you. You can at least give it a try.

VIRGO MEDICINE

Nature is a healing balm for a Virgo's soul; gardening and studying plants, organic medicine, and supplements are your things. Most of all, hiking or walking immediately brings you back to calm.

Virgo is the student—diving deep into science or agriculture, or studying the body and anatomy is your happy place. Reading a book settles your nervous system.

Quit the buzz of caffeine and the input of alcohol to see how much better you will feel. It's hard to stop the need for the buzz—your mind loves the increase of efficiency when you are sped up. However, you know that those substances actually make your anxiety and stress worse after the fact, and then you begin judging yourself again.

This sounds self-serving, yet astrology really is good medicine for Virgo. It doesn't take the inner critic away, yet it helps you understand your traits as endearing, which softens that negative inner voice.

Boy, do you like to change. It's so hard to stay too long with same/same. It's like a nervous twitch—you look for the latest superfood/product/person to solve your problems and give you new things to think about. Pick one thing—do it for a while until it's a habit. Then move on to the next thing with guilt-free cards.

Here's a mantra for you, Virgo: *I trust myself to get things done and I'm doing much better than I think.*

VIRGO'S LIFE LESSON

Virgo, your life lesson is to learn to stop measuring your life by how it looks on the outside. Instead, measure your life by how it feels. It's dangerous to live in your head. That's where shame, guilt, and sadness begin. Mother Teresa understood that she was here to serve, yet her journals revealed she had depression. It's easy for an exhausted Virgo to get cynical and not tell anyone (except, maybe, their therapist).

The world needs you. Your selfless service can result in happiness. When you are operating at your best, Virgo is a saint-like being, with an almost supernatural ability for helping and informing us of what we need.

VIRGO MOON

Virgo doesn't want to cry. Crying can be embarrassing and, even worse, inappropriate. That word follows you around. The emotional filter arrives, criticizing, taking you up into your head rather than into your heart. Virgo moon sees emotions as irrational, which bothers them. When a Virgo moon does get emotional or upset, they impulsively clean and organize. They grab a sponge and a vacuum and get busy.

The upside of a Virgo moon is how helpful you are. You will go the extra mile. Parents, healers, and friends who have Virgo moons are among the best at serving and caring because they have a strong natural impulse to be considerate and helpful.

MERCURY IN VIRGO

Mercury in Virgo is a great placement. Mercury rules Virgo so it's comfy here. This is someone with an organized mind that brings order and retains information easily. Great students, they make lists and spreadsheets effortlessly. You have a great memory that collects and retains information and data, even though you don't think so.

Mercury in Virgo is flexible due to mutability. You hold on to beliefs with ease until new data arrives, and then you are able to consider alternative views. For example, if you take a vitamin and later you are shown research against it, you'll change, just like that. Good solid data helps Virgo to move along. Mercury in Virgo is not ultimately stubborn like some earth signs are.

VIRGO RISING

You want to help. And yet you have a hard time reducing all the expectations. Virgo rising is crazy productive, yet painful. Can you be kinder to yourself, sweet Virgo rising? The Virgo soul is built to be in devotion. You have one job: service with a smile. Admit it, you love to help. If you are Virgo rising, when in doubt, give. This will provide a sense of fulfillment. Or, you resist that impulse. Letting your soul be in charge will help you find your way.

Virgos are good-looking people, especially Virgo rising. They carry a feminine essence. I once had the opportunity to do a whole slew of readings for stunning international models in Europe, many of whom were in *Vogue* magazine. No surprise, many of them were Virgo rising. They complained: "I have a mole on my left cheek." "My boobs aren't the same size." "My legs aren't thin enough." I would say, "Surely you realize how attractive you are?" They'd smile. Of course they knew it, in theory. It's not easy to receive compliments when you are focused on what is wrong. Virgo's inner critics are that loud. They don't see what we see. Best not to argue with them—they just think you are being nice.

Beautiful people with Virgo rising include Madonna, Dolly Parton, Janelle Monáe, Angelina Jolie, Nicole Scherzinger, and the supermodel Bella Hadid. Virgo rising men are lovely, too—Keanu Reeves, Timothée Chalamet, Michael B. Jordan, Chris Pine, Ryan Reynolds, and Paul McCartney. The outer appearance reflects the soul. It is the love within that makes Virgo rising so attractive.

Virgo rising, your work ethic describes your soul's fulfillment. Without meaningful work, you feel unfulfilled and endlessly critical of your efforts. That feeling can make your nervous system irritated so you end up thinking that something is wrong with you when there is nothing wrong. It's just the pressure you put on yourself, to constantly think you ought to be doing more, and with more effectiveness. That is a lot to carry. The pressure you impose on yourself will not increase your ability to get more done. It just adds a low-grade self-esteem issue that isn't even based in reality.

We love you, Virgo, for trying so hard. Anyone who hires you does not want you to leave. Your work ethic and willingness to learn cannot be surpassed. That's just the truth. Take in the compliment and allow your soul the good feeling of being Virgo rising.

SATURN IN VIRGO

Be methodical, cautious, and purposeful. Service toward others is your gift and contribution.

The beginning of your life is all about work, and as you mature, you will discover that being is as important as doing. Be patient. You are doing far better than you realize, even if your mind insists that you haven't done enough. It's not true. You have done enough, and then some.

Create a healthy routine and find holiness in the everyday. Make healthy decisions as a role model for others. Teach us what you practice. Practice what you preach.

Life lesson: Perfection is an illusion. We live in a perfectly imperfect world. The purity of your heart is the measuring stick of you fulfilling your purpose. Your sincere desire to help is why you are here.

MEDITATION FOR VIRGO

Help me see that I'm doing the best I can without the pressure that I should be more. My intentions are good. May I change my internal dialogue to be the voice of an angel with the kindness of a mother. I'm enough. I'm on schedule. I always get things done. My heart is pure.

THE ESSENCE OF VIRGO

Virgo wants to say yes when they ought to have said no. We appreciate that they always do the dishes after everyone leaves. They may not realize they could have asked for help. And that list they leave you, with all the books to read about your health issues, and the suggestions they wrote in red ink? Sure, you're grateful, although you wonder if Virgo realizes you do have your own doctor. It's a thankless job to always know everything. Virgo wonders, "What's so wrong with wanting to get it right?"

When clients come to consult with me as an astrologer, I have heard myself say: "You have a bad case of Virgo. You're unable to focus on the positive or receive a compliment. Even just looking in the mirror invites a host of gremlins in to judge you before you've even finished getting dressed." That's the result of Virgo's essence: just wanting to get it right.

Virgo energy is a gift to our world. There is not a better person to have around when suffering from bad news or an ailment. Virgo believes in double-checking and asking endless questions. It assures everyone that the details are covered. It's a great quality. However, Virgos judge themselves for forgetting that one thing that didn't even matter. A circle of judges lives in their head, and they work overtime. Can they please retire now?

Virgos understate their gifts. This makes it harder for them to move up the ladder of success, even though no one deserves it more. Virgo is useful, needed, and depended upon. There is no need to try so hard—if Virgo put in half the effort, they would still be the best at what they do. Virgo will not believe this. I'm so sorry.

14

The Psychology of Libra

WE BALANCE

Element: Air
Mode: Cardinal
House: Seventh
Planet: Venus
Body part: Kidneys—they keep your system balanced and clean.

If only you understood that my love for harmony, which I present as easy, isn't easy at all. I constantly wish that people were different. That they understood kindness. I don't understand people's need to talk over one another, or to get so loud and take over when we clash. Why can't everyone just have their turn and be heard?

I look for harmony in physical space. If your space hasn't been tended to, I notice. Please pay attention to where you put your books, your art, and even what you put on yourself. Why don't others have aesthetic awareness? It's not that I'm elitist or spoiled. I simply see the way life was meant to be—filled with beauty, color, aroma, pleasing to the eye and heart.

I came to Earth with a sense of belonging; I followed willingly. Over time, I realized I wasn't being my real self. Trust me when I tell you that I feel alien, even in my own family. I'm the one people talk about. I have ambition to go my own way and be a success. I make it look easy. People don't get that it's hard to always be the one who does the next right thing, takes the high road, forgives the unaware one, even when no one else does.

Why so much talk about Libra and relationships? It's all everyone thinks I care about. Stop calling me codependent. I'm actually not interested in any partnership that is not balanced and meaningful. When I find someone who can listen, has refinement, and enjoys art as I do, I'll consider them. Who will watch documentaries and read books that matter so we can have a great conversation? Too many misunderstand me—they think I'm so easygoing. What I long for is respect, equality, and a mutual appreciation for real harmony, from someone who isn't too sticky or clingy.

Most of all, don't tell me your interpretation of who I am or label me. I'm not interested. I spent my young years conforming to everyone else. I am so done with that. Nobody knows me like I know myself, although I long for someone who does.

I will admit to being a hopeless romantic who has never given up on the idea of true love. If I'm lucky enough in this life to achieve such a union, you'll know because I will age well and not complain about my partner. Leave me to my own devices in my art studio, with my instrument, or with my journal. I can do anything alone. However, I'd rather do it with someone nearby who respects my space, understands my dualistic nature, and shares my ideals. I'd love to find someone that I can be alone with so that I do not have to lose myself.

Please, don't interrupt me. If you are around all the time, I can't miss you. You need to go away for a little while. Just don't forget to come back. Closeness and space are my two favorite flavors.

If I appear wishy-washy at times, it's because I am. I have a hard time making decisions when the winds are just about to change. If you can be flexible, we will get along great.

Libra is a hopeless romantic. I can't tell you how many astrology sessions I do where people want to know, "Will I be in a relationship?" "How's my relationship?" "Am I in the right relationship?" It's a universal song, and also a gift because Libra energy is the primary source motivating us not to give up on love. Romance isn't the only Libra obsession, yet it is an important part of who they are. Venus, goddess of love, rules Libra. We all know the romantic, yummy feeling of being seen and understood and danced with by someone else. When we fall in love, we do just that—we fall, slipping on the juice of romance that drips off newlyweds that (as Libra is so aware) eventually goes dry.

However, the stereotype that Libra is willing to do *any* relationship, that they will sacrifice themselves, compromise, sell out, shapeshift, turn into pretzels, do whatever is necessary to keep the relationship working, isn't quite right. That may happen in the beginning of life. The young Libra looks for love in all the wrong places. That is the low road. What Libra really seeks is what we all seek: real, long-lasting love. Not the sappy, saccharine love of TV and movies. So few people in this world are gifted with true love. Every Libra wishes they were one of those people.

Once you get underneath the psychology of Libra, you will discover that the longing for love in all of us is really a longing for divine love—to know that you are worshiped, that the angels pay attention to you, that the spiritual world has your back, that you can make contact with the lost relative who really cared for you. That's what the Libra in all of us actually seeks.

This is different from human love, and that's what confuses Libra. Driven by the desire for love, looking for somebody to embody their romantic ideals, finding someone who has that kind of charge so they feel wanted or loved, someone they would die for—that's the Libra dream. However, when they get into an actual relationship with an actual human, reality sets in. No human can offer what divine love can offer, so human relationships never live up to Libra's expectations.

Libra's attractions go through waves. They want to be truly seen, yet at the beginning they can pretend not to have preferences. The romantic attraction is perfect because they try to please you. They are so charming and endearing. They have dimples, great hair, and often wear colors no one else can. They will spend hours looking for the right Hallmark card, the perfect birthday present, especially jewelry. They go out of their way to mail it to you or to present it to you in some creative way.

Then suddenly, the scales shift (scales are the symbol for Libra). They won't tell you that they're getting disillusioned. Instead, they will continue to look good, dance well, romance you, so you don't see who they really are. When they finally break, they are embarrassed. They want to be married, partnered, and dancing with the other—while also being left alone to pursue art, science, or whatever their aesthetic and intellectual passions require. It's hard to pin them down. They change easily like the wind. They're just so nice—until they're not. Once you become boring, predictable, or too clingy, they cut you off. Or you might not have done anything to cause those scales to shift. It's not your fault if you didn't live up to a Libra's fantasy. No one could.

Still, it's a great disappointment for both sides. Either the relationship continues unhappily, or it ends. It's the push-pull of "You failed to be what I imagined" and "Stay near me and tell me I'm okay because when you leave the room, I begin to doubt that I'm lovable, even if we do not get along anymore." Libra can present as confused, ambivalent, indecisive, and a shapeshifter in the name of love.

This is Libra's design fault: the never-ending pursuit of an idealistic love that ends in disappointment and pain. How many marriages end up in divorce? The statistics are staggering. That's not to say Libras can't have successful relationships. Many achieve this once they find the right person who understands their dualistic nature of wanting love and wanting to have space. If they have a solid grounding in their own identity, purpose, and talents, an older Libra can embrace freedom and enter into relationships with emotional wisdom.

Then again, they might be codependent, just like the cliché, because they are afraid to leave a relationship that isn't working. Many Libras just hate to be alone! Their opposite sign, Aries, loves to do things on their own. Both signs are inside each other.

Here we are, only talking about relationships, just what Libra doesn't like. Not every Libra is obsessed with finding true love. Many have given up completely after being disappointed too many times. I can't tell you how many single Libras I know who say, "I'm never getting into a relationship again."

There is much more to Libra than the pursuit of love, even if that drive is at Libra's core. Libra is the artist, the designer, the one with immaculate taste. They fight for justice, love, beauty, and idealize the world. They are the ultimate peacemaker. One of Libra's best qualities is their generosity and consideration for the other.

Or, they love their solitude and the pursuit of their art. You wouldn't be wrong if you thought of them as a little peculiar. They certainly ask a lot of questions, just like a lawyer; however, they have the kind of charm that allows them to get away with it. I think quirkiness is Libra's disguised best quality. They start by fitting right in, until they show up as their real selves. They are going to stand apart. It's the artist in them. Practical matters can be challenging for them. They may or may not be on time. That's just boring. They think doing the money and paying the bills will keep them from achieving success. That's someone else's job.

They can be a bit goody-goody and proper. They are quite witty and self-effacing with their jokes. They use language and humor to charm people. They know how to make all of us happy. And boy, can they tell a story. You get them talking, and they can go for a very long time. They are, after all, an air sign. They just want to make the world delightful.

They do their part to beautify, with color and good taste, immaculate outfits, everything matching. They seek balance, yet because scales are always moving, they never quite find it.

Guess who has a temper and won't own it? Libra can get stuck after being so nice for so long, collecting brownie points: "I was nice then, and I was nice then, and I was nice then," and suddenly they've had it. They want to cash in those brownie points. They get so angry if they don't get credit. They say: "For the last three months, we've been going where you wanted to go and doing what you want to do!" The person whom they've been catering to wonders what happened. Did Libra ever say anything about having an opinion? No, because they expected their partner to read their mind.

Libra, this is when you need to calm down, use your words, and accept that there is disharmony. All air signs look for a lighter experience in this life. They want to be mentally stimulated without getting into the messier emotions. Yet listen to this, Libra: you can do the therapy, engage your human side, get a coach, and stop the idealization of romance or art as the be-all and end-all. It is a proven scientific fact (Libra loves scientific proof) that the first flush of love, when we fall into romance, is a chemical rush. You are no longer in the free-will zone. Then, when the classic struggles arrive, and they will, the real test of whether the relationship can survive begins.

You can pass that test, Libra. Land, air sign. Come on down to the real world and do the work of relationship. That's the high road for Libra. You become a great mediator and therapist because you had to learn how to find peace within yourself and in your relationships.

The gremlins know Libras can be brought down by making them feel unloved and alone. The gremlins try to tell them no one really gets them. When that happens, Libra turns into an indecisive people pleaser, gossipy or clingy. They will get into a social group and be obsessed with knowing all the dirt on people and asking way too many questions. At worst, Libra feels alone in the middle of a crowd, disconnected from their favorite word: love.

Once Libra learns to speak the truth and reveal their vulnerability, authenticity arrives. Libra, there is no shame in being real. That's where true love lives. Your best friend doesn't need you to dress up or tell all your stories. You can quietly be your real self and be loved.

Truthfully, at best you are fascinated with life, which is why you are the interviewer, the journalist, the person who is trying to figure out what, why, and where. You ask all the right questions. You engage us. You bring out our best. You are, after all, a master of diplomacy, communication, and bringing harmony and justice to all.

No one tells you that in esoteric astrology, Libra is the most advanced sign. When evolved, Libra will let go of the well-worn bondage of traditional relationships. The evolution of relationships opens up to a new format where romantic idealization is no longer a human fixation, and Libra puts their attention on the divine. Sometimes it's a best friend, your colleague, your therapist, or your spiritual practice that you feel the closest to, not just a romantic partner.

This is how your life becomes art—the ultimate goal for every Libra. Thank you, Libra, for your beauty and sweetness. Your humor and the endless fascination you have with us is inspirational to everyone you meet. Keep asking all those questions. Let's make sure someone listens to you the way you listen to others.

PROFILE OF A LIBRA

When I first met Sting, I had no idea about the full measure of his success. I met him through his dear friend who had told him I was a good astrologer. I began by addressing his romantic life as a double Libra. I asked him what happened during his Saturn return—that was the year that his first big hit song, "Roxanne," came out and took him and his career to the sky.

It's a little-known secret that Sting has studied astrology, originally with the intention of proving it wrong, because he is a skeptic, as are all Libras. He delved into it and was asked to read charts of famous people without the names on them. When they showed him his wife's chart, he thought it must be the chart of Jesus. He was actually quite good at astrology, although he remained a skeptic, as only a Libra will do. Doubting Thomas is one of Libra's archetypes. He asks, "Is this real? Do I believe in it? Show me the proof."

Yet if you listen to his music, you will be teleported to a refined expression of spirit. I once nicknamed him Life's Instrument of Refined Passion. His relationship with his current wife, Trudie Styler, his soul mate, has handed him a partner who supports him (because she's a Capricorn) in raising millions for the Amazon rainforest and many other causes and charities, including Amnesty International and the Alzheimer's Association. The right use of Libra is collaborating. Sting has done that in his musical career, but most of all with his wife. They have generated money for so many positive causes.

He uses his artistic sensibility both for his own fulfillment and to inspire and help others. That included endorsing me as an astrologer, which changed the trajectory of my career. Libras are generous like that.

LIBRA LOW ROAD

The low road of Libra is a state of confusion between: "Don't go, don't go, don't go!" and "I want to be alone, how long are you staying?" Libra gets stuck in an ambivalent state of indecision. When they don't have a partner, they obsess about finding one. When they do have a partner, they hang on so tightly and don't admit when it's over. Or, they dump the person as soon as the romantic high is over and start again.

At worst, they want to make the other person wrong. "You're such a jerk. I knew it from the moment we met. I had a red flag at the very beginning. We never should have gotten married!" Really, Libra? You're blaming the other person for that? If you saw the red flag, why didn't you address it then? The low road is pointing the finger and blaming everyone else, looking for hard evidence to make them wrong.

When Libra gets silent, move away. A storm is brewing. The Libra who has given up, hardening their hearts to love, shuts down and plays hard to get. It's sad when they give up on love and turn it off for good—come on, Libra, there is always hope. Always.

THE LIBRA OBSERVER

When Libra learns to step outside of themselves and be objective, they can find peace. Relationships come in different shapes. Whether you find love with a romantic partner, or family, or close friends, or God, it's still love. It's all relationship. The observer gives Libra a new perspective on what it means to be hopeful rather than a hopeless romantic.

In esoteric astrology, it is suggested that blame, shame, and fear are the sources of all war, disharmony, and lack of peace. What Libra is really about—you won't hear this in most astrology systems—is the feeling of rejection and disconnection, and then healing that. The observer can show Libra how to take responsibility rather than blaming the other person.

I know that when you get emotional, you do your best to stay reasonable—until your hidden Aries (your opposite sign) arrives. The presence of your anger, while tamed, will be obvious in your energy. The observer can help you respond to your triggers by saying, "Don't get dramatic right now, we're having a conversation," or "Can't we just stop fighting and watch the sun coming up? This is just silly, fighting like this." Dramatic relationships may be fun for a minute; the observer helps you to see when there is too much drama or indulgence and it's time to move on.

There will be times in your life when you may need a break from relationships because you are disillusioned or feel cynical. Go ahead, you are allowed to feel that for a while—just don't give up, Libra. This is why it is so important to seek a friendship and let love grow out of that. That's a lesson learned in time. Find the version of love that makes sense to you in whatever shape that is.

LIBRA HIGH ROAD

Libra's highest road is to realize who they are apart from other people's reflection. They are no longer concerned with seeking approval at all costs, as the young Libra was. A mature Libra doesn't need a relationship to be happy. What would it be like to really find peace within yourself?

High-road Libra tells the truth willingly: "You know what? We're not getting along. It's you and me that's the problem. You're fine by yourself, and I'm fine by myself. It's our chemistry that's worn out. Now we've got a tension that doesn't create peace. I can't live in a state that is anything less than peace, so I have to go." They kiss, and leave in peace.

At their best, Libra prioritizes peace over pretending.

LIBRA MEDICINE

You feel best surrounded by beauty and pleasant aromas. Burn incense, light candles, use essential oil diffusers, use color to beautify your home. Your happy place is an aesthetically pleasing environment. Bring out your inner artist. Design your environment the way you love it, with your favorite colors and style.

You need someone to help motivate you. Find someone to work out with, start a project with, go to class with. For you, that's motivating.

Eventually you will learn that spending short periods of time alone is therapeutic for you. It may feel uncomfortable at first. You do so love company. However, the more you spend time alone with yourself, the more you will find joy in it, as you reclaim your individuality and spare yourself from constantly trying to please others and conform—what a relief. Do an experiment: Take yourself out on a date. Not to a restaurant—that's too much for a Libra. What about the movies? Try going to a movie by yourself. Just don't be alone for too long; isolation can cause you to lose your love of humanity.

As for your relationships, if you are seeking romance, the best medicine for you is to fall in love with *you*. I'm sure you have heard this in every spiritual book—because it's true. You are allergic to people who try too hard or who are highly emotional and illogical. That kind of behavior is a Libra nightmare. When you fall in love with yourself, you will understand better what you want in a partner, rather than getting swept away by the wrong person.

LIBRA'S LIFE LESSON

Your life lesson is to learn how to love and be loved without expectations or conditions. Believe in soul mates and establish a relationship with something higher than yourself, whether you call that God or something else. You are being asked in this lifetime to be an independent sovereign rather than living in the belief that you are incomplete without a partner.

Your highest purpose is to usher in a new age where men and women get along as equals, where our daughters and their daughters are free to be independent, and at last, the gender field is leveled. Imagine a world in which the thing most people seek is not power or money or influence. Imagine if love was the only goal.

Imagine a world where love transcends romance and relationship and even political concepts so that people prioritize equanimity and respect. Imagine a world where peace is the norm. Libra leads the charge into this new existence. John Lennon, the Libra, spoke the evolved Libra anthem: "All we are saying is give peace a chance." He also wrote the song "Imagine." A Libra specialty.

LIBRA MOON

This placement is uncomfortable because your emotions are not meant to be intellectualized. It's a tug-of-war between feeling and thinking. At worst, you can be cut off from an honest acknowledgment of your deepest feelings. The good news is you are especially good at friendships. You listen deeply to others, yet don't have good boundaries. You are a pleaser, even bending over backward to keep the peace. It's hard for you to know how you feel—you would love it if someone cared enough to try to investigate your mind by asking you a lot of questions.

MERCURY IN LIBRA

Mercury in Libra feels uncomfortable because Libra is indecisive and a bit scattered. You see so many options and possibilities. You try to understand all the points of view. You know what he thinks and she thinks, but you can't tell what *you* think! Your fascination with science and understanding big questions allows you to be interested in just about any topic—for a short while, at least. Your memory stands out, especially when you drill down and really take one subject into your awareness.

You tell a great story, filled with details. Everybody listens raptly. However, you can take on the poetic license to change the story just a bit to make it more colorful.

LIBRA RISING

It's easier for you to produce art and find harmony outside yourself than to balance yourself internally. You carry both male and female energies in your soul. You long to connect with God/spirit, yet the distraction of romance has you fixated on seeking "the one." Or you resist the soul's call and resist getting into a relationship at all. One day, you will hear the call of your soul that says: "You are the one you've been looking for. Release the pressure of finding 'the one' and let your soul guide you." Love may not look like what you expected. Has it occurred to you that you can be in love with your best friend, or have a soul-mate agreement with one of your children? Have you considered that romantic love and sex aren't the only paths to love? Because your priority is harmony, the question to ask yourself is: Who do I get along with effortlessly?

Physically, you are attractive—we all notice, and you work hard at it. Your good taste, style, and design sense are obvious. The question that plagues you is: How can I be true to myself while pleasing the other? Great question. Meanwhile, your soul calls you to change the old-fashioned notion of relationships.

Your soul seeks harmony, and when it isn't present in a relationship, the relationship probably won't last long. I have Libra rising, and I have all kinds of relationships. We all go through eras in life. Realizing this truth set me free. It took me many years until I finally realized that I am no longer the Debra who thinks she needs to be with someone—and right when that happened, I met someone! Nevertheless, I learned the lesson of self-sufficiency. I run my universe on my own. I see God in the eyes of whomever I'm looking at.

I've learned that what my Libra soul was asking of me was to learn how to love without expectations. Wow, what a gift astrology has been to help me not feel rejected by life during those times when I was single. Rather, I've learned to find love in all the right places and so can you, Libra rising.

SATURN IN LIBRA

The hardest lesson of all is relationship.

Saturn in Libra, you must learn how to say the big C word: commitment! Commit to being in a relationship. Commit to being in a body!

Commit to something. I know you don't want to, yet this is why you are here. Try making any commitment for just one month. It's a great lesson for you because you are here to learn about relationships. Therapy can help.

Study relationships. Your practice is to commit to something or someone for the short-term, then revisit that decision—you can always choose again. You are here to free yourself to change without guilt.

Life lesson: Relationships are the doorway to the evolution of the human condition. If you can stay true to yourself while honoring others, you will have learned your lesson. That's the goal for your contribution.

MEDITATION FOR LIBRA

I am self-sufficient. I do not require a partner to be myself. I can do whatever I want. I give myself permission to follow my own interests. I am an artist, and I can practice my art. My gift allows me to recognize myself as an individual who is inspired by the muse and has a relationship with beauty and love in its many forms. My soul is whimsical, and I can show up spontaneously without effort. My life is a work of art. I have the gift of effortlessly loving within the context of my human experience, creating divine beauty everywhere I go.

THE ESSENCE OF LIBRA

A lover, period. The essence of Libra is about sexual energy without taking your clothes off—the intimacy of knowing another, feeling them as a soul, getting to understand their uniqueness. Libra is unique—nothing like the others. They have taste buds that have us wanting to be like them. We hate it when they leave the room, and yet they seem to need so much space.

Libra has a refinement brought to us by music, art, fashion, gems and jewels, all the beautiful things. What's the point of a life that is not dressed up and in style? Why even do it? How could we not take advantage of a reality wrapped up in colors and scents that tickle our senses, and thoughts that make us ponder and then laugh hysterically?

Libra's joy is their gift—until we start to bug them, and then they just evaporate. When a Libra leaves, it's for good reason. Don't expect them to repeat their reasons to you. They told you once and you weren't listening. They, on the other hand, specialize in listening: to what you are not saying, to the expression of ideas, to the mixture of the elements in science or in nature that create art. Sharing what they learn from being passionate about what they do is such a Libra gift.

Libra thinks outside the box. Who says you have to get married just because you are in love? Who says you can't be in love with your best friend, your children, that song? Libra is in love with life itself. They are here to change our way of thinking and being—to update the concepts that are dated, especially contracts put in place through obligation. "Who says I'm obligated?" says the sassy Libra.

On and then off they go, like the light that they are. Lucky us, when Libra decides to shine on us. We are so grateful for their exquisite presence. They make the world that much more beautiful and kind, and we are so blessed to be in their sphere.

15

The Psychology of Scorpio

I DESIRE

Element: Water
Mode: Fixed
House: Eight
Planet: Pluto
Body part: Genitals—obviously, since they are all about sexuality.

If only you understood how my energy gets intertwined with yours once our eyes meet. If you did, you would know why I'm reluctant to look you in the eyes. Once we connect, I immediately feel you. You know how they say the eyes are windows to the soul? I believe it. They also say death is to be feared. That one is not true. Death is not what you think it is. I have studied death, and I can tell you there is nothing to fear there.

In fact, it is a great privilege to leave this world with your awareness on (in other words, at peace), accepting the end. I have been the witness to many endings, as I am sure you have. The breakup that shattered my heart, the death of my childhood pet, the disturbing behavior I witnessed in childhood, it all ended my faith in humanity . . . for a while. Yes, I've experienced re-

jection and heartbreak, far greater than I deserve. Apparently, as a Scorpio, I learn from the unfriendly teachers called Letting Go, Death, and Sadness. All those events made me a better person, once I allowed myself to process the pain. Can you say the same? Or is this exclusive to members of the Scorpio club?

Some describe me as a depressive personality type, or the mysterious, quiet one. I may look stoic on the outside. Inside, I experience incredible intensity. You wouldn't believe what it's like when I'm in my emotions, or up against a challenge, standing up for what I love. Then it's all hands on deck. I never do anything halfway, so if you are a flake or go back on our agreement, I'm confused and angry. I would never do that. I have no use for wishy-washy people—sometimes I think they're around just to irritate me. I know how to stay the course no matter what. I will never let my emotions stop me from growing.

I'm focused. Give me a goal and I'll fulfill it, come hell or high water. By the way, I can handle both hell and high water. I've seen what most would rather not know about: addiction, child abuse, the rejection of a child's love, just to mention a few. Tell me about the greatest human wounds, and I will show you my passport filled with stamps to all the lands most would avoid.

My superpower is to come back from sorrow or pain more informed. Then, I'll help you traverse those lands. I've witnessed pain to the nth degree, and I've learned not to interrupt someone's lessons. Pain is the soil where wisdom grows. If you are willing to be hurt and still maintain your faith, you will be healed.

I push people away, testing to see if they really love me. Most don't pass the test. The few that do are my loyal friends for whom I would do anything. I'm the person you want in crisis. When it's my time to lead, you won't have to look back. I will have thought of everything. Just don't talk too much about me, or to me. Show your love with actions, not flimsy words. I can't do small talk, although if you need someone to keep your secrets, that's me.

Please don't misinterpret my seriousness as anger or stoicism. I feel far more than you see, unless of course you are a fellow Scorpio. Then you see *through my sunglassed, secret look. See me. I long for someone to be strong enough to see me, handle me, and not shy away.*

Scorpio likes that feeling of being on the edge of their seat while watching or reading a thriller, a mystery, a scary story. The adrenaline rush stimulates feelings of being alive, whether that's jumping off a cliff, taking a strange drug, or taking a really big financial risk. Scorpio has excessive, extreme energy that might show up as sexual wildness, impulsivity, or substance abuse. It's the part in all of us that faces death bravely, looks directly at the psychological wounds people usually keep secret, and speaks to the unspeakable. Scorpio looks directly at the shadow without pretending it is anything other than darkness. How willing are you to face the truth? Will you walk through the fire? Scorpio will test you, at worst betray you, just to see what you are made of.

The Scorpio stereotype is associated with all things dark and sexual. While that's not always true, it does show up. Some Scorpios don't relate to these stereotypes—they avoid the dark, and they may not be all that interested in sex. This is why they reject astrology—the stereotype offends them. This can be explained—unlike any other sign, Scorpio has three representatives: the snake, the eagle, and the phoenix.

The snake is the Scorpio operating in the dark, fascinated with what happens after death, in a room with a Ouija board, studying the occult. It can also be the dark side, acting with devious intent—acting like a snake.

The eagle has a big, powerful energy aimed straight for the light. They don't touch the darkness. They fly above it. I call them blond Scorpios; they do not want to talk about anything dark or scary.

The phoenix, a mythical creature who is destroyed by fire then emerges from the ashes, has no fear on either side. "Yes, I'm in the dark. Yes, I'm in the light. I'm comfortable with both sides. No question: I have a dark side; I have a light side; I am free with my energy and powerful as a result."

What all Scorpios have in common is intensity. They listen deeply and display the outward drama of a fire sign. It's not surprising if you thought Scorpio was a fire sign. The difference is, their intensity is more like simmering water than fire. When dealing with scary topics like death or addiction, they comfortably share their depths. Not namby-pamby, vague personalities, Scorpios get straight to the point. In business, they bottom-line it: "How long will this take, how much money will we make, and who is in charge? Just give it to me straight and cut this board meeting short."

At worst they are self-destructive, self-sabotaging, even mean. They can't tolerate fakeness and have such a strong radar that superficial human behavior is unacceptable to them. They might even say, "Let's end it here. Let's kill this project/idea/relationship." Their words are harsh.

At best, Scorpio is a healer. Think of a surgeon cutting out the diseased parts of you so you can feel better.

In esoteric astrology, Scorpio is the only sign that will destroy their ego in the quest of their soul. Think about that sentence. It is what this book is all about. Let the ego focus on the soul, and everything is in order. If everyone did that, this world would shift, all in a moment. This is not a popular point of view. The ego seeks approval, and the soul doesn't care. Therefore, Scorpio is self-assured, which can seem intimidating. They move through the world with confidence and power, often with sexual energy that says, "I love being in a body." This is the highest version of Scorpio. They walk into a party and everybody whispers, "Who's that?"

They say when an actual scorpion is in a room, you feel it before you see it. Scorpio is just the same—their presence is energetically palpable. You won't have to wonder if they like you because if they do, you'll feel it. You won't have to wonder if they're attracted to you because they will stare at you. Scorpio stares without blinking and sees into your soul. Warning: if you never let your guard down, Scorpio—if you just play it cool and safe—you will miss out on intimacy. Don't mistake sex for love—even though I bet that's already happened. There are so many variations of sex. Just don't leave out the vulnerable, sweet kind. You know what I am talking about better than most. Let the soft part open when you feel safe.

What is surprising is how kind, loyal, and compassionate you are. Like all water signs, Scorpio has a connection with animals, children, and people who are down on their luck. They are empathetic and caring. You could even describe them as sweet. That's the seed of Taurus in you—your opposite sign. Taurus is gentle and willing to drop negativity to express the sweet kind of love, not the dramatic and the painful sort. That may sound like something you would love to be able to do. It's hard when you are in the midst of a lifetime of intensity. Still, you have that seed within you.

If a Scorpio loves you, you have won their hard-earned trust.

Scorpio's superpower is reading energy like an X-ray machine. They see right through you. Unlike Cancer, who makes a face when they disapprove, or Pisces, who runs away, Scorpio will stand face-to-face with what they perceive as fake and stare you down. They will judge you with a deadpan face.

When the pressure builds over time, if you do not take their insights to heart or acknowledge their point of view, if you continue doing business on your terms, they will strike. You don't want to be around when that scorpion tail goes up. Anger, honesty, bluntness, and ouch, that sting—this is Scorpio. They can be the hero who takes down the villain (somebody had to do it), then walks away, blowing the smoke off the end of the gun barrel.

Scorpio asks the hard questions. Fascinated by psychology, they make excellent therapists, healers, and surgeons. Scorpio could be a detective, or a mystery writer crafting a whodunit. They get underneath the story to the motives, all while noticing the smallest details and watching everyone closely from the sidelines.

In a crisis, they address the drama without any emotional involvement (until it's over). An actual scorpion can endure extremes of cold and hot and survive. Cool as a cucumber, they demand: "You do this, you do that, I'll handle the rest." You want a Scorpio with you when you need someone to stay calm—after the car crash, in the emergency room, after the diagnosis. When the crisis is over, let them go. They need to go off to be alone. Unlike other water signs, who show their emotions, Scorpio expresses privately.

I had a young Scorpio renting a space from me. Every once in a while, we would go for a walk, and she would bombard me with questions. I looked at her once and said, "Okay, Scorpio, mind your own business. You're knocking on a door that's not for you to open . . . yet." Over time, she won her way into my heart and is now one of my most trusted allies in this life.

Scorpio, you have seen so much of human nature that it becomes difficult to trust people. You hardly trust yourself. In your head, you say: "I want to stop eating junk food. I'm not going to have another drink. I'm not going to have the affair." Then you do *all* the things. The impulses that operate from the dark side of the human psyche stalk you.

The good news is, from your access to the dark side, you have gained deep psychological insight into human nature. What a powerful coach and healer you are.

By now, you ought to understand the word "transformation." In this lifetime, you took on the imprint of pain put in place during your childhood (Scorpios have horror stories about what happened to them). Have you done the healing that can help you turn that pain into wisdom? Please do therapy to get there. Stay with it, and don't pretend you've found healing when you haven't. Your clue will be that you are willing to be held, and can hold your partner without pushing them away.

Scorpio teaches us, as earthlings, that we have to go down first in order to go up. We learn the hard way, and Scorpio is the poster child. They carry the soul's urge to learn at all costs, to keep moving, to face all the hard stuff in life without turning away.

Thank you for what you have done for us, turning dark into light and healing the wounds that come with being human. Without you, we would have no role model for courage and fearlessness. I know it feels unfair that you had to be tested so young. My question is: Did you learn, and are you willing to share your wisdom with us? Scorpio, we need your guidance through the dark.

PROFILE OF A SCORPIO

Danielle was sexually abused as a child and never told anybody. She got married young to a wealthy man she met while she was drinking and partying, only to realize the relationship wasn't healthy. Then she became a fitness trainer and was well known in the town she was in because she was so intense. Her energy level was so far past everyone else's that they all wanted to emulate her.

She then became a publisher of a magazine. She made sure to know everyone so she could turn those people into clients. She was socially adept because it was work-related. Alcohol was always around, and she developed an addiction. She refused to go to AA or therapy. Like a true Scorpio, she named her addiction, yet didn't want help managing it.

After some bad decisions, she declared bankruptcy—the result of her well-kept secrets. She worked through it and changed jobs without reducing her intensity or addressing her alcoholism. She self-sabotaged throughout her life. No matter what happened, she wouldn't stop acting in extreme ways. At her second Saturn return, she changed her ways. Her addiction became a casual drink from time to time. Scorpios can do it their way and find peace. However, that is the exception.

SCORPIO LOW ROAD

On the low road, Scorpio tries to control the world on their terms. This is how Scorpios slide into addictions—the thrill of risk. Down they go to the low road, into behaviors that hurt them, self-sabotaging without even knowing it.

Scorpios do behave in ways that, at times, are hard to forgive. Their short fuse is awful—and their secretive nature leaves people out. They like to tell other people what is true about them. They can be so opinionated that it's hard to get a word in edgewise.

I knew a Scorpio who asked me to help him work with his shadow side—he didn't think he had access to it. "Really?" I said. "Think about it: your wife left you and will never talk to you again, your child is spoiled rotten and disrespectful, and haven't you noticed that people leave you behind as a friend with no explanation and never answer your calls? You can't see that your dark side is fully active in your life?" Sure enough—he was acting out in self-destructive ways and didn't even see it.

Scorpios too often keep secrets even from themselves. The more you address your shadow side with the help of a therapist or wise friend, the quicker you become the healer. When it's really bad, and you are suffering from pain that is unprocessed, you may experience some suicidal ideation. That's because some Scorpios don't like being in a body. The earth experience hurts. These are often the eagles—those blond Scorpios who refuse to do work on their shadow side. They stand back and pretend or deny until they can't take it anymore. Or this could be the snake version of Scorpio who becomes overly fascinated with death and near-death experiences and wants to go all the way.

In either case, if you find yourself thinking about suicide, please seek help! I know you don't like asking for help. Know that on the high road, Scorpio wants to live. They want to be the phoenix, moving through the fire to be reborn from the ashes. This is the evolutionary task: if failed, you have to come back and do it again.

You have the power to walk into the valley of the dark and make it back to safety. When you get back, you can draw us the map. Show us how to come back better for having had the journey. That being said, if you live with confusion about your shadow, or live in the underworld without speaking to it, you are on the low road of Scorpio, and depression and anxiety can haunt you. *Ask for help—therapy could save your life.*

THE SCORPIO OBSERVER

Scorpio knows silence. They can sit in a room full of people and be the only ones not talking. The observer is right there. They know how to listen and then rest in the observer. When someone has done the spiritual work, they become one of the wise ones of the zodiac. First, however, they must go to hell and back. Remember that design fault: we learn our biggest lessons from our mistakes. Scorpio specializes in this. Scorpio, you are a great student of life when you do the work.

SCORPIO HIGH ROAD

On the high road, Scorpio speaks blunt truth. "The door of evil will be sealed because I'm here," said an esoteric Scorpio. "I will not be driven by low impulses. When I see tricky personality traits in myself, I eliminate them. I will not engage with the frivolous side of human nature."

Scorpio on the high road has worked on their childhood wounds and is now able to say to their partner: "Please don't let me hurt you. I learned in my childhood that I can be mean. I don't want to do that to you. You're the best thing that has ever happened to me. Please help me be kind to us."

And so arrives the healer, the one you call on the crisis line. They get it because they have been there and back. Scorpio, at your best, you care so much it hurts. You are willing to go deep and not resist pain in order to bring others through it.

SCORPIO MEDICINE

You are healed by quiet. Let the people you love know it's nothing personal. "I love you so much that there are times I protect myself with distance. Call me out, I really do want to be close. I just need space from time to time."

Your threshold of pain is beyond most of us. You would do great in boot camp. You go the distance and do not stop. Skiing in powder, surfing big waves, rushing down a mountain on your bike . . . the rest of us are scared for you.

You can risk your money, taking on large investments. When you think something might be too much for you, that is your clue that you really want to do it.

I am sure when you were young, you found regular sexual release important. You carry a high libido. Tend to your sexual side—it is medicine for you. You might be a little kinky in your tastes. That's okay—just remember to hold consent as sacred! There's nothing better than when a Scorpio is satiated after the orgasm, after the workout, after the love affair, and finally finds internal quiet.

Because Scorpio too often represses the negative, it is medicine for you to tell your secrets, name your feelings, and open up to the healing process. Speak to your vulnerable side that you so often hide: "I'm afraid of losing you." "I have a drug problem." "Sometimes I want to hurt that person." Once you say it out loud, you can work with it. If you hide it, it festers.

SCORPIO'S LIFE LESSON

Scorpio, your life lesson is about obsession, fixations, and the desire to give your all and feel so much along the way. Careful with all that intensity—it controls you. This is a tall order for Scorpio.

If you have identified with failure rather than success, you will suffer, and your suffering becomes contagious. Once you study your mind, exercise, meditate (which is your specialty), even have a drink or microdose from time to time—there is relief. If you can keep your heart open, the world is yours.

SCORPIO MOON

Having your moon in Scorpio is not easy. While you feel and really care, you can get sticky. You attach and hold on. Dark emotions or moodiness, even depression, become your private companions. At worst, you are possessive and jealous. Once you turn on your observer, you can name what you are feeling, stand objectively, and stop the drama. Otherwise, your strong emotions steal your power, feeding the stubborn gremlins so they won't let you go.

The positive side of moon in Scorpio is a keen intuition, even psychic impulses. At best, you know exactly what is needed and what is happening with others emotionally. You have a long attention span, and you can read people's faces, energy, and goodness. You feel people deeply. Don't think you can fool a Scorpio moon.

MERCURY IN SCORPIO

This is a mind that runs deep. Students of science and psychology, your focus has you standing out no matter what your job. However, at worst, you can easily catastrophize and get trapped by negative thoughts.

Your gremlins can be insistent, like a broken record. You see the car accident before it happens. You imagine yourself getting robbed when there is someone walking behind you. You know where all the exit doors are, always preparing for the worst. You live with low-grade fear. The upside of Mercury in Scorpio is strong, powerful focus. With your mental energy, incredible endurance, and intelligence, you can do anything you put your mind to.

SCORPIO RISING

Who knew that intensity could be used for spiritual purposes? You ask hard questions. You focus longer than the rest of us. You are quiet, yet attentive to life's details. Unlike many other signs, you easily detach from your ego to seek the soul. You might like to study real estate, business, even spiritual matters like modern physics or tantric sexual practices. You can transverse into any world. Less and less interested in indulgence as the years go by, you find wisdom in your unique version of pleasure that no one else needs to understand.

Physically, you are durable and loyal. Your body is built for healing. You often move through illnesses and body issues like a soldier would: you take it, you heal it, you move on.

The question to ask is: Does the pain of this lifetime ever lead me to peace? This is the path to the soul. Once you realize that you have lived through significant and heavy lessons when young because you are the healer, you will find your soul's calling. There are means to get that toxicity off of you.

Listen to me: go do the therapy needed and you will quickly move to the next level. If you have never addressed your wounds and they lurk and fester, you can get stuck. If you live with unprocessed pain, you can go dark. However, no Scorpio rising ever has to stay stuck if they simply ask for help.

As an evolved, soulful Scorpio rising, you will be the one who leads people through darkness into light, because Scorpio rising, at best, is fearless, calling out the pain instead of pretending it is all okay. It just takes a lot to get you there—your pain threshold is so high.

What a gift to be the seer.

SATURN IN SCORPIO

You tend to be in denial about your dark side. You resist it.

Saturn asks you to embrace your dark side. It's important to ask yourself about betrayal, addictions, and sexual encounters. Your gift is to go deep, and your greatest challenge—it's a huge challenge for you and you won't like it—is to learn how to trust and let go of control. You are not in charge. That is a nightmare to you. Yet, whatever is occurring in your life, Saturn's lesson is to trust. Good luck with that!

Do you trust? Or do you feel victimized? Do you hold on for dear life because you think you're losing control? Guess what: you never were in control to start with. Life is not superficial to you. If you're in pain, if you are suffering, your job is to find the light at the end of the tunnel because otherwise, the darkness will overwhelm you. The only way out of the darkness is to go through it. You are built for pain and learning about death, and you will know if you have learned your lesson, which is how to turn pain into wisdom.

Life lesson: Embrace the shadow. If you can learn to let go and grieve while feeling your feelings, you will master this energy. It's not easy.

MEDITATION FOR SCORPIO

My gift is my capacity to feel. I've come into this lifetime to learn the lesson of vulnerability and openness. I'm learning to love this part of myself. I accept that I am more intense than most. That's why I don't use many words. I am a truth teller. I am empathic. I feel who people are and I know who to love. I am learning to accept the range of human nature without judgment. Yes, I love the dark side. I also know the path to the light.

THE ESSENCE OF SCORPIO

"I have always loved this sign," said every therapist who gets to watch someone change right before their eyes. They see the person who had an addiction and once was a wrecking ball transform into a compassionate person with a voice that soothes others who are only just starting their recovery. The first time someone reveals a private secret about trauma, abuse, or internal pain, and offers forgiveness for what happened to them, the process of transformation begins. Until they tell the story of their childhood or their shocking experience, until it is left behind like a pile of ashes, the next life can't arrive.

Scorpio is here to do life in a big way—none of that flaky, kinda-sorta stuff. They play hard ball, seeking pleasure and longing for more. The sky is the limit in the name of success or money—bring it on. This is the part of us that deserves to eat dessert first, for all that has happened and been endured. Scorpio has the ability to walk through the fire, burning that suffering away to emerge like a phoenix.

Loyalty is not a common trait in our modern world. It is for Scorpio. When they commit, it's a long-term promise. If you don't follow through with a Scorpio, be prepared for anger. They feel betrayed. They may abandon you. All of this happens without words. If you are deemed unworthy, you no longer exist to them. Just be glad you didn't get stung on the way out. Or maybe you did.

This life is meant to be intense. We are here to ride big waves. "Get a life," says Scorpio, "and if you don't, go to hell." Heaven to Scorpio is to play hard, cry in privacy, make love, have a great meal, then do it all again. Leave out all those excess words that have no meaning. Just do it. Scorpio says, "If only everyone just listened to me, everything would stay in focus and this world would get along just fine." At their best, Scorpios don't argue. They keep their eyes wide open and speak truth with words and without.

16

The Psychology of Sagittarius

I SEEK

Element: Fire
Mode: Mutable
House: Ninth
Planet: Jupiter
Body part: Thighs—the freedom of movement and running is Sagittarius's specialty.

If only you understood my need for freedom. The call to go, leave, change follows me around most of the time. At some level it bugs me, yet I can't do anything about it. I want to settle down into householding or a professional life without being in doubt that I made the right choice. Even when I'm playing my role in my community or at church, I am thinking I should be somewhere else. I'm a moving target. To be at home with what is, as all the spiritual books suggest, is a wonderful theory. In practice, I'm not so sure.

Speaking of theories, I hear all this talk about karma, yoga, past lives, and the new lingo about Gene Keys and modern astrology. Yes, I have studied them all, and still nothing is better than a trip on a plane with some good friends to a retreat somewhere—second only to microdosing, to give me access to the world anew. Now that's my kind of a spiritual trip.

I am not built for same-same. I love novelty. My goal is to liberate myself, as an ego, and also to liberate myself from the karma I've been sent here with as a human. I have a greater role to play.

I know I can appear immature, like a kid. My sense of humor and my need for freedom have me saying the wrong thing at the right moment, jumping off a cliff, and cracking you up with one-liners so you realize how funny this whole life really is.

I have to laugh. Please don't misinterpret that as disrespectful. I'm loud, I'm crass at times—I am trying to wake you up! I see how contrived this reality is. So I say the thing that we are all thinking. I am the one with the courage to stand out, step up, maybe even present as a bit obnoxious so that your comfort level will shift.

Disruption is the way of the shaman, asking you to look again at what you thought you knew. I love to challenge the status quo. That's why you keep me around, because I am the medicine in the form of humor that allows us to free ourselves from bondage. You're welcome.

I am waiting for the time when we let go of the differences in our society that separate us so that we can see this world as one shared home. That spiritual theory is real: all we are doing is trying to remember who we work for, to have a relationship with spirit, how we can serve better, and how to enjoy every minute of this wild ride. I'm so glad to be here. I am the ultimate optimist that says: "Have another, a bit louder, turn up the fire! We have only one life to live!" Or, "On second thought, maybe we are a reincarnating species that is evolving. Of course we are! If we all just keep our eyes on the joy of life, we will fulfill our purpose."

Sagittarius believes the best way to deal with a problem is to pack your bags, take a trip, change the scenery, and let go of what is bugging you.

If you can't talk about it and get results, just leave. It's okay to outrun or avoid problems. They wear rose-tinted glasses that accentuate the positive, eliminate the negative. This is the part in all of us that is the seeker, asking big questions: "Why are we here?" and "What's the meaning of life?"

Do you know the part in you that just wants to be happy all the time? We all want to have fun, make life easier, and feel good about why we are here and what it all means so that things aren't as bad as we think. Sag, when things aren't going well, you want to run away. Some of your favorite phrases are "Don't fence me in" and "The grass is always greener." It's hard for you to say the word "commitment," much less act on it. You can commit for a while and then . . . well, life happens. There is always something or someone better just over the horizon, isn't there? Life is a change machine.

The stereotypes suggest Sagittarius loves to travel, study philosophy, spirituality, and is the quintessential know-it-all. In truth, not every Sag loves to travel. For some, staying home reading travel magazines is enough. Others are literal vagabonds. At some level, Sag has the impulse to go and study far-away cultures, new languages, new ways of thinking, especially about God. They are not just philosophy majors, they are students of other cultures and languages, as well as other religions.

What most Sags have in common is optimism. Blunt and uninhibited, sometimes rude, they specialize in fun—hello, Sag, the life of the party. "Let's celebrate!" Sagittarius is an expert at the feel-good one-liners: "It will all work out. Everything happens for a reason. We are all here to learn. We create our own reality. Everything is unfolding exactly the way it's meant to be. The universe has your back. The good guys always win. It will work out. Don't worry, be happy! Have a drink or a toke and relax! Let's talk about something fun, like the nature of reality!" These can offend people who don't think Sag is taking their pain seriously.

At worst, they have a feisty reactivity that comes with a bad temper, especially when their idea doesn't get chosen, or when people don't agree with them. This is when you may hear broad, sweeping generalizations like "People are stupid," or "Few can handle the truth," or "Most people don't think for themselves." This comes with the implication that, of course, *they* are not stupid, *they* can handle the truth and, in fact, know what it is, and that *they* most definitely think for themselves. At times, their self-righteousness can become a problem. They can be very judgmental, disguising that as spirituality. They may believe in conspiracy theories because this helps them explain why this world is as it is.

Perpetual students with a passion for knowledge, they can be the jacks of all trades, masters of none. They study a little of everything, then they move on. Or they may be the ones who study deeply. Either way, they will have an opinion, whether it's based in reality or not so much. They speak with authority and conviction. You might want to fact-check them.

People get mad at Sag, and Sag doesn't know why. Is it because they have no filter and offend people with the volume of their voice? They don't realize they're being so loud. Is it because they laugh at their own jokes? Their appetite for life is exciting and passionate. They bite off more than they can chew.

They are optimists. "Climate change will be fine, we'll figure out a solution. You'll see. The latest war? Don't worry, it will pass. Really, if you just ignore these issues, they'll go away." This attitude can offend people who take the problems of our world seriously.

Sagittarius is the luckiest sign in the zodiac. What is LUCK? I think it is Living Under Correct Knowledge. If you have studied metaphysics, you know there are some universal laws for harmony, one of them being gratitude. Sag is often so grateful and positive, it's no wonder things work out for them. To a lot of us, that doesn't seem like such a sure thing, so we are suspicious of Sag's rosy world view and how luck shows up for them all the time, although maybe not always in relationships. As an astrologer, I'm handing you a guilt-free card for your first marriage, Sagittarius. It's in your nature to just jump in and then realize you made a mistake. You are allowed to start and stop your plans—just keep your eye on your goal. This is how you will find your success.

It's okay to redefine success according to your values. After all, you came here to give us a fresh perspective on being human. All the spiritual material that we find so fascinating, you have been studying for years. I bet you have been reading either astrology books or spiritual texts for a very long time.

You have a library of knowledge, and are often a few steps ahead of the rest of us. Therefore, you have the potential to be a great teacher. Be patient with us. We don't all know how to be so open-minded yet. We are learning not to get bogged down in this reality.

Yet let's be honest—there is something delightful about the person who gets on stage, grabs the microphone, and makes everybody laugh. There is something irresistible about someone who can always see the silver lining. They are so uninhibited that they can convince us, even if just for a moment, that everything is going to be okay. It's hard not to love them. They inspire us to find joy. Despite their escapist tendencies, what a great role Sag has in this life.

Thank you, Sagittarius, for your contagious laughter. No matter what happens in this life, you continually find joy. How do you do that? How do you find pleasure in the simplest of things? It's a gift. Thanks for sharing with us so willingly.

PROFILE OF A SAGITTARIUS

At a young age, Jeffrey displayed musical ability. He went to an art school, got discovered, and was signed to a record label. He had his bout with drugs, and youth, then traveled to Israel to discover his Jewish heritage. He was committed to the faith, studied in depth, then returned to the US to make spiritual music.

Back in the US, he talked about religion a lot. Yet his practice lost the intensity it had when he was in Israel. Eventually, he left Judaism behind, all the while secretly wondering if he should have stayed in Israel. He married a woman he met in a spiritual group, and once again doubted his choice. He became very successful as a musician, yet he never left behind Doubting Thomas. The endless questions about honoring his spiritual lineage, compounded by a sense of a past-life memory from his time in the motherland, left him in a state of confusion.

Years later, as he matured, he harbored secret regret, always wondering what his life could have been if he hadn't done what was expected of him. That feeling is familiar to so many: Did I follow my spirit, my ego, my purpose, or what came easiest? The constant wondering and wandering and questioning—"Should I have done that differently?"—saps the happiness out of life, and happiness is Sag's ultimate goal.

SAGITTARIUS LOW ROAD

Sag on the low road indulges without the off button and loses the plot. They suffer from never deciding what to do in this life, floating around and never getting grounded. They are in a dance between indulgence and abstinence. When they take their ideas too far, they start to sound silly. Do you really believe life can be reduced to a pithy phrase? A superficial Sag knows the sayings, yet the weight of their words falls short.

They can lie by telling themselves a story that is not real and convincing themselves it's true. When you interrupt with reality, you become the bad guy. This is the party animal that just will not grow up and take responsibility.

THE SAGITTARIUS OBSERVER

When Sag turns on the observer, they learn how to read the room and become empathetic to the fact that their emotional body is not like the person in front of them. They might even ask, "Did I offend you? Did that make sense? Help me see your point of view."

Once you become aware of how you deliver your truths, you will find people who love your humor. You learn to keep quiet around those who don't. It becomes easier with the observer to censor yourself once you are aware of the impulsive nature of your mouth. If you don't take responsibility for your bluntness, it can be alienating.

You have probably heard since you were a kid: "Tone it down, why did you say that?" With the observer on, you won't have to take the feedback personally. It's just that we are not all fire signs. Without the observer, Sagittarius can override others with insensitivity.

SAGITTARIUS HIGH ROAD

The high-road Sagittarius has the ability to explain, in words that truly comfort, how tragedy is an opportunity to learn. They turn pain into lessons. Sagittarius at its best is capable of achieving a shamanic-like understanding of how astrological signs have been given to us, angels are here, and we don't need to worry. They speak with earned conviction.

They interrupt us with non sequiturs that snap us out of our funk, turn off the autopilot, and bring us back into the present moment. When someone feels down, the best thing to do is to find a Sag who can uplift and remind us that this too shall pass, with parables and lessons that really are filled with wisdom.

SAGITTARIUS MEDICINE

Learning mediation or yoga or mindfulness will serve you greatly. Sag benefits from feedback; you don't always see yourself in a realistic light. It's a good idea to ask your family members advice on how to approach situations, what to say, or how to repair the hurt you caused. Just as you give advice so freely, it's good for you to take some. That is not easy for you.

Speaking of medicine, Sagittarius is fascinated with plant medicine. First in line for ayahuasca ceremonies, magic mushroom journeys, any and all drugs—they love an altered state. Why? Because it takes people out of their stuck patterns. It interrupts the mind, gets you out of a slump, opens up new perspectives.

The easiest way for you to change the energy of being stuck is to plan a trip. Travel is great medicine. You punctuate your life with retreats, trips, and gatherings so you do not get stuck in the mundane for too long. If you get away, you shift! Give yourself something to look forward to. That will keep you more motivated for when you're doing the necessary, boring parts of living.

The mundane has never been your lane. For the sake of your finances, find someone who is good with money. Even though it may feel restrictive, it will serve you in the long run. You are good at taking instructions from those you trust.

I really shouldn't have to tell you this: most important for all fire signs is to make a regular practice of outdoor activities. You were born to be outside; you are in love with Mother Nature. There is no greater medicine for every Sag than the outdoors. Ski in the winter. Surf in the summer. Ride a bike, play tennis, you name it—you have energy to jump into fun. If you have left behind your love for sports and physicality, think about why. Your activity level will influence your aging process. Sag can stay young when they keep moving.

SAGITTARIUS'S LIFE LESSON

Your life lesson is to be okay with people being mad at you for telling the truth. Don't let the judgment of others beat you down because you think nobody wants to hear what you have to say. Yes, you often offend and get in trouble. That is the fire sign delivery system. There is a way to learn how to speak to hard topics that makes them easy to hear. You have that gift, and it is your life lesson to find it. Embrace being human in all its truth: the good, the bad, and the ugly. When Sag faces the negative without running away and shows others how to see the good, they have learned their lesson.

SAGITTARIUS MOON

The moon in Sagittarius is one of the best placements. You can't get depressed when this is your moon. A wonderful optimism controls your emotional body. It's kind of silly, yet it lifts everything and everybody up. You always see the positive. You can't stay too long with your negative emotions—there is an ambivalence about anything heavy. You are an emotional escape artist, and that's okay because it helps you stay cheerful, and that's contagious.

MERCURY IN SAGITTARIUS

You are blunt, funny, and sarcastic. You live in the no-negative-thought zone. Keep someone around to be a checkpoint, to balance out the false positivity you can conjure up. Your mind seeks escape. It's hard to satisfy you, so you might take uncalculated risks. The kid in you can be daring and unrealistic, justifying anything you want to do.

My friend Eric, whom I use as a business consultant, who has Mercury in Sag, is always advising me to think bigger. My Mercury is in Taurus, so I like same-same. He says, "You're here to try things and make mistakes, it's good for you!" I say, "I don't want to make mistakes!" He says, "Go for it!" Then I remember I'm talking to a Mercury in Sag, and I wonder why I even asked his opinion.

SAGITTARIUS RISING

You are a natural coach, teacher, or mentor who began spiritually seeking at an early age. Your life experience includes education or traveling, and you collect stories that inspire others. When you speak the truth, who can argue? Seeking the truth is your soul's calling, and your loud, blunt nature is hard to argue with. Or you may resist your rising sign, resist that call from your soul to seek truth, or resist sharing what you have learned.

You have the ability to trust life and encourage us to do the same. You can speak from experience and with authority. Having been to so many places and having taken so many classes, you are educated. You study the laws of this reality and model them: positive energy begets positive energy. That laugh of yours rolls off you so easily.

I have had clients pay me to tell them what time they should have their baby via C-section (time of birth determines the rising sign). I always pick Sagittarius rising. A soul that came here to have a party, laugh in the face of it all, be optimistic, turn everything into light, study, travel, be financially abundant? Who wouldn't want that for their child? This is the luckiest rising sign.

SATURN IN SAGITTARIUS

Be honest and don't hold back. Be blunt.

You have to be all right with making waves. You are here to wake us up. You need to have the courage to be disliked because of your extreme honesty. You also tend to be indulgent or self-righteous about whatever you believe in.

Can you speak your truth without degrading the beliefs and truths of others? That is how your message gets through.

Life lesson: It's okay to disrupt. Speak to the unspeakable and listen to the opposite point of view to make sure you have cultivated humility.

MEDITATION FOR SAGITTARIUS

I will forever be devoted to the creator in my way, and always find myself in gratitude for the delicious, abundant, magnificent life that's been handed to me. Please help me to stay humble and remember to say, "Thank you." Help me to remember to listen. Help me to see that yes, I know a lot. I just don't know it all.

THE ESSENCE OF SAGITTARIUS

Sagittarius was born under a lucky star, which means that whatever happens in this lifetime, they have the ability to reframe it—with a softer heart, big questions, and a spiritual angle. Change is Sag's middle name. They punctuate their lives with journeys, external and internal. They take such joy in life that they can neglect the boring, mundane world, which means they aren't always able to achieve what they desire. Yet their great appetite for life and meaning is larger than most.

The gift of optimism allows them to see a world that is generous and benign. "The spirits, those that watch over us, have our backs, even if the lessons with our names on them seem impossible." That is such a Sagittarius thought. "'Impossible' means 'I'm possible,'" said the Sag.

The essence of Sagittarius is the result of lives well lived. They are so blessed, having been long-standing students of the history of humankind. Only a Sag gets to open the alchemical formulas for long life, written on paper-thin chronicles inside the chambers where God's name is spoken in so many different languages and tones. Only the Sag is willing and able to translate all that history.

Sag is the one who loves long stories, is open to continuous lessons, and smiles all the way home. They show us, by the way they live, how to stay positive no matter what.

17

The Psychology of Capricorn

I USE

Element: Earth
Mode: Cardinal
House: Tenth
Planet: Saturn
Body part: Knees—because they need to learn humility and drop to their knees to ask for forgiveness (not that they will do this easily).

If only you understood how much there is to do. Not everyone notices what is required in order to be always on time and organized. Someone has to take care of the schedules, guarantees, insurance, safety protocols, profit margins. Someone has to organize a governmental team to put all that in place and enforce it. Life requires organization and rules!

Nothing gets done without me. I'm the first to stand up and say, "Here, let me do that!" I hire, fire, and maintain the company's mission. If I am okay with who I work for and with, and they are competent, maybe even excellent, I will hold down the fort. I cannot do a half-assed job. Period, full stop.

If I am merely materialistic, seeking the top awards at the expense of those in pursuit of the same, we will end up in a society that looks just like the one we are in—a world that is crumbling before our eyes. I cannot be solely materialistic without losing my soul. The high road for me is to create a new way of doing business.

It may appear that I am without emotions—do not mistake that for heartlessness. I am the overseer, president, decision-maker bound to this world in order to fulfill my purpose. That doesn't mean I don't care. I work hard for the benefit of all concerned. I am often at the helm of the ship—it's no surprise that I will benefit monetarily along the way. What's wrong with that?

I am a leader with a purpose. How does anyone live without a purpose? That makes absolutely no sense to me.

Every company must have a leader who is (we hope) benevolent and willing, at times, to take on the role of the bad guy, the corporate voice, the governor, to make the hard decisions that will benefit all. That's me. I'm the head of the office, the captain of the ship. I'm not in it for merely the credit. I'm in it for the results, to reach success and be the best I can be at what I do. Every Capricorn knows the only direction is up. That's how you make enough to eventually own the place. Call me old-fashioned if you like, although I'd rather you call me a classic, timeless success story.

Seek excellence and the money will follow. That is my advice to all. Money can steal your free will, burden you with red tape, and at worst, leave you guilty of tax evasion. It can't be the only goal. I aim higher than just the profit margin. I have my own integrity to answer to. I will climb toward the goal, as I encourage all of us to keep looking up, striving, and giving all that we have.

What has changed my life is the spiritual thought that I listen to my soul and put my ego second. If I can succeed with humanitarian goals so that my hard work was useful, that to me will be true success. I'll win this game *called life and find peace. Watch me. The older I get, the better I get, and with all my effort, I will summit the mountain because my work ethic is my strongest gift.*

This sign is all about ambition. Capricorn is willing to seek constant achievements with the goal of being the best at whatever they are doing. They want to win, whether it's the Olympics, graduate school, getting the promotion, or getting straight As. They organize and structure schedules and know how to do strategic planning. They speak the language of business effortlessly. The CEO wearing the nice suits, the expensive shoes, who pays for everything? That's Capricorn. They can even be ambitious to a fault—they totally get *The Godfather.*

Why doesn't everyone prioritize work, see work as a virtue, and feel badly if they aren't working? Capricorn can't imagine. Ruled by Saturn, Capricorn wants us all to follow the rules, and gets upset when someone doesn't. Classic designs, old-fashioned ideals, and trustworthy business structures feel right to a Capricorn. They don't think it will be easy to take down those boys' clubs of old, and they're not sure they should. Even Capricorn women seek to rise up in the ranks by following the old rules and doing things the old way.

Some say Capricorn has impossible standards. You may have had the father who looks at your report card and says: "A, A, A, A-minus . . . so tell me about this A-minus," or who says, "You're not very good at that." One of the annoying traits of a Capricorn is their bluntness. They are so to the point, and all too often, they are right. They tell you not to do something, and then you do it and it goes wrong, and they say, "I told you so." They get a little thrill from that.

There are understandable stereotypes that people misconstrue as heartlessness. There is an idea that Capricorns don't really care about you as much as they care about their work and their bottom line. "All work and no play" is the Capricorn way. They can be materialistic at the expense of compassion. That is one version of a low-road Capricorn, although it definitely doesn't describe every Capricorn.

They often act like know-it-alls because Capricorn is so smart and successful, and knows they are in a league of their own. They benefit from learning humility so they don't constantly outshine others. They can present with kindness rather than arrogance. It doesn't always come naturally. They are not aiming at being the center of attention, although they are often the person standing behind the front man, making sure he is following the rules.

I had a Capricorn client who told me that when he was young, he was in a race in middle school. He realized he was running much faster than the rest of the kids. He found this embarrassing, so he stopped running as fast as he could just so he wouldn't be known as "that fast kid." As an adult, he still holds back from standing out. Capricorn isn't ruled by their ego alone. They have a sense of propriety.

As the years go by, Capricorns sometimes lose the energy to try. A Capricorn who excelled as a child, was identified as the one who would most likely succeed, and worked harder than everyone else might burn out at thirty-five or forty. They often retire early. Or, if they were hurt as a child—the father was absent or harsh in expectations—they can lose their ability to exert effort or care. Some never even try to achieve success. They lose themselves and forget their purpose.

Capricorn is one of the most extreme signs: it is all or nothing. Either they are the best, or they don't try at all. They are working ten-hour days or sitting on the couch eating potato chips and scrolling through videos. If they can't be the best at something, they would rather not play.

Purpose is a topic for a lot of people. "Why am I here? How do I describe myself in functional terms? What should I do? Where did I come from?" Capricorn knows the answers to these questions. They build the scaffolding for society. They put values and rules in place, and they won't be happy with you if you break the rules. They collect the fines and take you to jail. "The rules are here for a reason," says Capricorn.

They aren't warm and fuzzy, or interested in small talk or superficial anything. They are interested in order. They tend to be serious and they don't usually look like they are having a good time. Once you get to know them, you might discover their subtle, dry sense of humor. They can be witty under their breath and love being around people who can bring out their lighter side.

However, when it's time to work, it's time to work. Don't bother telling them to work smarter, not harder. For them, working harder is the only way. They like to walk uphill. They want to reach the top of the mountain. Once they get there, they want to know where the next peak is. They will only walk down so they can walk up again.

Capricorns are old when they're young, and young when they are old. If they no longer have a goal, they don't know what to do with themselves. Then they don't do well. It's the energy of men who retire and die early because without a role, they feel useless. They turn bitter. To a Capricorn, if you don't do what's expected in society, if you don't perform your function, you're not useful.

Be warned: secretly, Capricorns will judge you, almost as harshly as they judge themselves. They carry a measuring stick to determine your excellence: the car you drive, how attractive your partner is, how much money you make. Do they want to go deeper and figure out if you are happy based on inner experience? Not really. As an earth sign, they are instinctively oriented to the material world first. As they age, their deeper selves may emerge. However, if their measuring stick is based on the external, it is unlikely they will find true peace. The outer world does not guarantee happiness, nor fulfillment. It can take Capricorn some time to figure that out.

Capricorn is made to struggle, feeling like they have never fulfilled their purpose, or didn't get to the top of the mountain on their terms. It's hard to be an earth sign! However, Capricorn, there is no question that when you are interested, you are a good student. We all know you have what it takes to be the best. Just don't forget why you are so ambitious: because you believe excellence is the highest cause—unless you've found your spiritual path. Then you know there is an even greater cause than worldly achievement. It's called an inner life.

Thank you, Capricorn, for always getting it right. For trying too hard. For carrying the team and the family. Thank you for taking care of those you love. You are so many people's grounding force. It's challenging to play savior, wisdom keeper, and the one who fixes and makes things better. You are not just willing, you are truly capable of doing what it takes to get anything done you put your mind to.

PROFILE OF A CAPRICORN

One of my dearest friends started a successful college. The model he used went across the world. On the surface, he appeared to have a heartless personality. However, watching him go through a divorce and seeing the kindness he showed changed my mind.

While his soon-to-be ex-wife was assassinating his character, even to the shareholders, trying to get them to see him as a bad guy (which was 100 percent not true), he never took the bait. He went to extremes to remain kind. He ended up being friends with her, and has a good relationship with her and his children. I watched this man extinguish the charge between himself and his wife, which allowed them to raise their children together peacefully. They celebrate all their family holidays together, without a hitch. He created an advanced example of a healed Capricorn man who, instead of seeking vengeance, sought peace, all in the name of his children. When Capricorns have a purpose, they can do anything. They can handle any amount of pain.

As a Capricorn, what matters more than practicality is a higher ideal. It is only a Capricorn who can compartmentalize in this extreme way—he managed to lead his wife gently to a peaceful ending of their relationship. This is the highest road. Most people don't know how to end things.

He is a profound example of a Capricorn who accrued great wealth and did it with integrity every step of the way, defied a traditional response to a spouse wanting everything, and created an entirely new way of being. We can learn from him. Capricorns are teachers.

CAPRICORN LOW ROAD

Low-road Capricorns don't have a soft spot for people, or at least they don't know how to show it. They care about end results. Their best friends are work friends, and they "talk shop" over dinner. They're always at work, mentally if not physically, always focused on the goal. They can't stand mediocrity, so they come off as elitist and choose their friends according to status. At worst, they can become arrogant, even mean. They are workaholics, judging those who don't work as hard as they do.

When a low-road Capricorn gets caught doing something wrong, they blame someone else and feel entitled to superior treatment ("I shouldn't have to pay a fine—do you know who I am?"). Or they deny wrongdoing ("I didn't think that was wrong."). They become stoic.

Some Capricorns peak when they are young. They excel, then something happens and they don't get their needs met—or they don't get their greed met. They begin to feel the victimization complex common to Cancer (their opposite sign), and they never excel. All that potential goes to waste. They get addicted to the struggle, and they self-sabotage so they never succeed. Then they complain about it and blame their circumstances for their lack of success on other people or situations. This is someone who doesn't want to be too soft because they themselves have been hurt so much. They become scorched and thick-skinned.

At their worst, low-road Capricorns believe the ends justify the means. They may do unethical or even illegal things to achieve their goals. Think of Richard Nixon, a classic Capricorn. He literally said, in a famous interview with David Frost, "If you're the president, you're allowed to lie." He believed that whatever he did was justified because his motives were in the best interest of the country. Really, Capricorn? Where have we heard that before?

THE CAPRICORN OBSERVER

Capricorn, you are just so serious! Your observer helps you to lighten up a bit. Can you laugh at your overly ambitious, critical, judgmental self? When you realize it's all a shtick, some of that extreme pressure you put on yourself and others lifts off. You have the devil's sense of humor (the Devil is your tarot card). Step outside of yourself and see what you do. With a wink and a sardonic grin, your observer shows you that you don't always have to be so extreme. Once you realize how much influence you have over people, you become gentler, less punishing, and more compassionate.

Perhaps you are not sure you want to turn on the observer? If so, I am amazed you got this far in the chapter. You have *no* good reason to keep reading a book of this type if it doesn't serve you, and the observer is not about serving you. It is about you serving others. You need a good reason to learn something spiritual and new. The observer may help you see what it is. Billionaires use astrology—does that inspire you? Let's just say a book like this has your best interest in mind. You'll gain an advantage over the others who do not have this kind of insight and information. It will be profitable—spiritually if not materially, and quite possibly both.

CAPRICORN HIGH ROAD

Capricorn, whose ultimate aim is humanitarian, who elevates people based on their gifts rather than just their profit potential, can evolve into a benevolent leader rather than a dictator. They have integrity and answer to their soul's standards rather than their ego's appetite to stand out for prestige. They take pride in their significant abilities while still taking it easy on people who didn't come here with the same drive they did.

High-road Capricorn doesn't make excuses or try to justify bad behavior. When a Capricorn can admit straight up, "I made a mistake," that's evolution. Capricorn, try saying: "I'm sorry, I was wrong. Help me." That shocking humility becomes disarming because Capricorns usually keep themselves so high above everyone else that the expression of need is rare. This is how Capricorn becomes the teacher.

CAPRICORN MEDICINE

Practicing humility is such good medicine for you—and a hard pill to swallow. Capricorn rules the knees, and if you get down on your knees in humility, accepting that you don't actually know it all, you will understand how powerful this medicine is. Ironically, humility makes you even more powerful.

You feel most comfortable in beautiful, high-class living spaces. Is that so wrong?

You are one of the longest-living signs (Betty White was a Capricorn and she lived to ninety-nine). Take advantage of your natural longevity by taking good care of your health. Unlike some who can't keep up with good habits, your natural discipline and follow-through give you an advantage.

CAPRICORN'S LIFE LESSON

Your life lesson is to be in service to something other than your own personal gain. It's easy for you to believe that the ends justify the means, yet what are your ends, Capricorn? If you don't see beyond your desire for status and money, you will be unfulfilled. You can seek a life of service while still maintaining a deep belief in your own dignity, your own worth, and your own somebody-ness. You produce the highest-quality work. You keep going when others are tired. Be proud of what you produce.

The question is, can you accept the flaws of the human and know that you, too, make mistakes? Can you be humbled in the presence of the wisdom of something higher than yourself? Yes, Capricorn, there really is something higher than yourself. When you operate at the level of your soul, you will achieve purity in your expression and in your work.

You don't believe me? Let's get clear on one thing, Capricorn: you did not come here to achieve some notion of fame or success. We all come here to Earth for individual growth and to assist the species in its evolution. You may not know that yet, so I'm educating you. I'm telling you that if you would be willing to learn a little bit about why you're here on Earth, besides material success, being practical, and getting your goals accomplished, you might have more compassion for other people. If you understand that not everyone works the way you do, things will go better for you in this life and the next.

CAPRICORN MOON

This is a difficult placement for Capricorn. Who wants to have an emotional body that cannot feel? Dare I say it: Hitler had a moon in Capricorn. Capricorn moon struggles to find compassion. You are goal-oriented to the point where you turn off your feelings in order to get things done. It's easy for you—not necessarily for the person working for you. You have little tolerance for mediocrity. When people get emotional, you get judgmental, even arrogant.

A classic Capricorn moon saying is: "People are stupid." It's so easy for you to play the superiority card. A Capricorn moon might be perfectly nice when they aren't emotionally triggered. Once they are, watch out.

Unlike many moon signs, you are less intuitive than you are edgy, and super practical. You give good business advice, but you won't take direction without evidence. It's like you carry around a sign that says, "I already know." Yet nobody gets more done.

The upside is that you are a reliable, loyal friend who gives good advice not influenced by emotions. You did not come here to indulge your feelings. You came here to work, to assist us and teach us, and give us detailed instructions on how to put emotions aside in order to get the goal accomplished. That can be a useful skill.

MERCURY IN CAPRICORN

This is a great placement resulting in a single-minded thought process available for utilitarian goals. You have intention: collect information, memorize it, ask the right questions, and apply it. Every Mercury in Capricorn I've ever met has the potential for genius, with great retention and an organized mind. Of course, it depends on how that planet relates to the rest of the chart.

Shortly after my kids moved out years ago, a young man moved into my downstairs. He was a student in my astrology school. He had *seven planets in Capricorn,* including Mercury. He came upstairs every Tuesday night to study with the astrology group I was teaching. It was so interesting to watch his mind. He worked harder than anyone to learn the entire system perfectly. He memorized charts and asked the most intelligent questions. Six months later, his mother called me and said, "We don't know what you've done! He is so much nicer! He used to be grumpy all the time." This is the transformative power of spiritual study, especially for worldly Capricorn. No one absorbs and utilizes complex information like a Mercury in Capricorn.

CAPRICORN RISING

You are physically strong. You can perform any task requiring muscle and determination. Capricorn rising has endurance, longevity, and if properly played, they age well—gray hair included. You look good gray. If only we could get you to see your beauty.

Because you are an ethical hard worker who goes the extra mile, eventually that pays off. Capricorn rising will not stop until the job is done. This is the farmer, the industrious businessperson, the organizer, the manager who says, "I have one thing to do, and that is to complete this job the best I can." Who wouldn't want to hire this person?

You live to produce. You push yourself, and then you get tired. You may be extremely ambitious for years, until you hit a wall and stop. Then you feel awful. This is not an easy rising sign to pace, which would make all the difference. Instead, it's all or nothing. Because you are operating from a soul urge as the selfless server, this effort is instinctual.

If only you valued yourself the way we do. Wow, are you ever hard on yourself, Capricorn rising! There is a never-ending narration going on in your head that can hurt you, and it never stops—not until your last breath. You underestimate your worth, deny your power, and live with an inner critic that challenges you to *never* rest on your laurels. You think you don't ever do enough. You ruminate.

When you use your work ethic for the benefit of others, and for humanity in general, you answer your soul's calling. Still, we have to wonder why you are so hard on yourself. What is the upside of that, Capricorn rising? It's an old pattern that doesn't serve you.

In esoteric astrology, Capricorn is the savior. When that is your ultimate goal, you will be a success by any measure. Just give it your best. You are the designated driver and the executor of the will, yes. Now, what do you do for fun? Can you stop for a minute to take a breath and realize how extraordinary you are?

SATURN IN CAPRICORN

Stand up and be the leader in your life.

You may either be completely focused and living your life with purpose, or you may be waiting for someone to give you direction. You are a late bloomer. However, you need to realize that you can take charge of your life, and you should remember to be gentle with others. You're only the boss of yourself.

You learn through taking responsibility, walking the walk, making stuff happen, and building a solid system. Define your own idea of success and go for it. Make the rules and then follow them. Don't judge yourself for being on your own timeline.

Life lesson: You are the one you've been waiting for. Once you take on the position of the director of your life, your longed-for success will come your way.

MEDITATION FOR CAPRICORN

I release the pressure of achieving and seeking in exchange for the recognition of how well I've done and how much effort I've already put in. I recognize that this life is a long movie. I will make it to the top, and I will enjoy the journey. I will give myself a break when I need one. I will remember that there is no rush.

THE ESSENCE OF CAPRICORN

Capricorn is a hard-working human whose concern is simple: do your best. The pursuit of excellence follows them around, even when that isn't what they're aiming at.

They have such a gift of determination. They are not someone who studies astrology, or anything for that matter, without asking: What is the purpose? How can I sincerely help someone with this practice? *And . . .* how much can I make doing this?

Motivation is not Capricorn's issue. Focus is not their issue. They have to have a vested interest in what they are doing. If they don't, they won't excel and, eventually, they'll burn out. Capricorn can learn how to pace themselves and have fun, even in the middle of the work cycle. They can celebrate their achievements, stopping and smelling the roses, before they walk straight into the next challenge. As they become more conscious about how dutiful and responsible they are, they can choose to add fun and joy to their to-do list.

Aren't we all grateful to Capricorn for showing up as they do, always giving it their best, and holding us to the standards that will allow our world to flourish? Even if it means hard work and consistent practice for all, Capricorn is a great role model for what matters most for humanity.

18

The Psychology of Aquarius

I KNOW

Element: Air
Mode: Fixed
House: Eleventh
Planet: Uranus
Body part: Calves and ankles—they try to stay grounded, yet their wobbly ankles reveal how difficult it is.

If only you understood that I don't understand you. I am not of this world. I play smart. I talk. I study. My intelligence makes me stand out and apart— that's only because I have come from the future. I am here to show you the map to get to where we are all going. I'm not in the same time zone as you are. You people fascinate me and remain a mystery.

From a young age, I stood out as different. Was it that I was such a good athlete, musician, writer, performer? Honestly, there is pretty much nothing I can't excel at if I choose. Still, this game of life has me puzzled. I study science and remember the details. I read books and am intrigued with the philosophy behind many kinds of teachings. I have always believed that we ought to live and let live. I share much in common with you, though I don't think we are the same species. That's obvious. What's not so obvious is that I can read your mind.

So I step off the grid. I think differently. I have a different sense of time. I wish that you could just let me be. Instead, I notice that I am not in sync. I try, and then I stop trying because I can't make it work. I have an on-again, off-again relationship with a lot of things.

Maybe you've noticed I have a strong personality. I'm not here to bend or pretend. On the other hand, I know what you need, and I give it to you exactly as you requested. This is how I did so well in school. I know how to get you what you want, even though it's probably not what I want. What is it that I want? I'm not sure, although I know it's something brand new. Something incredible. Something nobody has ever seen or thought of before.

I am a good doctor, healer, scientist, builder, or extraordinary anything, really, because I focus on what has been done, learn it, and then take a rocket ship and go further than ever before. I don't need to fit in. I would never join a club that would have me as a member because I know that I am not what you think I am.

It's good to stand apart, to detach from ideas that most of society takes for granted. I'm used to it now. I live by my own rules. If you are interested in my thoughts, I'm happy to share. Mostly, I have questions for you and your world. I love inquiry. I want to know about the assumptions you all have. I want to remember all the details you reveal.

I wish I could just jump on a spaceship and go back home. I can't do that just yet because I have not completed my humanitarian mission. There is still too much suffering for me to abandon Earth. I'll stay here and report back to the mothership. In the meantime, I'll use humor as my medicine to comfort me in this strange place.

I love astrology because I remember when we all got along and were a *family. Do you remember that? It's when astrology first arrived here. You probably don't remember. It was in the future.*

I'll see you there.

Aquarius is intrigued by the experience of life and the challenge to fit in and feel comfortable as a human being. They are curious, inquisitive about what matters and what is just pretense. "Can someone tell me what part of the multiverse we're in right now? Are there different species out there? Of course some of us come from another planet. Let's question the idea that we are all earthlings. What does the future hold? Will there be an AI revolution? Are extraterrestrials willing to intervene? Is science fiction really fiction?"

Aquarius, you have a natural interest in all things science and technology. You want to know how to utilize all the gadgets on your cell phones, the smart home systems, and how to communicate quickly and efficiently. On the other hand, just because everyone is headed that way doesn't mean you are—you are interested in going against the flow. You constantly wonder about humanitarian issues and long to have a life that influences the world. Aquarius knows they don't fit into this world. Even dating and getting married seem awkward. All the assumed "norms" our society demands must be questioned, right?

Aquarius is an air sign and can seem suddenly flighty or noncommittal. They are not. Because Aquarius is a fixed sign, they are stable. When an Aquarian commits, they're really in. They do love to surprise us, though.

There is a stereotype that all Aquarians are weird—the ones with blue hair, tattoos, and a pierced nose, vaping, standing apart, watching everyone from a distance. This is somewhat true, yet their weirdness may be hidden in an effort to fit in for a while. Their close friends know that their humor and off-the-wall comments are coming any moment. They behave like an odd duck. Why? Because Aquarians don't care what you think about them. They are just themselves. Standing apart at the party with their unusual friend, they can't help marching to their own drummer, listening to their exotic music, and going against the mainstream. Aquarius is a rebel.

Oh, how they love science and abstract thought. Mathematics, technology, astrology, engineering, architecture are right up their alley. They have excellent memories and are on the front lines of anything new. The Aquarians are often the first to show up in the latest styles. It's like they can see the future and start the trends.

What's remarkable is that whatever they try, they are good at. The range is wild—all the way from politics, like Aquarian Abraham Lincoln, to genius inventors, like Aquarian Thomas Edison. They say there are more Aquarians in various halls of fame than any other sign. Think Mozart or Oprah Winfrey—they break the mold. They might do physical feats in a way that no one has ever done before, like Michael Jordan being the best basketball player, or the famous Wayne Gretzky, who has no fire in his chart. Whoever heard of a hockey player who didn't want to fight? And someone explain to me, how did he always seem to know where the puck would be from way across the rink? I think it was ESP.

Think brainiacs built for engineering or advanced science. Whatever they do, they are capable of mastery and demonstrate what we call genius. Because they will not participate in following, they step away from "normal" expectations and then wonder why everyone is so impressed.

The Aquarian ego is not like ours. It contributes to them doubting their success. They don't aim for fame. They simply act according to their brilliance. They wonder why everyone likes them so much. They are secretly socially awkward. You will not be able to tell when socializing for them in an ordinary setting will become like nails against a chalkboard. You can't tell by looking. They prefer to be in a group with a cause, a function, a purpose. Otherwise, what's the point?

That doesn't mean they don't have friendships. They need their "peeps" and they stay loyal even more than they do with their own family. When they bond, they are fiercely loyal, although they have a hard time in romantic relationships. They try, they definitely flirt. They love to watch the response they elicit, and then they wonder: Does that person even like me? How could they? I haven't shown them my real self yet.

Aquarians wonder if they've ever known true love. They often get married late in life (Oprah never has), then wonder what made them do that. They enjoy being in the company of friends, at a dinner party where no one is exclusively focused on them. When they do get into a committed relationship, it has to be with someone who makes them laugh and is a good conversationalist—to take the pressure off having to lead all the time.

Just like Leo, their opposite sign, they easily make best friends. Unlike Leo, they don't want people to follow them, and they definitely will not act differently just for the spotlight. Aquarius doesn't have Leo's ego. They are confused when everyone wants their attention. "Why would you follow me? Do you think I know something you don't know?" Actually, Aquarius, you do.

Life is both strangely foreign to them and strangely familiar, like they've done all this before. "Excuse me," says the Aquarius, "I have some questions. Why are we doing this . . . again? What are we learning? How is this supposed to go? Do people really have to cheat, or not play upfront? Who decided it was okay to act like that? Why are we all dancing around like this? If this is the game we're playing, I'm going to do it my way, so get ready for the rules to change. I'm going to make this my own. You can count on me to collect information, interview everyone, ask the hard questions, learn everything, and do whatever is possible—or impossible—to make the most out of this experience."

Aquarius loves animals and children because there is no need to explain their emotions. They instinctively know answers to our questions without knowing quite how they got there. They fill in sentences before you finish talking. There are some who have photographic memories, or are fourteen steps ahead, wondering why we are all so slow. In elementary school, we learned the times tables. Aquarius asks, "Didn't we do all this last year? Why are we doing it again?" Because not everyone is like you, Aquarius, with that memory of yours. Your mental body is at an intellectually advanced level. When you listen, stories stick. You model the updated operating system most of us haven't upgraded to yet. You do things better.

Aquarius comes in many versions: (1) straight as a pin and will follow like a soldier; (2) a groupie hanging out with the hippies because they are a dropout; (3) an inventor who had a download and then proves it with science; (4) a self-taught musician/artist who writes lyrics that are both poetic and rhythmical. Those are just a few examples of how Aquarians might express themselves. One thing is for sure: there is not a better team player—if they've bought into the mission. Aquarian Ronald Reagan, once a committed actor, was called to be a statesperson. He left his old identity and offered his life in service.

While you may not have wanted to be the teacher or the leader, we want you to teach us. But Aquarians don't like teaching—they think people should figure it out for themselves. They have a desire to help humanity, and they are willing to abandon their ego to be helpful to the whole. There is not a kinder, more considerate sign when it comes to a larger cause.

You bring us into the future, and we can't wait to follow you there. Just be patient with us, Aquarius. We haven't quite caught up to you yet. Thank you for bringing the humanitarian desire to make a difference here on Earth. Even when we think you're "different," you just keep giving. You stand out because of your tenacity and commitment to kindness and friendship. Thank you for being willing to step off the ordinary stage with your family and our society. Because of you, we will be headed in the right direction, toward the future, no matter how strange it may appear to us in the meantime.

PROFILE OF AN AQUARIUS

Born a natural actress and performer, my friend—I'll call her Anne—with four planets in Aquarius was singled out as a "spiritual giant" when she was young because she asked so many questions in church. She sat in the front row and studied what the minister said, making a list of everything that didn't seem correct or that required further explanation. She left the church with a great deal of knowledge. She entered into her career, hoping to become an actor, only to discover it felt too fake.

Instead, Anne became a writer, finding her niche as a ghostwriter for successful people doing interesting things. This meant her name was never front and center. She didn't mind. She was more fascinated by the subjects of the books she wrote and the knowledge available from the people she met. Asking questions and learning about topics that spread information and wisdom to others was the part she really loved.

One day, after years of work, Anne realized what an amazing success she was. That was never her intention. However, she also wonders if her success is really valid. The secret of every Aquarian is that they ask themselves, "Am I really that good?" So what if, as a collaborator, she has eleven *New York Times* best sellers to her credit—that wasn't even hard, she thinks. Is that really success? Everyone else thinks she is successful. She still wonders—and keeps writing.

AQUARIUS LOW ROAD

Low-road Aquarius is rebellious, just for the sake of rebelling. They cannot help disagreeing.

You ask a question: "Are you eccentric?"

"No," they immediately answer.

"Oh really, Aquarius? Then why do you have all those tattoos, and why was each one designed by a different artist?"

"Oh, everyone has them."

They can't agree at times, even when they want to. At their worst, Aquarians live in their heads. They are cut off from their emotions, and yet like to get everyone else riled up. They move quickly and judge others for being slow, less smart, and having no style. They can be oppositional, a rebel without a cause. It's no surprise they feel separate and alone.

Their favorite lament is "No one understands me." They think that they are the only ones who can design the world the way they like it, and that they probably aren't getting paid enough. Not that they really care. Aquarius isn't about the money. When they detach, it's not to turn off their hearts. Yet the pain and sadness that come from feeling alone can create a deadness, a settling, so Aquarius stops seeking their dreams.

They harbor secrets thinking being human is not a healable diagnosis, so why talk about it? They think they'll only be appreciated after they're dead, and isn't that sad? They feel so ahead of their time that they are lost in time.

THE AQUARIUS OBSERVER

Aquarius is comfortable with the observer; they are watching everyone from a distance all the time anyway, which is what contributes to their feeling of separateness. This is not the natural state for the rest of us. It's like they are an anthropologist or a social scientist who stands against the wall at the party and whispers, "This party is interesting. Look at what these people are doing. How curious." Stop it, Aquarius. You're a person at the party, too. Come back to reality. You're not separate. This is not what the observer is for. The observer is not an escape route. It is a point of view you can use to gain insight about yourself and others.

The danger of standing apart is that you miss an important part of the human experience: feeling. And while you can cry for humanity, you can be cut off from your own emotions. This explains the detachment you so easily slide into. Standing apart has you asking: What makes me do what I do? Why is my personality so different? Am I unique? How do I best understand other people? This is why astrology is a natural fit for you. In fact, all metaphysical topics make your heart sing.

Aquarius might benefit from turning *off* the observer once in a while and just hanging out. Give it a try, Aquarius. See what it feels like to be emotional. You probably won't like it. Just know that humanity uses feelings to be human and learn about healing and pain. Strange, isn't it, when you think about it: Why do we have to feel to learn a lesson? That's the operating system we came with. Aquarius may try to change it. Sometimes, Aquarius, you have to work with what you have. The observer will help you once you realize this is your shtick.

AQUARIUS HIGH ROAD

At their best, Aquarians are creative, hard-working, and versatile. They are curiosity machines, in a laboratory (literal or metaphorical), in an art studio, writing scripts, trying to invent and update, always trying to get more information for the collective good. They ask questions without prejudice. Think social scientists with a gift for standing apart from judgment. Think artists who never care about following the trends. They can be raw and honest when someone is really listening to them.

High-road Aquarians' humanitarian urge motivates all their decisions. They are fascinated by other people who don't fit into the mold— the disenfranchised, the artists who have the ability to see the world in a new way, the people who dress strangely or say surprising things. The more eccentric, the better. Homeless people can feel more relatable to an Aquarian than the wealthy.

In esoteric astrology, Alice Bailey said we will know the New Age is here when science and metaphysics meet and converge. That is the goal of the Aquarian, who is fascinated by quantum mechanics and metaphysical principles. They are here to prepare us for the future. They are always pushing the envelope into the next rendition.

AQUARIUS MEDICINE

Aquarians don't think they need any medicine. Why go to the hospital? Everyone is sick there. They don't believe in complaining about emotional issues. It's too repetitive. The smartest kid in school doesn't think they need any help because they think they don't have any problems. Yet Aquarians tend to be cut off and compartmentalize. With effort, they can learn to make those boundaries more porous.

The best medicine for Aquarius is to try on emotions for size. I know, you don't want to do it. Do it anyway. It will make you feel more human.

Having a group of friends is medicine for Aquarius. They thrive when surrounded by a lot of favorite people, even though, from time to time, they are so sensitive about feeling separate from those same people. They are often the sounding board for out-of-the-box ideas because they understand the concepts immediately. They like to hear what other people have to say.

If you didn't have kids, or didn't stay married for very long, don't think that's wrong or bad. This lifetime, you took the road less traveled. Somebody had to go that direction, and although you may not remember, you volunteered.

AQUARIUS'S LIFE LESSON

The Aquarius life lesson is to study the emotional body. Begin to notice the words you use to refer to emotions. Do you often use the word "think" as in, "I think I'm angry" or "I think I'm sad"? That's because you are so mind-oriented.

The truth, Aquarius, like it or not, is that emotions aren't about thinking. They are about feeling. I know it's a leap for you (more or less so depending on the rest of your chart), but it is something you can practice. Consider the exploration of emotions as a scientific experiment that will help you better understand humans.

AQUARIUS MOON

Moon in Aquarius is a difficult placement because the moon represents emotion and Aquarians are so resistant to emotions. You often say, "I've heard about that," or "I'm researching that." You have a mental list of all the human feelings, although you haven't necessarily felt them. Negative emotions in particular, like anger and sadness, aren't really your thing. "Why would I waste my time feeling that or talking to you about that?" Instead, you are thinking about futuristic ways of creating. Your creations, whether you write, draw, or design, aren't about evoking emotion. They are about innovation—doing something that has never been done before.

MERCURY IN AQUARIUS

Mercury is exalted in Aquarius. This is where Mercury is most comfortable. You can look at something you decide is important, and it will stick in your mind. You remember hard data and numbers without any problem. You are really good at astrology. Any good astrologer has a natural capacity for pattern recognition and understanding esoteric concepts. They don't make things up. They are based in facts. They study. They remember, and they are curious about human nature and the notion of time. That is the realm of the mind. You like it there.

AQUARIUS RISING

Who in the world can keep up with you? Your mind moves as fast as lightning. You are an expert at anything you decide to focus on. You are the best parent. You learn how to address your children on their terms. You are a great partner because you accept the personality of your partner, knowing them better than they know themselves. You are such a good friend, perhaps one of the best. You can tell exactly when someone needs you. And then there is your love for community, inviting everyone to your house, encouraging each of us to be our wild selves. You know how to throw a party.

What a great body you have for any sport. You excel at physical challenges with little effort. What is it like to be so good at everything?

You are nonjudgmental and endlessly curious. You know so much and ask, "How can I be of service?" You honestly want to save the world, right there in your own neighborhood, enlisting all your friends and family. You share your wealth far beyond others' expectations. If only others could see and agree on what you already know to be the right answer, we would be closer to a world in which we are all kind, generous humanitarians.

You are a soul who is a know-it-all in the best way, and it would serve all if people listened to you! If you resist your rising sign, as people so often do, you may shy away from taking a leadership role in changing the world and bettering humanity. You may want to stay in a close circle of immediate family and friends. Yet that is not your destiny. You can lead us into the future, even in a small way. Take the leap, Aquarius. You have the vision.

SATURN IN AQUARIUS

Accept that you are different.

You don't fit in and it's okay. You are allowed to be yourself in any context. You may disrupt or disagree in order to stand apart from the group.

Give yourself permission to be contrary without explanation. It's your right to be an individual.

Life lesson: Freedom is giving yourself (and others) permission to be unique and true. Challenge the old way to bring new solutions for humanity. Humanitarianism is the keyhole to your purpose.

MEDITATION FOR AQUARIUS

May I find comfort in standing out, knowing that my promise in this life is to bring the new, updated humanitarian ideas and the gift of open-mindedness to the world. When I feel separated or misunderstood, I remember that I am ahead of my time. Others long to understand me, even if I don't always see that. It's okay to let others into my world.

THE ESSENCE OF AQUARIUS

Remember being a teenager and following the cues from your friends to fit in? Aquarius does. Then one day, they got in trouble because they couldn't follow. They had to step away from expectations and sneak away from who they were pretending to be. They were rebellious, and eventually discovered that while conformity is easier, it's not better.

Thankfully, the Aquarian ambition never tires. Aquarius gives everyone all that they are, and so they excel. They are surprised and slightly uncomfortable about the praise and acknowledgment they get for being so good at everything. The Aquarius thinks, it didn't take that much effort, so why is everybody praising me? They find it hard to accept recognition for what comes so naturally.

There is a time when our contrived, acceptable reality will wear out. Everyone and everything has an expiration date. For most of us, it hurts when things end. Not so much for Aquarius. Their emotional body knows how to cut off when needed. The conversations in which people are mean, unfair, or boring go right over an Aquarian's head. They skip the human part. Design and art and their work, whatever it is, has to make their heart sing. When it does, they go for it.

Truthfully, being alive, while it is entertaining, even fascinating, is overrated when you feel like you are alone. Even in a crowd of people, or around friends and family, Aquarius feels like the odd man out. One day, they will realize their function here is to bring an updated version of humanness so that we all question our own assumptions, just as Aquarius already does. You need to be apart from the crowd to see that.

Aquarius may not have children, or stay married, or even get married. They can't follow what is expected. They might change their careers and enter into a wild new frontier, just because they desire it. Why? Because they need novelty, and besides, they never quite believed they ever reached a level of mastery. It takes time. One day, Aquarius will see their younger self with compassion and let them off the hook. No way they were ever going to take the short ride to "normalcy." No way.

Aquarius came here to show us how boring, stupid, and dated this consensus reality is. They stand apart, their head held high. Since they can't follow us, we will follow them, even if they don't want us to. Aquarius helps us to get rid of the mean-spirited, warrior-like qualities that live in our bad operating system. They are the new version of human.

19

The Psychology of Pisces

I DREAM

Element: Water
Mode: Mutable
House: Twelfth
Planet: Neptune
Body part: Feet—because that is where the soul (or sole . . .) lives.

If only you understood how confusing this place is to me. You would never know by looking. I dress nicely, I perform appropriately, I've watched enough movies and can follow along so that I can act normal. Truth be told, I'm just pretending.

I sing. I create art. I remember my dreams and recite the recipe for ice cream. I think in poetry. I don't often speak because of my awkwardness. It shows up in my feet; I have the strangest big toe. Apparently, Pisces rules the feet. Think about it: the bottom of your foot is where your soul is. I am soulful.

I think about the purpose of being human. Why don't we all know how to assist the mind straight to a connection to the soul? We ought to learn that in elementary school. What a lofty thought. Are you following me? Aren't we all here to express creativity with a higher purpose, a soul-filled urge? Creativity: Isn't that why we are alive?

Pisces rules the imagination: dolphins, mermaids, and pixies, to mention just a few. Movies, classical music, and all things magic. I wish it were safe to tell you about my relationship with topics that are not socially acceptable, like talking about dead people and how close they are to us, or that I believe in past lives. There is no question about that; I know in my bones that the stars rule us. Don't you agree that altered states and the dreamtime can appear more real than this reality that we have been sold on? I do.

I want to say all this out loud. I won't because I'm sure you won't understand. You don't have to understand, just believe, we are spiritual beings having a human experience.

I wish we could jump over the moon and make it feel so real that you would leave behind your logic. We cannot. No wonder you are confused—you should be—who thinks like that? Truth be told, I am an expert at anything I really put my mind to. I can blend this world with the next. It's like dancing with the abstract. I bet you didn't expect that. I blend flavors others do not, which is why I am an eclectic artist, cook, painter—you name it, I can do it.

I wish you understood how hard it is for me to stay on the same page with other people and just act normally. To me, normal is a setting on the dryer. It's a place my family lived comfortably, so I followed them even into their dysfunction, as all good kids do. Don't be fooled: I always knew something was wrong.

I have always thought that if a spaceship landed, I would be the first onboard. There I would be, standing in line, as I whisper in the ear of the person next to me: "I always knew we weren't from here. Glad to be going home."

The truth is, I will, as all grown-ups are expected to do, find some semblance of normalcy, and give up speaking with my poetic voice. It's exhausting to fit in. No wonder I want to escape, to be alone, to have quiet. This is one reason I love sacred medicine and altered states so much. They feel normal to me.

I hope someday you will find out, as I have, that this charade of life only exists to remind us all of what is truly real: the stars are real, magic is real, *the esoteric truths are real. I know that we are just egos dressed up in outfits camouflaging our soul. The soul is real. Truth be told, ideas about who we are and why we are here need to be updated and unpacked to make this life worth living. That's why I'm here. I can help if you only ask me. Otherwise, I will be standing here, daydreaming, hoping the world will catch up with the reality I wish we all lived in.*

Pisces has to escape. Taking a nap in the middle of a party, eating banana cream pie for breakfast, or watching that comforting old movie again alone on a sunny day with the shades down—for Pisces, rules do not apply. They get a little spacey, confused, and self-conscious, like the teenager who doesn't want to go to the party and also wants to go to the party, then gets to the party and tries to camouflage themselves because they are socially awkward, so they drink too much. They live with a feeling that they don't know how to be a grown-up, no matter their age. Getting lost in fantasies makes them happy. Then they don't have to deal with this boring, contrived reality. Pisces is comfortable with alcohol, drugs, movies, music, social media—anything that takes them out of this world. Then again, there are some who are not going to touch any of that. They stay in reality, in disguise, acting the opposite of all their natural inclinations, just to feel like they belong. That's the Virgo in them—their opposite sign.

The stereotype of Pisces—that they are irresponsible, don't follow through, aren't reliable or accountable, that they don't finish things—is not exactly true. Sure, they are dreamy, spacey people who at times don't pay attention to the details of what they're doing, which is why Pisces gets a bad rap. Yet their creativity is limitless, and so is their focus when they are doing something that truly engages them. There is no greater artist or scientist than the one who will read and study and create for a very long time without remembering to eat or drink water.

There is a great story about Einstein walking in front of MIT. Supposedly, some students stopped him to chat, and after they finished, he said:

"Was I walking toward or away from the school when we started this conversation?" He couldn't remember if he was going to teach his class, or if he had already taught it. I don't know if this is a true story or not. Either way, it's an appropriate representation of a Pisces.

Surprisingly, it's hard to spot a Pisces. They shape-shift so effortlessly, playing the role of the regular person, that you may not be able to pin them down. It's the insurance agent or the businessperson or the doctor committed to protocol and details, who secretly reads science fiction or metaphysical books when no one is looking.

Think of Elizabeth Taylor, a Pisces with those otherworldly purple eyes, and her talent for acting. She was obviously a hopeless romantic, married eight times, all the while struggling with addiction. She was close friends with Michael Jackson, whose mastery could be associated with his full moon in Pisces. He also suffered from addiction. Both had talent off the charts, and were secret keepers who left us confused about their characters.

When you talk with a Pisces, you might well feel confused. You wonder, "Is there anybody in there?" It feels like they are hiding from you or distracted. They say, "I'd love to get to know you," then leave without putting their number in your phone. They dress with style, all the while remaining incognito—you never knew they were a clothes designer or a famous artist because they are private and unassuming.

They're reclusive. If they seem flaky or uncommitted, think of Pisces as two fish going in opposite directions. One, they are in water, where it's hard to communicate because it's so murky and unfriendly to the human. Two, they are pulled by opposing forces, creating incongruence. No wonder they are so confusing.

Don't be fooled: their soul is all in—they're just not quite as focused on the more practical aspects of reality, as truly soulful people often aren't unless it's required for their dream to come true (and they have some earth in their chart). They are the mystics—the ones who transcend the rules of this world in exchange for a connection to the other side. The ones who value spirituality first, and the practical world as an afterthought.

Yet not all Pisces are spiritual. That's another stereotype. Some are even scared of things that are "woo-woo." Most feel more comfortable during their dreamtime. Then there are those who claim not to buy into the whole concept of dream language.

They have a natural ability as dancers, creative writers of science fiction and/or poetry, and scientists. They are the mad scientists. They seek out ways to enhance the mundane or to step into a more interesting reality. They might be deeply religious. They inherently know how important the concept of God is, and they have known that since they were young.

We all know of someone who says they can see spirits in the room or even talk to dead people. Edgar Cayce, known as the Sleeping Prophet, a double Pisces, was a psychic who could diagnose illnesses while in a trance state. He was known for being able to leave time and space, entering into universal consciousness where he received answers to people's questions. This is so Pisces-like.

Pisces rules classical music—think Vivaldi, Chopin, Handel, Rossini, and Ravel, all Pisces. They have a refined, odd quality about them. They can be contortionists, like the performers in Cirque du Soleil. Watch those bodies, listen to the music, and ask, "Was that real? How do they do that?"

They practice. They focus. They stay the course. Not every Pisces is inconsistent. Dreams and reality can get intertwined, so they ask: "Which world is real?" This is how Pisces gets lost: too much dreaming and not enough reality. They scare themselves with negative thoughts. "I am not very good at anything." They lose sight of their own gifts. This begins the imposter syndrome, which is scary. One thing for sure is that Pisces requires structure and ritual to keep them grounded. Otherwise, they might just float away on a dream or a philosophy.

Their opposite sign, Virgo, of course, is hiding inside, adding self-critical thoughts. Pisces says: "I don't know if I really exist. However, if I just follow along, no one will notice."

Anyone vulnerable—pets, the underprivileged, the person who needs them—will feel safe and good when they are dependent on a Pisces. Being of service is so healthy for Pisces. Thank you for your ability to care so much. Thank you for bringing us art and mysticism and beauty. While it can feel as though this world is harsh and insensitive to you, the animals thank you, and so do the people you have helped. Take the time to let yourself be appreciated. You are loved.

PROFILE OF A PISCES

My dear friend Tom is a Pisces. He is poetic, spiritual, and highly sensitive to the point of sometimes being unable to function. He went to India twice, and both times he came back more distraught than when he left. Sometimes he couldn't stop crying. On his third trip, he became enlightened. He returned home with an incredible, transcendent sense of self. Everybody wanted to talk to him, yet he withdrew. He couldn't handle all the people. He moved to a cabin and doesn't talk to anyone. He remains reclusive and internal.

My aunt is another great example of a Pisces. We called her Annie Franny. She was the youngest of three sisters, very pretty, and she loved animals, as Pisces does. She used to lie in the sun with tin foil under her face to increase her tan. She always had a drink in one hand and a cigarette in the other. She had children and dressed them well, although she wasn't a very present mother. She was vague and uninvolved.

As the years went by, her financial situation changed. Ignoring this, she kept spending money. She had closets full of clothes with all the tags on them because she never wore them. She was always talking about dead people—she scared us as kids because she'd see ghosts. She would say, "My friends are here. They've been talking to me all day." Nobody understood what she was talking about. She was very exotic. She sent us all birthday cards, every year. She wrote rhyming poems inside.

Eventually, she went bankrupt—she was oblivious to practical matters like finances. She had no boundaries or sense of consequences. She lived in a transitory state. They evicted her because she wasn't paying for the house. She ignored the notices. She just kept living in that house in complete denial, up until the day they made her leave. She was in la-la land. I helped take care of her financially until she died. At the end, she told me she wanted to die, then kept changing her mind when the end seemed near.

PISCES LOW ROAD

On the low road, Pisces is scared of the invisible world, as well as being scared of reality, dead people, and divination, to the point where they refuse to believe in anything off the beaten path. This is how they think they are protecting themselves. They deny their preferences and their real self, just to fit in and be acceptable.

At worst, they love their addiction or escapism more than they love the truth and reality. They ask the people in their lives to accept their addictions and escapism, to pretend it's okay for them to be that way so they don't have to face the truth. It's not okay, Pisces. You have a high road available to you. The observer can show you.

THE PISCES OBSERVER

Pisces can have a hard time with the observer's unbiased, clear gaze. Your emotional body is distracting, second only to Cancer, so that makes it hard to turn on the observer. To avoid the observer, Pisces gets slippery and refuses to understand the concept. They come in and out of reality without distinguishing their inner critic from the observer.

The observer never criticizes—it merely reflects what is. Pisces can harbor a secret critic that never leaves them alone. They suffer from becoming incapacitated by their emotions. They think they are doing things wrong or catastrophizing every moment. Once they can let go of the ego mind and allow the soul to liberate them to their real self, they will see their patterns if they turn on the observer: "Oh yes, there I go again making the other person wrong and justifying my fear and my impulse to escape what is difficult."

The observer helps to cultivate discernment for Pisces. There is nothing more powerful than the tears of a Pisces who has called themselves out for their confusion, or their love for someone, or the betrayal they admit to. We all melt and find their honesty so powerfully inspiring. The observer insists on honesty. The observer says: "It's okay that you just changed your mind, disclosed your vulnerability, admitted to feeling things other people didn't notice. Stop pretending you're normal when you're not, Pisces. It's a gift, not a liability."

It's okay not to be of this world. Take care of yourself and do what soothes your nervous system while you get used to this reality a little bit at a time. Just watch out for addiction. Call yourself out when you know you are using too much. Listen to the cues. You get signs all the time.

You can feel and manipulate energy. That can become a great strength rather than a source of suffering. This is the powerful part of you that can surely manifest.

PISCES HIGH ROAD

On the high road, Pisces radiates unconditional love. They role-model how to turn the other cheek. They don't just forgive, they forget. It's over for them after the "sorry." They make it easy for others to cry and to care about animals and the less fortunate.

It's a great trait to know how to let go because you are not attached to worldly things. You are a free spirit. At their best, Pisces on the high road is evolved, with spiritual gifts from past lives like psychic powers, artistic ability, musical ability, the ability to invent, or the gift of healing.

Pisces on the high road makes beauty everywhere; they can channel pure creative impulses. Pisces is a conduit for higher knowledge. They can become visionaries and geniuses, operating successfully in the world in their own way.

PISCES MEDICINE

Meditation is natural for a Pisces—off you go to another realm. For you, meditation gets you to the same place drugs and alcohol do, without the hangover. You cannot live without some form of spiritual practice or communion. Is it God, Buddha, plant medicine? Whatever form works for you, find your path to something higher than yourself, then share the map with us showing how to get to where you are.

Your dreams contain answers. Write them down and study them. Look for patterns, recurring themes, and symbols. You can learn a lot about yourself through your dreams. It's a profound language that requires sincere inquiry and follow-through.

When you feel far away from reality, rather than trying to escape, look in the mirror, into your own eyes. Say, "I need help. Give me access to my observer to get me out of these deep emotions." Tell yourself, "I love you." This will elicit your soul's presence. When you can establish a real, live relationship with your own reflection, you'll achieve a whole different relationship with reality. This exercise can put you back into your body.

If I were you, I would make a schedule and stick to it. Medicine for you is to have some semblance of consistency in your days and weeks. Start with taking a regular yoga class or working with singing bowls or spiritual practices. Anything you do with regularity will help you feel more grounded. Find your calm by being in or around water, putting on music, and being with animals and children.

PISCES'S LIFE LESSON

Pisces, because you have such a relationship with the invisible world and all things imaginary and magical, you have the ability to walk into the future. You can show us the way into the realms we haven't seen yet, the way you've seen them. With the observer on, you can accept that you don't know what's going to happen, and you can stop pretending that other worlds beyond this one don't really exist. You know they do, and you can walk straight into them without fear. Pisces is here to learn how to fall in love with their fate, to accept what was handed to them in this life. This is their greatest challenge. Learn how to stay the course and follow through. You are our ticket to eternity.

PISCES MOON

Moon in Pisces is not easy—the moon is emotional, and Pisces is, too. It can be too much. It's redundant. You have a tricky emotional body. You suffer from overreactivity. You can sense things before they happen, although only after you train your emotions to be under your dominion. Otherwise, you get swamped and have a hard time functioning.

"I feel everything!" I know it hurts as you are assaulted by a barrage of emotions that may not even be yours. You can be a sponge. No wonder you love to be quiet. You want people to leave you alone. A good question to ask a moon in Pisces is, "Where do you go when you go away?"

The upside of extreme emotional vulnerability is a special connection with animals and the ability to communicate with them. Spirit will find its way to you if you stay the course and work with meditation or a teacher who can help you.

MERCURY IN PISCES

Mercury in Pisces is also a difficult placement, although you can be a genius in science, poetry, writing, and religion. You might be able to recite the periodic table or the book of Psalms while having no idea where the car keys are. When you become obsessed with something, you go down the rabbit hole. You get lost on the internet, spending hours learning about something that seems relevant in the moment but that will be irrelevant tomorrow. You have trouble making decisions, especially about practical matters. The real world scares you. Other realms fascinate you.

You are a natural mechanic, carpenter, or builder. It's almost like you have a relationship with inanimate objects. You can merge with a task and get lost so that when someone calls your name for dinner, you don't hear. You focus intensely when interested. Spirituality is a natural way to bring peace to your mind.

PISCES RISING

You are the empath, so sensitive and tender. I don't want you to cry. Yet when you talk about your soul, it's bound to happen. You absorb other people's pain. Large groups, airports, and concerts aren't your favorite places to be. You need to discern who to be with and how to manage your energy.

Of course you love astrology. You love all things mystical and religious. You are a student of life—when you focus. Truth be told, you don't have very many needs, as long as you are with your people, your pets, and your spiritual "stuff."

When you join this world with both feet on the ground, your inner artist shows up. Just be forewarned: you love to escape, or not follow through. When you aren't grounded, you can get depressed or anxious at levels that may require external help. Otherwise, you can get swamped with emotional pain. It's not a curse—it's because you care so much.

What a gift you bring us with your colors, art, jewelry, and beauty! Now let's get practical: please say no when you mean it. Don't shape-shift to please us, or just to feel connected. You are connected. You know that spirit has your back.

Eventually, you may end up alone, which you like and at the same time do not like. What a contradiction. Here's the trick: accept that we need you on Earth, with both feet on the ground. Don't leave yourself out by escaping. That is what contributes to the loneliness you hate.

At worst, you live in a dreamworld. At best, you create dreamworld. Do you want to get out into this life? Then stop the Netflix and go skiing, go to other countries, take airplanes—even if it all seems dangerous. It's usually you who does the work to get us all well planned. You can sure plan a party, creating joy for all. After it's all in motion, you may not want to stay at your own party for very long.

Best for you to learn about meditation, crystals, and doorways to bring your heart to peace. We love you, Pisces rising. Your inner beauty reminds us of what matters most: the love for life itself and all the beauty in this world and beyond. You love this life in small doses, on your terms. Find your comfort zone and decorate it with all things spiritual. Will you invite us in? What a gift you are to our world.

SATURN IN PISCES

Your issues are boundaries. They are either too weak or too strong. Can you live in the real world and not complain about it?

With boundaries comes wisdom. The sooner you admit to being vulnerable and emotional, your authentic ability to know what you need and do not need will show up. Once boundaries are intact and you have your emotional honesty, you will realize how deeply wise, empathetic, and compassionate you are.

You are allowed to express your deep emotions. Because you are a sponge for energy, you have the ability to channel and heal for the collective and yourself.

Life lesson: Either you are captured by your own sensitivity or you are cut off. In either case, the exploration of your feeling body will assist you to evolve and be who you really are.

MEDITATION FOR PISCES

My faith is seeking me. I am safe. I am encircled by angels. I lean into my higher self. I let myself steel my mind. I take deep breaths to reduce my fear. I find calm. I get downloads and insights, creative inspirations, and I find it effortless to manifest. I value the refined parts of life that make me feel centered. This is how I find my peace. I give myself permission to design my world so that I can return to wisdom whenever I need it.

THE ESSENCE OF PISCES

When a being comes in with a deep calling, it's hard to resist, even if the world demands that Pisces play on the same turf as everyone else. They can try, but Pisces must learn to bridge many worlds: the movies they love, the dreamtime, the hopes that humanity will evolve.

They are concerned about the less fortunate. The kindness in their hearts is a well-worn badge they received because of past lives when they paid their dues. This lifetime, they are testing themselves to see if they really did learn anything. They most likely do not remember this consciously. If they look at their natural response to help, to create, to write the script, the story, they will see the depth of care they have.

If life doesn't comply with what Pisces thought was going to happen, if their dreams were not fulfilled the way they expected and their life does not resemble what they wanted, this is their test to love life just the way destiny asks. They are capable. They have a spiritual backbone, even if the world doesn't always make them comfortable.

Pisces's essence is spiritual. They are willing to do what is needed based on spirit's call. They have all the magic and angels a being could need—when they trust the magic, they will see it reflected back.

20

The Thirteenth Sign

When one is in a mess like you are, one has no right anymore to worry about the idiocy of one's own psychology, but must do the next thing with diligence and devotion and earn the goodwill of others. In every littlest thing you do in this way, you will find yourself.

—CARL JUNG

I'M CONFIDENT THAT YOU SPENT a good part of your time reading this book focusing on your sun sign (better known as your ego), identifying with your quirks and unique traits. Maybe you read about the sun signs of your kids or your partner. That is why every astrology book is written—so you can understand and be understood.

Esoteric astrology is a little different. It grabs the attention of your ego while quietly seducing you toward your greatest lover of all: your soul. It is a circuitous route from the ego all the way back to your soul.

This is why I prefer esoteric astrology, and why (as you have learned) this book has esoteric astrology at its heart. You are a soul, dressed up in an ego, with stars and planets, endless stories, heartbreaks, gifts, and a list of lessons that were specifically assigned to you. It's a full meal deal, batteries included, without an instruction manual—well, until now.

As you begin your study of astrology, the good news is that your ego has a powerful function in facilitating your growth by setting you up for repetitive lessons. By now you know that your astrological chart is filled with indicators determining your life lessons, and the timing of hardships and blessings. If this book served you at all, you are closer to your real self.

Let's talk about the opposite of your ego. While unlabeled and hard to identify, it is the part of you that waits in the wings—call it your higher self, your soul, your awareness. This part of you must be deliberately invoked. We now know that the ego takes over everything—your mind, your unconscious, your urges—without a supervisor or a governor to bring you back to your soul. I am suggesting that your soul is your chaperone to get you to the thirteenth sign.

This is the voice that is often found only after profound longing, or enough crises to drop you to your knees, leading you to seek comfort, praying for help and soul-filled wisdom that softens pain. Yes, the voice of the thirteenth sign is established through hardship. This voice is grown in the soil of pain. You know this story. It's a major theme in this book.

Two possible doors to finding this voice are:

1. A series of crises revealed by Saturn's clock (Saturn return, or a seven-year Saturn cycle).
2. You were lucky and worked hard in past lives, from which you inherited wisdom. Was it through a dream, great parents, a medicine journey? Maybe it was an introduction to a spiritual teacher or path? However you got there, just know this voice is waiting for you.

For me, astrology is the doorway to this voice. A voice that is not easy to find. Let's be clear: this is the part of you that is in love with your essence and has been from the first moment of your existence.

I hope after reading this book, your ego feels seen and understood. I hope you have found it illuminating to read about your rising sign, Saturn, the planets, the houses, and everything else in this book about astrology.

Well, enough of that! Here we are at the end of the book.

This is the most important topic: the thirteenth sign, a flimsy, non-linear concept that accesses the quiet zone, the silent cave, the perfectly colored sunset, where everything is at peace, at one, untarnished. Call it home base, where your ego comes to rest and you stop the efforting—you just are.

This has been called by many names in many cultures throughout human history. In ancient China, they call it the Tao; in India, they call it the Atman; in the Jewish Kabbalism, they call it Einsof; in Buddhism, they call it Nirvana. All these words describe something that cannot be described. We are heading toward the realm of the ineffable where words fail.

Think of it as the place in the chart where all planets, houses, and signs come together. If the thirteenth sign could speak, it would say, "Okay, spirit, if in this lifetime I came here to be this exact personality, to fulfill the karma I have been assigned throughout my lifetimes, and now I have this chart in this lifetime, help me to stay neutral enough to ask and inquire, to question my thoughts, to be the governor of my mind that knows how to filter out the unhealthy gremlins that are keeping me from you—my true self. Assist me to be a conscious vehicle, a wise being, responsive to my chart with grace and ease."

It's almost funny that you just read a book distinguishing all the astrological signs and their countless permutations, trying to help your ego find its heart, giving words and concepts to describe your character, informed by an ancient tool called astrology—with all that science and math. And now, I want to send you into a far greater space where you are so much more than your name, or your face, or your sign, or your childhood wound, or those shattered pieces of your heart you left behind, or any logical thoughts that have you thinking your mind would be the key to enlightenment. Trust me—to get to the thirteenth sign, you have to leave your mind behind.

"Perfect timing," said the astrologer. We need assistance in a time when we as a species are so vulnerable and confused. "There is a profound awakening occurring for the entire human race," said the astrologer. You can feel it, the exponential changes circling our globe—I only have to say "AI," and many of us shudder. What are the implications of such a gargantuan technological advancement? The possibility of a dark technological future conjures up terror because we all know that our world is shifting.

There is no need to be scared. It's better to be prepared, conscious, and awake. Warnings are helpful in eliciting grace during such change. We all have a choice: to move into this new era with a calm nervous system and to hold the peaceful acceptance of what is, or to be scared, anxious, and unprepared.

There are obvious indicators beyond astrology that describe these changes. It starts off simply. Never before have there been eight billion people on our little blue rock in the middle of space, overwhelmed with implications of modern technology. Without the partnership and capacity for emotional and psychological wisdom, coupled with the skill to turn on the thirteenth sign, we should be scared.

We just left behind the Piscean Age that included masterful teachers such as Jesus, Buddha, and Muhammad. According to astrology, these cycles change approximately every 2,100 years. In the 1960s we witnessed an era shift. As an astrologer, I would be remiss to not confirm: we are in the Aquarian Age! The Aquarian Age is echoed by the entrance of Pluto into Aquarius. The most obvious indictors are the environmental and geopolitical changes. Do I even need to name them? The climate, the wars across the world, and dark technology.

I will be watching the astrological influences starting in the summer of 2026 onward when all the outer planets enter fire and air signs. The last fifteen years were all earth and water—a time of business as usual, stay the course, the old boys' club, the governments who pretended to have our backs, all in an attempt to create stability and consistency. Now they are all moving into fire and air—starting in 2026, we will have Saturn in Aries (fire), Uranus in Gemini (air), Neptune in Aries (fire), and Pluto in Aquarius (air). This is a huge shift: fire and air contain combustive energetics that fuel change and newness. We must become aware of choice as we recreate our societal values.

I want to address the implications regarding Pluto. Pluto is the smallest planet in our galaxy and yet the most powerful. As I mentioned in chapter 5, its discovery coincided with the discovery of nuclear power (such an obvious influence of Pluto's signature). World War II, Hitler, and Freud all introduced us to the unconscious powers of either good or bad during this moment in history. Now Pluto is changing signs and has the potential to change our world beyond recognition, like it does every 240 years. The last time Pluto changed signs (1777), America had just become a country. Think about the implications for our world. Pluto now enters the sign that represents astrology and all things futuristic—hello, Aquarius.

Will we choose kindness and compassion steeped in sharing and caring? Nothing else will let us cross over the timeline from one age to another with greater ease than a heightened humanitarianism. Or will it be AI creating a new iteration of humans who do not resemble what came before?

There will be choices! Your ability to utilize the thirteenth sign to reduce your ego's confusion, to anchor in faith and trust, to realize that we have been made by our creator, placed here to embody divinity—this is the highest version of Aquarian energy.

Aquarius: freedom, uninhibited authenticity, the generosity of a divine human who really cares, loves, and is kind. Go ahead and read about Aquarius. Ask yourself: What kind of humanity do you want to leave behind for our children and the future generations?

We have to accept that these radical changes are upon us as we enter into partnership with AI and advanced technology, which hopefully will be informed by both our heads *and* our hearts. This will make all the difference—if we can accept the changes while keeping our attention on the voice of peace and compassion.

Now is the time to come off the chart with me, up to the heavens, to the land that has no name. This place defies gravity and language. Stop right there; your mind has no right in this place. Fear is not welcome here. FEAR: Forgetting Everything's All Right.

Let's default to love and welcome these changes as conscious beings who know how to calm their nervous systems, and let's celebrate the changes, no matter what they may be. No one knows for sure what's going to happen—not one astrologer, seer, or prophet can prepare us for which way we will go.

What is true is that you are safe. The thirteenth sign floats through reality, never bumping into any semblance of pain. It has nothing to do with the human race. The thirteenth sign lives far beyond the mind's attempt to make sense of this place.

The "real" thirteenth sign has actually been discovered in space. A story has resurfaced about how NASA discovered a thirteenth zodiac sign—Ophiuchus, or the serpent bearer, as the astronomers have called it.

But I'm not talking about that. I'm talking about the thirteenth sign that has no name. It stands away from measurements like time and space. It rises above stilted language. You cannot perceive the thirteenth sign until you surrender, close your eyes, and listen with your heart.

Do you know the part of you that is eternal and was so willing to take on the human plight? The part of you that loves every single aspect of this experience? The part of you that slides willingly into eternity, leaving behind your form with no desire to draw lines of separation or speak with words? A floating decimal point, a wave, a particle? It doesn't matter what you call this place. The thirteenth sign is the part in all of us that stays as far away from human understanding as it can get.

Surely you know its opposite. Your ego has been described in detail. You know the part of your mind that longs to be special, different, ego-identified, sitting there with this book, absorbing and learning? While I love that part of you (it compelled you to buy this book!), that's not who I'm talking to.

I am talking about the unconditional love in you that never stops, and is just waiting in the wings to be activated.

Think about the sun and its never-ending compulsion to chase the moon. Think about your heart, activated from the moment of conception. This is the part in all of us that is trustworthy, stable, and never-ending, as constant as the North Star, untarnished and healed. We are loved beyond measure by the force that moves the planets every single day through eternity without ever stopping.

Death has nothing on the thirteenth sign. The thirteenth sign exists across all time. This is our ticket to eternity. If only you understood that your mind must stop, your nervous system must relax, and then you get to come home.

This is why this chapter is so short and abstract. When the future arrives, and it will, your relationship with concepts like calm, quiet, and safety will determine everything. How good are you at adjusting your nervous system, taking deep breaths, meditating, trusting God above all else? This is the last stop in order to enter the sacred chamber of peace. Words don't describe this place because words instantly dissolve upon the face of God.

So close your eyes and relax. You have a home, where gratitude lives in you constantly and your heart smiles. This is where we live forever—they call it eternity.

Do you know why we live forever?

It takes that long to say thank you.

Appendix I

DEBRA SILVERMAN RESOURCES

Applied Astrology School | Join Our Waitlist and Get Your Free Gift
Debra's Applied Astrology School teaches the language of astrology through a psychological lens. Applied Astrology has helped thousands of students from all over the world, all walks of life, and all ages get an education in the fundamentals of astrology.

There's a track for everyone, distilled into bite-sized modules. You could train to be a professional astrologer, or simply learn about your chart as a self-help practice.

Applied Astrology enrollment occurs twice a year with limited spots available. Join our waitlist now to be among the first to know when enrollment opens and to get access to our enrollment packages.

Plus when you join our waitlist, we'll gift you our *Reframe Your Quirks Into Your Gifts* series, so you don't have to wait until school starts to unlock insights into your astrological chart and how your personality challenges are often disguised as your best qualities.

Join the Applied Astrology waitlist and get your free gift by heading to: http://appliedastrology.me.

Progressed Moon Guide | Understand the Seasons of Your Life

Timing is everything. Imagine **knowing what season and cycle you are in, according to your chart, so you can flow with the cosmic influence** rather than *against* it. Are you in an introverted, homebody phase, or are you feeling extroverted and ready to socialize? Is it time to be creative and productive, or is it time to relax and enjoy? Everything goes in seasons.

There's a quick and free way to see what cycle you're in through **understanding your Progressed Moon. Debra has made unlocking these insights simple and easy, yet so profound!**

With the Progressed Moon, you can pace and manage with wisdom the era you are in, plus prepare for what's coming.

Simply visit https://debrasilvermanastrology.com/progressed-moon to get started!

Tell Me a Story | Rewrite Your Life's Story

We all have stories—triumphs, tribulations, and everything in between. In your mind, your story gets eclipsed by negative internal dialogue.

There is great liberation when you can stand in your observer—the part of you that is objective and kind—and look back at your stories with compassion. This writing course (which requires no skill as a writer) is a chance to tell your story through the eyes of love. **Join us in our element-based writing course, "Tell Me a Story."**

You will be guided by a trained and trusted TMAS facilitator. There is no astrology knowledge needed for TMAS to give a return on this investment in yourself. Nothing short of a miracle occurs when you can look at your life story from your soul's perspective.

Who knew a writing class could be so impactful? Join our next session: tmas.co.

Certified Astrologer Readings | Book Your Astrology Reading

If you're ready to **feel seen, understand your uniqueness, and dive**

deep into who you are through the lens of the cosmos, it's time to **book your astrology reading with one of Debra's certified astrologers**!

Each certified astrologer has been through a rigorous training program designed by Debra. Using her iconic method, you will receive a transformational, life-changing reading.

After sitting with one of our certified astrologers, you will know yourself better than ever before. These sessions address timing, a personality assessment, your purpose, and answers to your deepest questions.

Find out more and book your reading today: https://debrasilverman astrology.com/certified-astrologers.

4E Immersion | Instant Access to Relief Through Elemental Embodiment

Decades ago, Debra discovered that when the wisdom of the four elements is synthesized beyond words and theory into an experiential method of application, people found therapeutic relief. 4E reduces the stress of the broken record you live with. In other words, 4E can change your life.

Join a free week-long immersion where Debra will introduce you to the four elements by interviewing wisdom keepers and those new to the process. Get a taste of how the four elements provide wisdom and medicine.

This is for you if you want an introduction to the power and curative nature of the four elements. Get access by joining for free at http:// elementalimmersion.me!

4E Sessions | What Element Is in Your Way?

There are many voices that live within your head, some of which support you and some of which sabotage. Let's take you on a journey through each of the **four elements to discover who the culprit at the scene of the crime is that is interrupting your fulfillment.** You will get one-on-one support from a Debra Silverman–certified 4E facilitator.

This is an element-based experience using Debra's 4E process that

is unlike any other therapeutic offering available, where you discover potent insights and therapeutic introspections that can change your life.

This is perfect for you if you want to do something practical that is related to astrology but far simpler.

Book your session today at http://4elements.me/certified-sessions.

Intensives | A Piercing Look into Your Soul's Agreement

Spend a day and a half with Debra to reveal the karma of your lifetime. Be prepared to tell her your life story, as she poses the question: **What did you sign up for in this life?**

Using the concrete evidence of what has actually occurred throughout your lifetime, and your astrological chart, **Debra will objectively acknowledge the challenges you've been through, the triumphs, and most important, the lessons that you signed up for**.

This is a very intense and time-sensitive program for those who are at a critical juncture, about to make big decisions, or who have lost their love for life. **This is a one-on-one healing process that will be waiting for you.**

Book your session today at https://debrasilvermanastrology.com /services/intensive-breakthrough.

If anyone is interested in supporting financially challenged individuals to attend these classes, we have nonprofit status in the United States so you can donate and receive a tax benefit. I always imagined how different I would have been if I had found this school at a young age. But could I have afforded the classes? That's why we have a scholarship fund. In honor of my father, I have called this the Milt Silverman Astrology Fund, which is hysterical because he didn't believe in astrology. I can only imagine him rolling over in his grave and saying, "What's the name of the nonprofit?"

Appendix II

FIND YOUR SATURN SIGN

Find your birth year below to discover what sign Saturn was in when you were born. (This is not a precise description—please go to Astro.com, put in your birthdate, and they will tell you exactly where Saturn was. Retrogrades do occur from time to time, so you must check.)

ARIES: September 1939–March 1940

TAURUS: March 1940–May 1942

GEMINI: May 1942–June 1944

CANCER: June 1944–August 1946

LEO: August 1946–September 1948

VIRGO: September 1948–August 1951

LIBRA: August 1951–October 1953

SCORPIO: October 1953–October 1956

SAGITTARIUS: October 1956–January 1959

CAPRICORN: January 1959–January 1962

AQUARIUS: January 1962–December 1964

PISCES: December 1964–March 1967

ARIES: March 1967–May 1969

TAURUS: May 1969–June 1971

GEMINI: June 1971–August 1973

CANCER: August 1973–September 1975

LEO: September 1975–August 1978

VIRGO: August 1978–September 1980

LIBRA: September 1980–December 1982

SCORPIO: December 1982–November 1985

SAGITTARIUS: November 1985–November 1988

CAPRICORN: November 1988–February 1991

AQUARIUS: February 1991–February 1994

PISCES: February 1994–April 1996

ARIES: April 1996–March 1999

TAURUS: March 1999–April 2001

GEMINI: April 2001–June 2003

CANCER: June 2003–July 2005

LEO: July 2005–September 2007

VIRGO: September 2007–July 2010

LIBRA: July 2010–October 2012

SCORPIO: October 2012–December 2014

SAGITTARIUS: December 2014–December 2017

CAPRICORN: December 2017–December 2020

AQUARIUS: December 2020–March 2023

PISCES: March 2023–February 2026

ARIES: February 2026–April 2028

TAURUS: April 2028–June 2030

GEMINI: June 2030–July 2032

CANCER: July 2032–August 2034

LEO: August 2034–July 2037

VIRGO: July 2037–September 2039

LIBRA: September 2039–November 2041

SCORPIO: November 2041–November 2044

SAGITTARIUS: November 2044–January 2047

CAPRICORN: January 2047–January 2050

AQUARIUS: January 2050–January 2053

PISCES: January 2053–March 2055

Acknowledgments

I probably shouldn't tell you this: I had zero interest in writing this book. I made the mistake of using the word "never." I learned my lesson.

I remember telling my best friend: "I will never write another book." The truth was, my ego mind didn't want to write—that lazy little voice—however, my soul had an assignment and I eventually answered the call. You're holding the result in your hands.

One of the bottom lines of this book is to listen to your soul. That's not easy. The soul speaks in a cryptic language, through dreams, strange opportunities that arrive, endless invitations that we overlook or even resist. After years studying human nature, I realized this is one of the greatest pains of the human condition: to leave this life without fulfilling your mission.

Luckily, that did not happen to me, because so many people are seeking wisdom from the ancient doorway called astrology. I am so grateful.

For over five decades, I have been studying. I've looked at tens of thousands of charts, enough to realize that human nature, when supported by the soul, will present similar issues over and over again, waiting for you to catch on. *Oh, you want me to write a book? You're asking me to share what I know?* I did finally realize what was happening when the message became so loud that I could no longer resist. I want to say thanks to those who deserve acknowledgment.

It started with a friend called Jolie who said: "If you were ever to write again, I know a woman who could help you." They called her a ghostwriter. For me, she was wholly present, embodied, and brilliant. So much for ghosts—she was a superhero who studied astrology with me and had the gift of writing it down. Thanks to her four planets in Aquarius in the first house, she was built for the job.

Let's start at the very beginning, by thanking the people who permitted my soul's existence: my mom and dad.

I learned through my dad, Milt, the stoic Capricorn, to see through to the soul, to step over the outer personality, and to pay attention to someone's integrity, to pay attention to their word, and the softness of their heart. My dad had a heart of gold, especially when it came to me. He now lives in the foyer of my inner mansion. The first thing you see when you come all the way into the chambers of my heart would be Milt. He resides there and will continue until we meet again. Truth be told, I miss him all the time.

From him I learned that the soul supersedes the ego—but only after we realize that love is all that matters. Not that he wasn't a crook, emotionally stunted, and deeply flawed by his 1930s karma. That story is not the one I want to share with you. What I want to share is simple: he demonstrated unconditional love, up close and personal. I found out that love transcends the outer world. This is evident by the way that love's presence lasts long after the person who loved you leaves this world. True love can never age.

My mother, on the other hand . . . as a Leo, she demonstrated a loud, wild ego. Her hair, her nails, her jewelry defined her. She was quite the opposite of my strange, soulful father. I was introduced to the impact of both the ego gone wild (hello, Tillie) and the soul hidden behind a disguise (hello, Milt). And so began my fascination with contrasting energies, which has never left my awareness: the soul versus the ego. The outer world demands attention while the inner sanctuary whispers, "Come sit with me." And as all well know, they are at war.

I hope when you finish this book, you will feel that neither the ego nor the soul needs to be alienated or judged as better or worse. They are just different. This is the ultimate invitation: you have been asked to rest in the inner world of the soul, which is your guiding light, your true north. The soul is the source of fulfillment—not the personality and the ego, which are the transportation devices that get you to the soul.

My next gratitude is for my son. Evolution continues throughout time. Once you see the long view through the study of astrology and metaphysics, or geology or astronomy, you realize the next generation is evolving, and hopefully they will be an upgrade to what came before. Thank you to God for sending me a son who has taught me so much. It is because of Daniel that my faith has been reignited. His relationship with Christ reminds me how safe we all are once we find our divine promise: the soul's calling and the willingness to answer the call. Daniel, I am so grateful for the God-loving man you have become. Our lineage continues to evolve because of your presence. In fact, all our ancestors thank you. Daniel is yet another teacher in my life who has contributed to this book.

This is the family line that has influenced me to become the writer and astrologer that I am.

There is my best friend, Laurel. She has held my heart as if it were gold, providing stability like an anchor of a tree under which I find shelter—anytime, anywhere, and for as long as I need. She is home to me. Every night, her voice is the steady-eddy loyalty that made space for me to write this book. Yes, as I've said, I resisted writing, but she challenged me. That's what friends do. They ask the hard questions, track you, and keep you on your soul's mission.

And so I surrendered. The soul's command came through a friend who knows me better than I know myself. Thank you, Laurel, and thank you also to your husband, John, who has had to deal with the endless Gemini phone bantering and hysterical laughter on too many nights to count. This book happened because I knew that Geminis have to talk and write. I was just being myself.

I have a crystal-clear knowledge that friendship is real, and that neither time nor space will ever stop true love, sister to sister, and from my dad, and from my son. I rest, deep in the marrow of my own bones. I relax into the truth: that I am safe, loved, and cared about by these people. This is one way spirit shows up and provides safety: through love and friendship.

From here, other souls have taken up the call and answered their own destinies and purposes. My cowriter, Eve; my agent, Alex, who kept us on track and willingly introduced me to publishers; my team at work who hold down the fort in my astrology business/school; my assistant, who plays mom for me and tells me what to do; and all the other people whose hands touched this book: I give thanks for you.

Then there are my other best, lifelong friends, whose ears I borrowed to listen to me get it wrong, and whose generous patience allowed room for me to clean it up, and get it wrong again, and only then to finally find my voice. You know who you are, Carla, Lynn, Ashley, Mimsy, Lee, Sarah, Parker, Eric, and those who are not here: Judy, Tim, Kevan, and so many others whose names I do not know. I have made friends in cyberspace with souls all around this world.

"I don't want to write this book," said my lazy ego, yet my ambitious soul, who is in love with her boss (God), refused to stop until it was done.

"Just know," said the astrologer, "when you follow your soul's voice, brought to you in myriad ways, you will be able to die softly, having completed a life well lived." We are here to fulfill a vague promise, put in place beyond conscious memory, hidden within Egyptian hieroglyphics, written inside an astrological chart that delivers your agreement. It waits for your approval, and most of all bides its time until your memory is finally activated, at last recalling that your soul said *yes* to the very life, just as it is right now! Your ego may resist this truth, but if you do your daily prayers—"Let me be of service to my soul, to fulfill my promise, to embody love"—you, too, will erase the word "never" from your world, so you can do whatever life asks of you next.

Here is what life asked me to do: write this book. I did it and truly, I feel so good that I can check that off my soul's to-do list and leave here fulfilled. Next stop? We shall see. Spirit always has another assignment for those who say yes, who keep saying yes, who keep going, and who learn the lesson that "never" has never been a word we needed.

About the Author

Debra Silverman holds a bachelor's degree in psychology and dance from York University and a master's in clinical psychology from Antioch University. At the age of twenty, she met an astrologer who changed her world forever. Debra is known for her honest and direct style, plus her fun, nontraditional way of communicating. Her goal is to connect with you on a deep level to heal while making you laugh, so you can fully accept who you are.